11 12-19

To Taylo

Thanks

Listen-ing !

This Is
AirTalk

Larry Mantle

To Taylor,
Thanks for
listening

[signature]

This Is
AirTalk

20 Years of Conversations on 89.3 KPCC

Larry Mantle

Foreword by Patt Morrison

To Kristen and Desmond,
for all your love and support.
—L.M.

Contents

Two amazing radio careers began in California in 1985. One was that of a fellow named Rush Limbaugh. The other was that of a fellow named Larry Mantle. One decided to use his microphone as a bully pulpit, usually with him as the bully; the other chose to use it as the kitchen table, as a town hall, as an education by ear. Rush's bellowing makes us blink; Larry's engaging curiosity makes us think.

If the only energy you want to expend when you listen to the radio is the effort of switching it on, Larry Mantle's *AirTalk* is not your program. What calls itself talk radio nowadays is really shout radio, harangue and bombast that burn up all the airtime and oxygen available, considerately saving the listener the trouble of doing anything—including thinking—except perhaps uttering a feeble "ditto" of endorsement.

Talk radio—real talk radio—isn't for the lazy-minded. True talk radio should properly be called thought radio, just so there's no confusion with the other kind. Marshall McLuhan created that famous temperature gauge of media, but his intellectual thermostat seems to go all haywire when it comes to radio. When he lumps it in with television, it's "hot"—meaning the audience are couch potatoes, sofa spuds doing nothing but passively receiving. But if he were to consider *AirTalk*—Larry Mantle's thought radio show—it's "cool," requiring the audience to engage mind and imagination with what they're hearing. I wish Larry could have gotten McLuhan across from him in that guest chair to ask him about the contradiction.

For those twenty years, *AirTalk* has introduced millions of listeners to thousands of guests: some of the finest minds and deepest souls and most curious characters that Southern California and the nation have to offer.

Those thousands of guests have been narrowed down here to twenty-one, and they are doozies, exemplifying both the broad reach of radio into the grand arena of ideas, and the intimacy of two minds and two voices in conversation—never mind the tens of thousands of ears listening to them.

Milton Berle confesses to Larry that "Mr. Television" himself doesn't watch TV comedies (this, after standing next to Larry at the urinal in the KPCC men's room, and handing Larry a good cigar). Walter Mosley, the California author who delivers social consciousness with striking characters and plot lines, tells of being a young boy who comes home one night during the Watts riots to his house in West Los Angeles to find his father drinking and almost crying—not because the man is afraid, but because he understands, because "I know why these people are mad, and I want to do the same thing." Frank Gehry tells Larry that he agreed to give his all to the Walt Disney Concert Hall during a rough-and-tumble game of ice hockey with the former mayor of Los Angeles, Richard Riordan.

There are interviews with Hollywood and Washington figures, and here's something that's curious but true—I know it from my own broadcast interviews—the hardest people to interview are the ones who are used to being interviewed, the pols and the practiced celebrities. Here's why. Ten minutes may sound like nothing to you— perhaps you spend that much time at Starbucks, ordering a coffee and waiting for it. Ten minutes in broadcasting is a good chunk of eternity. In 1968, the average sound bite allotted to a presidential candidate on the CBS evening news, which was then the gold-standard network, was forty-three seconds. Look at your watch. You can say a good bit in forty-three seconds. By 1996 the sound bite had shrunk to eight seconds. Look at your watch again. More a sound nibble than a sound bite. What can you say in eight seconds that doesn't sound like a bumper sticker or a refrain from a country-western song? Comedian Mark Russell suggested this multipurpose line: "It's great to be here in [fill in the blank]. New Hampshire. Jobs. Jobs. Jobs. God bless you." Click.

Remember, we're talking about people who have had their candor genes removed, and who want to stay on message no matter what. So they trim their sound bites to fit the time allotted. Suddenly, they're on with Larry Mantle; they have ten minutes, maybe even longer! That means two things: one, the speaker who is accustomed to getting by on autopilot for the length of his standard-issue sound bite finds it soon runs out, and there are at least another nine-and-a-half minutes left to talk! And two, as a result, the listener gets to hear perhaps some of the first authentic, spontaneous words that this public figure has uttered in public in a long time.

This happened to Larry early on in those twenty years, when he interviewed Gary Hart, the Colorado senator and Democratic presidential candidate who had all but dared reporters to follow him around. Hart dropped out of the race after photos surfaced of him aboard a yacht, the *Monkey Business,* with a blonde in his lap. His handlers had warned Larry not to ask about the incident, but Larry approached it elliptically, asking what Hart regretted about how he operated his campaign. The question elicited a thoughtful, painful answer that was more honest and frank, his staff said later, than anything he'd even told them. And *AirTalk* listeners got something they couldn't have heard anywhere else—not some elaboration of scandal, but an intimate understanding of politics and hubris from someone who had been in the white hot core of the volcano. Sad to say, the recording of this interview was lost, precluding its inclusion in this book. Happily, the conversations that *are* printed here are just as revealing.

Having occupied Larry's chair from time to time, I can attest to this, too: the easier it sounds on the air, the harder it really is. Not because of glitches—silent mikes, guests whose phones go dead, although those happen. It's hard in part because an interview is really a conversation with a purpose: to engage and enlighten the listeners but also to engage the guests with questions and ideas they might not have heard before. A radio host is both a referee and a polite provocateur. And as vital as listeners' calls and questions are to the very fabric of *AirTalk*, some of Larry's best interviews are the ones in which nobody out there in Listener Land calls in with a question or a remark. They are so rapt, so intent on the singular conversation between host and guest, that they don't want to miss a word, nor break the subtle, elusive spell that the voices have cast.

Don't think of this sampling of twenty years of interviews as a retrospective alone. Think of it as an inducement to at least another two decades of such significant voices and ideas, and to the kind of radio programs and radio stations that believe in them.

So go ahead, open these pages and turn on the radio of your imagination. Hear the host and the guest, evoke the tone and the color and the depth in their voices and words. As McLuhan would tell you, have a hot, and very cool, time.

—Patt Morrison

Introduction

"**T**his is *AirTalk*. **I'm Larry Mantle . . .**" Every weekday morning as I sit down at the mike in the KPCC studio to introduce our topics and guests, I feel the excitement of talking to thousands of Southern Californians about the most important issues of the day. It never gets old. I feel incredibly fortunate not only to have the honor of talking to the best listeners in radio and to fascinating guests, but of doing this in a region brimming with innovative ideas. This book celebrates my twentieth anniversary as host of *AirTalk*, Southern California radio's longest continuously running interview/call-in program.

The show launched in April 1985, with a half-hour interview with Pasadena Mayor Bill Bogaard. As I write these words, he is still mayor (though not continuously since 1985) and I am still in the host's seat. I don't know whose luck rubbed off on whom.

The format of *AirTalk* is special; it's rare in the broadcast media for a host to have the luxury of time that I have with each guest. There's no better way to get a sense of a guest's personality and motivations than in a half-hour to one-hour interview, sans commercials—the listener comes away with a strong feeling for who that guest really is. This format allows me to conduct interviews in a style that is quite different from the norms of commercial media. These kinds of longer conversations are much less prevalent than the verbal wrestling of commercial radio and cable TV talk shows, where the form now seems more campy than newsy. The pressure to compress every argument into a simplistic talking point has turned the *art* of broadcast conversation into the *science* of keeping and attracting audience by appealing almost solely to emotions. That has further polarized our public debates into extreme and unyielding opinions that are not opened up for closer examination. People feel that they do not have to defend their positions, assuming "right" is on their side.

At *AirTalk*, our intent is to serve the highly curious listener who is not satisfied with unexamined arguments based on emotion or self-righteousness. It's far too common in our society that people fall prey to such arguments. I'm not implicating any one side of the ideological divide. I see this as a syndrome affecting the closed-minded from a variety of camps. Fundamentalism is not exclusive to religious extremists. It has led us from the ugliness of Clinton-hating to the zealotry of demonizing Bush, neither one a very productive strategy for enlightening or bringing about change. *AirTalk* is a forum for strong arguments from a variety of perspectives that can help all of us better converse across ideological, religious, economic and cultural divides. If we lose the ability to listen to each other with open minds, we'll further Balkanize ourselves and make shared values and social progress impossible. One of the greatest compliments I get from listeners is when they say they've listened to an *AirTalk* segment and heard new information that made them reexamine their beliefs.

To facilitate that process, I ask myself before every *AirTalk* conversation, "What are the strongest possible arguments challenging the opinions I'll hear on today's show?" My goal is to probe guests in such a way that I can get them to truly ponder their positions. It's very satisfying when that happens, whether with a comedian, a U.S. president, a sex worker or a world-renowned author.

I believe so strongly in the power of conversation because it is what I've always valued most in my life. Even when I'm by myself, I carry on a constant internal conversation. It's how I organize, understand, and relate to the overwhelming stream of information that washes over me, and all of us. It's how I work through issues that confuse me. It's also how I constantly try to intellectually challenge myself.

AirTalk's most crucial role is to dig beneath the conventional arguments to a place where we can talk about underlying assumptions, comparative measurements, and even the history of a perspective. Looking at these and other deeper aspects of familiar debates allows us to better talk with each other about what our differences are and why we have them. Does an opinion we hold come from the way we were raised? Whether we've had much money? Our religious beliefs? Our prejudices? Or is it based on serious, open-minded questioning, with the possibility that we can modify our view with new information?

Why is this so important to me? My upbringing helps explain a lot.

I am a fourth-generation Angeleno, born in downtown Los Angeles, delivered by my physician grandfather. My mother, Carole, became pregnant with me at age fifteen by my sixteen-year-old father, John. My grandparents helped my parents raise me early on, but Carole and John didn't need much assistance; they were extremely mature for their ages. As I grew older, my parents fostered in me an open-minded approach to the world. Non-dogmatic and highly curious, they always encouraged me to be true to my nature and interests. We spent countless hours as a family exploring the world of ideas—after all, they were almost as young as I and we shared the same tastes in music and popular culture.

My grandfather Dr. Verne Mantle was an important role model for me. He not only practiced out of two offices, but was house doctor for the historic Bullock's Wilshire department store and a sexual dysfunction clinic in Long Beach. I have discussed on *AirTalk* many of the same medical issues he'd bring up during our drives to house calls when he'd let me ride along. Grandpa Mantle also helped make me comfortable talking frankly about a variety of sexual issues. Family meals often featured his comments about why some couples have difficulty with intercourse, or why young people should masturbate regularly so they don't feel pressured to have sex—not your typical dinnertime fare.

I grew up surrounded by intense family discussions about politics, science, religion, race, the nature of fulfillment, and how best to relate to others. I loved being with my parents and grandparents, talking with them about the world. This probably explains why I'm an expert at nothing, but interested in everything. I remember being four years old and relating to the world as a questioner. I've always wanted to know who, what, where, when, why and how.

My strong interest in politics emerged when I was nine, an age when few of my fellow fifth graders at Inglewood's Centinela Elementary School shared such a passion. In 1968, after I asked our teacher to hold a mock presidential election, I volunteered to be the surrogate for Hubert Humphrey and another student offered to represent Richard Nixon. We each made our pitch, playing more to emotion and the stereotypes of the two parties than anything else. The classroom divided its vote exactly down the middle. I was hooked.

Later that year I was elected student body president. My campaign featured emotional appeals about student empowerment that culminated in a lunchtime rally during which my classmates carried me from one side of the schoolyard to the other. The refrain "We want Mantle! We want Mantle!" is still vividly stored in my brain.

After my family moved to Hollywood, my interest in politics and social issues continued at Le Conte Junior High. I became close with a group of friends who shared my interests. We would discuss issues such as the environment, welfare, nuclear disarmament and even California ballot initiatives. It became a point of honor to know all of the major initiatives. Given that this was early 1970s Hollywood, most of the kids and the teachers were liberal. I was bothered by hearing only this one-sided perspective—something was missing in our debates, and I decided to do something about it. I became the self-designated conservative.

I read Barry Goldwater's *The Conscience of a Conservative,* and started listening to anti-communist radio shows such as *The Voice of Americanism,* hosted by Glendale minister Dr. Stuart McBirnie. I came to class talking about the communist menace and how foolish liberals were to downplay the desire of the Soviet Union to dominate the world. I would quote Goldwater and his reasons why Social Security was a terrible idea that insulted the ability of Americans to save for themselves.

My teachers looked at me as if I had become possessed—they weren't sure by what. I could hear my classmates who didn't know me well ask each other if I was serious. At lunch, I still debated my friends on all the usual topics, but I'd take the conservative position.

They kept trying to make me laugh and break character, but I was insistent about holding on to my role as the dissident right-winger. Oddly, the longer I kept up this conservative role, the blurrier my own beliefs became.

By the time I got to Hollywood High, I had retired my conservative persona, but my interests in social issues and debate were as strong as ever. I traveled to high schools all over Southern California to compete in speech and debate tournaments, and thoroughly enjoyed arguing assigned points of view, regardless of my own.

When I attended Southern California College in Costa Mesa (now Vanguard University), I found almost the opposite of my junior high experience. In an attempt to balance classroom debate, I was often one of the few students espousing liberal views. Thankfully, despite the image some have of an evangelical Christian college, the faculty at SCC was very open and quite balanced.

So from an early age, there was politics and debate . . . and there was radio. I had been addicted to the medium since age five, when I used my own money to purchase a transistor radio—the first thing I ever bought for myself. I was a voracious listener, to many different stations and formats. In high school, I participated in an Explorer Scout program that let me hang out at KTTV television and KLAC radio, even getting a one-time chance to host a half-hour public affairs program, *Southland Close-Up,* on KLAC-AM. In college, I managed our student radio station for two years. Nothing gave me the pleasure and satisfaction of radio.

So why didn't I pursue radio as my career from the outset? There were a few reasons. First, I knew that it was extremely difficult to break into radio in a market as large as Southern California. You usually have to start out in smaller markets at low pay, prove yourself, and work your way up to a larger station or city. I had no interest in a career that could force me to move away from Southern California. Staying in the region was also important because of my strong personal and familial connections to the area.

Beyond my desire to stay close to home and my concerns about the radio business, there was something else: I was determined to enter the ministry. I had had a significant religious experience and felt a strong connection to God. At the time, ministering to a congregation seemed to be the best way for me to talk about the issues I thought were of greatest importance to a significant group of people.

However, my ministerial intentions weren't getting me very far. I began my studies at SCC majoring in Biblical studies, only to become so interested in my psychology classes that I switched majors. Then after graduation, I started on a master of divinity degree at Fuller Theological Seminary in Pasadena, only to realize once more that I wasn't connecting with the coursework. Fortunately, my first wife Constance set me straight. As I was trying to figure out what I really wanted to do as a career, she emphatically reminded me of my love for radio and urged me to pursue it. I can't imagine what I'd be doing now if Constance hadn't been so insistent. Ironically, shortly after beginning my radio work, I realized that what most attracted me to church ministry was what would most satisfy me in my broadcasting career.

I started at KPCC as a volunteer in 1980. I began by writing news stories, reading them on the air, and then doing some fill-in anchoring. However, my heart was set on being a sportscaster. So I did some color commentating and worked my way up to play-by-play man for Pasadena City College football and basketball, UCLA women's basketball, and assorted high school games of the week—all the sports KPCC had to offer. But after a year, I started losing interest. This was the same thing that had happened before: Whenever it came to specializing in something, my enthusiasm seemed to ebb.

KPCC then offered me a part-time job as local host of *Morning Edition.* I enjoyed the work, despite struggling with the early hours. Having a daily radio gig made me happy, and confirmed that news was the area with a range wide enough to hold my interest.

I left KPCC late in 1982 for a full-time news anchor position at CBS affiliate KPRO in Riverside. It was there that I met Steve Julian, the current local host of *Morning Edition* on KPCC. Steve and I not only co-anchored KPRO's three-hour afternoon news program, we became best friends. My time at KPRO was short because KPCC called me in early 1983 to offer me the news director job. I took over as producer and anchor for our nightly drive-time news program, *Evening Edition*. I was very proud that the half-hour *Evening Edition* won a number of awards for journalistic excellence, despite being staffed by volunteers and Pasadena City College students.

My life changed dramatically in early 1985, when General Manager Bob Miller asked if I wanted to do more than anchor *Evening Edition*. He thought I should be showcased on a more personality-driven vehicle. I jumped at the chance. We discussed the possibility of an interview/call-in program focusing on both current issues and interesting guests. I knew our listeners were so intelligent that they would have a lot to offer a call-in show. But at the time, the attitude among public radio managers was that talking with listeners was stooping to commercial radio's level. Program directors thought public radio should be the place where experts talk at the audience, not interact with it.

Fortunately, Bob was a college administrator unencumbered by public radio orthodoxy. He loved the idea of a call-in show, and asked how soon I could have it on the air. Once we had a telephone interface and seven-second delay unit, we went on the air April 1, 1985 with the first edition of *AirTalk with Larry Mantle*.

What began as a half-hour show with me as host and producer, has evolved into two hours produced by a wonderfully gifted staff of four. A bigger team and more resources mean we can respond immediately to breaking news. We strive to be the news/talk program of record for Southern California, while never sacrificing the depth that public radio listeners crave.

It's not just the ideas we debate on *AirTalk* that I treasure, it's the KPCC environment as well. I wish you could hear the conversations we have when the microphones are off. We passionately debate many topics at length before we even finish lining up the guests for a segment. This discourse continues with other members of the KPCC staff, all of whom are very smart and deeply committed to the station's mission.

This almost perfect intellectual atmosphere inspires each day's *AirTalk*. On these pages you'll read some of the rewarding conversations I've had over the last two decades. Given how fulfilling my work is, I'm hopeful I'll be talking about Southern California's most important issues, with the region's most interesting guests and the world's best listeners, for at least another twenty years. Thank you so much for listening.

JANUARY 2005

P rostitution is not only one of the most controversial topics a talk program can discuss, but it is the source of almost endless public fascination. Many of us want to understand what would lead sex workers, beyond the money involved, to offer themselves up in this way.

There are many reasons behind that decision, and there is a wide range of women attracted to the work, according to former Harvard Medical School student Alexa Albert's study of prostitutes at the now-closed Mustang Ranch in Nevada.

Albert's book, *Brothel,* is absolutely compelling in its accounts of the Mustang's legal prostitutes. My conversation with her is also one of the segments I'm most commonly asked about by *AirTalk* listeners.

Larry Mantle: Share with us your idea behind doing this. It sounds like your family, your husband, your friends, thought "Oh, that's nice; what a novel idea." It was only when this actually became a possibility that they freaked.
Alexa Albert: Exactly. It wasn't easy getting in. It took me three years to persuade Nevada's legal brothel industry, their representative, George Flint, to let me inside. I originally went to do a condom study, to look at how the women were using condoms, and when I finally got in, what I found was this fascinating, mysterious world, this isolated community of people. It was beyond my expectations and I felt compelled to learn more, and that's what this book, *Brothel,* is about. It's about the people who work in this business, who live in this business, and their secrets.

LM: I've driven by the legal brothels that are along 95, the road between Vegas and Reno. Those are the only ones I've even seen the outside of, but they all look like very little, almost mom-and-pop kinds of businesses. What you describe in the Mustang Ranch, though, is a big operation. A lot of women were working there.

AA: Basically, the Mustang could contain up to ninety women. They tended to cap at seventy-five because, you've got to remember, they're competing with each other. You don't want too many women there because it makes it hard; it makes it very tense as an environment, depending on how many people are actually coming in. You raise a really interesting point. It's a very diverse business; you have the huge Mustang Ranch, and as you say, there are also small brothels scattered throughout the state with maybe two or three women working them, and very small little houses run by one or two people. It's a very eclectic combination.

LM: Let's talk about the women who worked at the Mustang Ranch, because many of us have this stereotype of the prostitute who comes from a sexually abusive family background, a woman who is very cut off from her sexuality as a result. How does the reality differ from that view?

AA: The women were all unique, their stories all very different. They represented all different races, all different religions. The youngest was eighteen years of age, the oldest was sixty-three, and she hadn't started prostituting until she was fifty-two years old. She had been married and her husband left her, and in the book I describe how they had a complicated marriage where she wasn't enjoying sex. It sounds as if he was not terribly sensitive to that. When she became a single woman again she was raising two kids, and to get them through school, to pay their tuition, a friend recommended, "Why don't you sell sex? There's a place you can do it safe," and "safe" was a really important thing to her. She wanted somewhere where she was allowed to use condoms and she wasn't going to be hurt, as many people are hurt who sell sex illegally on the streets.

LM: Is that the biggest draw to working in legalized versus outcall or street prostitution, the safety factor?

AA: I think it's a huge piece of it for these women, and to answer your earlier question, this is a job for them. These women are there to earn money. They all are supporting someone else, a partner, a spouse, children, even their parents in some instances. And how they deal with it is again, very individual. Some shut their eyes and think about other things during the sex, and some actually reported to me they enjoyed the sex. It was a very individual experience for each woman. In terms of histories, there was much less sexual abuse than you see in other populations. It existed, but it exists among the general population as well. It just wasn't remarkably significant among this group of women.

LM: We also tend to think of prostitutes having a very high rate of drug addiction and alcoholism. Did you see evidence of that at Mustang?

AA: Drugs definitely existed and alcohol definitely was drunk there, but I didn't see women supporting their addictions by prostituting. Women experimented with drugs, but it wasn't everybody doing it. It was more representative of drug use in our mainstream society.

LM: It seems it would have been difficult to be a heavy drug user within the legalized brothels, because the women are there for such an extended period of time. Talk about their schedules.

AA: I think you're totally right. The houses are very much regulated. Their women work twelve-hour shifts during the week, and over the weekends they work fourteen-hour shifts. There are rules; there's a floor maid, who is responsible for them and is supervising them, and there's a chef there who's running the meals. If the women aren't eating lunch on time, they miss lunch. It's run like a business with a real time clock to it. I think for women who have drug addictions and are trying to support their habits by selling sex, it's hard to comply with a lot of the rules and expectations put upon them. I think a lot of them who come in hoping to work end up failing to survive there.

LM: Now when these women are on shift they spend day after day within the brothel, correct? How long do these terms typically last where they're working every day and don't leave the brothel except maybe on quick runs to the store with an escort?

AA: Again, every story was different. Some of the women are locals, so maybe they're there for just a couple days of the week and then they go home during the early part of the week when business is not typically as busy. Some of these women are coming from out of state, from as far away as Florida, Maine, Nebraska, so financially it makes more sense for them to come for a stint and stay for a couple weeks or months at a time and then go home and go back to their life. There was a graduate student there who was paying her tuition during the school year, so she just worked during the summer, three months solid.

LM: And she obviously made enough money to get her through the school year as a result.

AA: Exactly.

LM: Let's talk about the money made. At least at the Mustang Ranch, the women split fifty-fifty with the house.

AA: The women work as independent contractors, which means they negotiate their own prices, and prices can vary from each customer. So if a customer comes in who's really drunk and the woman doesn't want to service him, she can inflate her prices and basically opt out because hopefully he won't pay those prices. Typically, sex seemed to run somewhere between one hundred fifty dollars and five hundred dollars. If business is slow, women might reduce their prices. If there's a really heavy demand—the parlor's full of potential customers—women may up their prices.

LM: So it's a mini free-market economy. What might be the average a woman would make in a week's worth of work at Mustang?

AA: I'll tell you what they can make in a day, because it's easier to envision. A woman could make somewhere between three hundred dollars and fifteen hundred dollars a day.

LM: Can a woman who might be considered less attractive by the general population still earn a lot of money?

AA: It was remarkable watching the lineups. Just to make it clear, I've spent about seven months in the brothels of Nevada, not just Mustang Ranch, but a number of the other ones. But I lived at Mustang Ranch when I was there, so day in and day out I was sitting there. I would eat breakfast with the women in the cafeteria, I'd sit in the parlor with them on the couches with the clients, sitting at the bar with the women, just watching. And you'd see the lineup is a terribly diverse population, I mean, different sizes, different races, different ages, and the women all got picked. If they didn't get picked the women didn't stay. They were having to pay a small daily rent to stay there, so there was less incentive to stay if you weren't earning money.

LM: As you describe it, in many ways it sounds like a dormitory, because all the meals are taken there and there's a woman who handles the floor where the men come in. It sounds like so many other legit kinds of experiences but in a totally different way, because it's all about sex.

AA: Exactly right, and I think that was one of the biggest surprises for me: that there is a community and a sisterhood among the women. You also have this fierce loyalty and protectiveness exhibited by the ancillary personnel—the bartenders, the maintenance people, the laundry help. Then you have these other people from the community who somehow made their way into the brothel. There's a man who has a retired Greyhound bus that he drives from brothel to brothel selling clothes. One of my favorite stories, which is really quite poignant, is about a Vietnamese woman who comes in and does the women's nails. She came in very fearful at first, and she's become the women's confidant in many ways. It's a small subculture. It's utterly fascinating for that reason.

LM: Alexa, take us through the process. A customer walks in the door looking for sex. What happens?

AA: A customer is either dropped off in a cab or pulls up in his car or semi. There's an eight-foot electrically-controlled gate that encloses the entire brothel—both Mustang No. 1 and Mustang No. 2, which is just across the way and considered more of an annex. There's a sign posted on the gate stating that condoms have to be used; condoms have been required since 1988. The customer rings the doorbell on this gate, and somebody in the house is checking out the window to see who's at the door. Women aren't allowed in, and they're also assessing whether this person looks at least eighteen years of age. They'll buzz this customer in. The women in the house, in turn, have heard the doorbell, and by the time the customer has reached the front door the women have lined up. Some days there may be ten women in the lineup, on busy weekends there may be up to fifty. There's also a hostess who welcomes the customer and then says,

"Ladies, please introduce yourselves." And one by one the women give their names, all working names, and the men just stand there, just gaping, just staring. It's quite a spectacle to see this many women lined up in various degrees of undress, this many different physical types; it's quite awesome. Some men pick immediately; some go to the bar. If a man goes back to the room with a woman, that's where they negotiate prices. The women are not allowed to talk prices or sex acts in the parlor area.

LM: And that can be overheard, that negotiation?

AA: Correct. That is primarily so the house basically knows what prices are being set, because the house is expecting to get half of the money. So the woman talks prices, she checks his genitals for any signs of disease, any visible lesions, and then she will ask him to undress. Then she'll take the money up to the front cashier and deposit it before any sex occurs.

LM: The house doesn't want the women to rip it off and be taking more than their fifty percent cut, so the negotiation is overheard through a microphone in the room.

AA: Hidden, correct.

LM: And that supposedly is turned off once the negotiation occurs and the money is deposited with the cashier.

AA: I never heard people exploiting the microphone. When I heard there was a microphone, I thought people must be listening in. But it didn't happen.

LM: It probably gets pretty old in a hurry.

AA: I think it does, and I also think it serves a security purpose. If somebody's afraid that something is not going right in a room, if they haven't seen a woman come out of a room, they can flip on the mike and hear if the woman is okay in there. There's also an ATM machine there, which boggled my mind. There's this little ATM accepting most credit cards and bank cards, and it comes out with Nevada Novelties at Mustang Ranch. Most of them have some sort of euphemism or something innocuous as a name.

LM: You had an opportunity to observe the men, too. What are the types of men who are willing to pay this amount of money for sex and go to all the trouble of going to a brothel? Why do they do it?

AA: It's interesting. The men were truly as diverse as the women. Mustang actually serviced about 325,000 men a year. On the same day I saw a group of Japanese men coming off their bus with their interpreter on an organized sex tour, a professor from my medical school came in the door. So it's a very diverse family.

LM: That must have been an awkward moment for him.

AA: I didn't actually know him, but he knew I was there and he was very private. This speaks to a number of the men's experiences. This is a secret business; there's tons of stigma. It's legal in Nevada but that doesn't mean it's terribly legitimized, although I think it's better there than anywhere else in our country. We don't just shame the women, we shame the customers as well, and he was very nervous that if he shared where he worked with me—which hospital back in Boston—I might out him. But at the same time he wanted terribly to share his story. That's what this book is about, these people's personal stories, because they all want to be understood. They want to not be judged, but they want their story told.

LM: Is the shame that the men feel more related to the fact that they have to pay for sex that they're not getting in relationships or in the dating world, or does it come from other kinds of insecurities that maybe led them through the door in the first place?

AA: That's a really good question. I saw so many reasons men were going there. Some of these men, you think, aren't capable of having relationships on the outside, and in my book you meet a number of people who are virgins. There's a group of men on the Internet; they call themselves the cyber-whoremongers. It's a fascinating group of people. They invited me to one of their annual conventions, and a few of them confessed that they were older virgins in their forties and fifties and they chose to lose their virginity in a brothel. I think a lot of that came from a lot of fear of being unable to have a relationship on the outside. In the book I also describe the day a young virgin comes in with his father. It's a really interesting story about why his dad chose to bring him to the brothel. Then you have a professional golfer who has a girlfriend but is afraid to ask her for the kind of sex he wants. There were also men paying women just to talk, just to cuddle. Some of these men had partners at home. For them, being intimate, being vulnerable, crying, chatting, was not what they were doing with their partners at home. I walked away feeling that we still have so much trouble communicating our sexual needs and desires, and that's what these men seemed to be doing at the brothel. Somehow they felt safe to do it there but had terrible inabilities to get these needs met elsewhere.

LM: That story about the father who brings in his nineteen-year-old son is very poignant, because while it's not the typical example of a visitor to the Mustang Ranch, it is so sad. He brings in his son, who is experiencing what appears to be the early signs of schizophrenia, and he has been, among other things, teased by his fellow college students because he's a virgin. So dad, not looking at the other psychological problems that the son is having, thinks, well, if I can only get him laid that's going to solve the problems.

AA: Correct, and he was a white-collar gentleman who said he had never been to a prostitute before, but felt they were safe. He'd seen it on one of our television shows, I think *60 Minutes,* and he felt desperate to try to fix his son's problems.

LM: And the young man couldn't perform with the woman.

AA: That apparently is not unusual with some of the young men who come in as virgins, but what makes that story most poignant for me is the women's sense of pride in their work. I describe at length that woman's experience with this boy, whom she doesn't know has this psychiatric history until after we meet up at the end to talk about him. She just saw him as a young virgin who had trouble fulfilling the entire act, and she took her work very seriously. She extended his time, trying to make sure he had a satisfying experience. That amazed me. I hadn't expected to see the women take their work that seriously. I envisioned these were wham-bam-thank-you-ma'am, cold, heartless people who were just selling sex and not caring about who their customers were. That is not at all what my experience at Mustang Ranch was.

LM: You point out that in talking with the women about what they would be doing professionally if they weren't doing this, they name professions like nursing and teaching and caregiving kinds of professions.

AA: From daycare work to being a nurse or a doctor, jobs that were people-based. These women are doing a service in most of their minds.

LM: At one point a client with a particular fetish request that involved two women agreed to let you watch.

AA: The invitation to go into the bedroom stemmed from the women's sense of pride in their work as a service they were providing to these men. The woman who invited me in is one of the women I was very close to, and she wanted me to see what it was like to do the work they do in the bedroom. We have all these stereotypes, and I spoke earlier about my assumption that it was just this hard, impersonal sex. I don't want to give too much away and it's definitely described in the book, but this one particular man had a fantasy to be dominated, and he hadn't felt comfortable getting it satisfied anywhere else. He was in town for a convention. I don't even know if he was sure that he would actually do anything back in the bedrooms, but he overheard some of the women talking about the range of men's sexual desires and fantasies and said, "Gee, maybe I could." He went back to the room with one of the women and she said she could do it, although she had never done a dominance party. She invited Baby in, who was the woman who then invited me in to watch, and the two of them engaged in this event with this man.

LM: You mentioned it's not uncommon for a less-experienced woman to ask a more experienced one to come in and help in a particular type of scenario.

AA: Exactly, there is a lot of teaching that goes on from the more experienced women to the younger women, and again, that speaks to the sense of community in the house, and the work ethic. A lot of the women who have been in the business for a long time have a true sense of morality about how the business should be run, how professional it should be, and how safe it needs to be.

LM: So how was this for you? Was it the same as watching an adult film—was it that distant? Or was it a much different experience sitting there and seeing these three people engaged in sex just a few feet away?

AA: I definitely went through many different experiences in that instance of watching. There were times when I felt I could distance myself, but to have him smile at me, eye to eye, staring at me in moments which added to his fantasy of being watched and not being shamed by this fantasy, brought me immediately back to the moment. I felt terribly aware of where I was. It was pretty intense, the sex that this man wanted, and I'd never seen anything like it before.

LM: There was some pain that was inflicted. He says to you at the end of it, "You look like you need to lie down."

AA: I'm sure I did.

LM: So that was your first experience. The second time you witnessed sexual activity in one of the rooms was with another one of the women who wanted you to see a very different kind of sexual act play out, one that was much more conventional. And this is rather poignant because the man who's the customer still lives with his mom. He's apparently a very insecure guy who actually believes, or it's his justification psychologically, that he is helping out this woman by coming to visit her regularly.

AA: Even more interesting was that he thought he was doing her a favor because she wanted me to see that sex wasn't just these dominant fantasies, but that men were coming in to be treated tenderly and it was intimate for them. He allowed me in because he thought he was making her happy, and that was so important to him. He was terribly enamored of this woman; she was his girlfriend.

LM: It sounded like he may have never had a girlfriend in his life.

AA: I think he had seen a number of women in the brothels, but I agree. His father had brought him out to the brothels many years before, and had since passed away. This was where he had relationships with women.

LM: So in having these two experiences of observing, did that fundamentally change your perception of the work?

AA: I guess it just gave me a deeper understanding, which is the whole point of this book: to speak to people and hear their assumptions or preconceived notions about prostitution and present the real, complicated, human and controversial aspects of this business. This is the first book written by an outsider who spent time inside, so it's the only way that we know what this world was like.

LM: Given the access that you were granted, it sounds like the industry was hoping that having someone with respected academic credentials come in without an ax to grind might in some way validate legal prostitution. That had to be their thinking.

AA: I think in large part that fueled their support, eventually. Again, it took three years for them to let me do my original condom study. I also want to say that Nevada's brothels are a remarkable public health story. The women have been getting tested for HIV since 1986, along with other sexually transmitted disease tests. To date, there has never been a case of HIV among any of the women in the houses.

LM: And that's with, what, almost two-thirds of a million customers throughout the state each year?

AA: Exactly, and we're talking about three or four hundred women getting tested once a month. I think at this point there are over forty-two thousand HIV tests that have been run there.

LM: I know it's impossible if you're not in the room with every particular business transaction, but as far as you could tell, was there universal compliance with the condom mandate?

AA: That's what I tried to confirm with the first condom study. There really was. These women are very informed about what their risks are, and again I think a large incentive for being in the brothel is the opportunity to practice sex safely and know they have support, institutional support, in doing that.

LM: I want to talk about the women's relationships with the men in their lives. It seems that there's a very high incidence of women who are in relationships with men who, for lack of a better term, are largely shiftless.

AA: The relationships the women had with people on the outside, their partners, were very complicated and somewhat disturbing for me. Some of the women had the stereotypical pimp. I had been shocked to find in a legal industry there that you'd see the typical street pimp as you see him portrayed in the media, with multiple women working for him.

LM: If you're going to be a pimp with a stable of women, why would you be splitting their take fifty-fifty with a legal house of prostitution?

AA: I think it's very enterprising, actually. I think most of these men were not Nevadans. There's a notorious set of twins in Oregon who have multiple women who all look very similar, like *Seventeen* magazine cover girls.

LM: All of the women think that one of the twins is in love with them and looking out for their best interests.

AA: And they may not know he's got other women working in different houses; he may be working women up in Oregon on the streets. But the ones they send to the brothels, they're very well-maintained and controlled. These men don't need to worry that they're going to be picked up by vice on the streets in Oregon. They don't have to manage them day in and day out, so it made sense to me why they'd be willing to give up some of the money to give them more freedom.

LM: So why do the brothels cooperate with these pimps? It sounds like the brothels are very complicit in this.

AA: More so in the past. For the last ten or twenty years the brothels have become much less supportive. But in the old days when prostitution was operating in Nevada as a tolerated business in the Sixties and was first legalized in the Seventies, pimps actually worked to the advantage of the owners. The pimps managed the women and "disciplined" the women.

LM: So they were the hammer?

AA: Exactly. If one of the houses had difficulty with the women they'd call the pimp. The pimp would call to make sure the women were working, either by threatening them or some such sort of push, and the houses didn't have to worry about it. But philosophies change. The owners I met aren't supporting these pimps. They recognize these men are exploiting these women, and frankly it complicates the business. Time and time again women get into these huge brawls on the telephone with these men, and some of the women just pack up their bags and leave in a rush. That is not good for business, according to the owners.

LM: You make a point about the men who are in relationships with the women who work at Mustang Ranch, that some of them are pimps, but others are boyfriends and spouses who have very ambivalent feelings about the woman in their life doing this work.

AA: Correct; in my book there's an instance where I have the opportunity to speak with one of these husbands at length, and to hear about his ambivalence about what his wife does. My sense of the relationships—and let me just say, unlike some of the men who are partners to these women who don't hold jobs, who are managing the children at home and the women are earning the bread and butter—a lot of these men had full-time jobs. The one man you meet is basically an accounts manager at a manufacturing company; he works full-time, very long hours. I met a federal agent for the INS who's married to one of these women.

LM: And he gets stimulated from her describing her activities with the customers during their sexual activity.

AA: It plays into their intimate sexual life. So again, I found a very wide range of men. Let me say one thing: the women were enablers. These women are the providers, the breadwinners, the support people for their families, and time and time again I had to remark to myself about that. It made me wonder in some instances if the relationships were difficult because the women were choosing dysfunctional relationships. Then when I met the husband who is the manufacturing accounts manager, and he spoke to what his difficulties with her working were, I wondered how much of it was secondary to the fact that she was away from home for weeks at a time.

LM: In the case where you had a meal and spent an evening with one of the women at Mustang and her husband, they got into some pretty heavy stuff about how this had affected their sex life. When she got home from her extended stay at Mustang she was not up for sex. It was as though she just turned off that part of herself when she got home.

AA: I think a lot of it is just recuperation. These women are tired after working these hours and being away from home for periods of time. That's not to say all of them had trouble sexually at home, but some of the women did. What was interesting to me about that was her sharing that what worked for her sexually was not being the director, but being seduced by him, because she was used to running the show in the brothel's bedroom. It spoke to my assumption that these women were terribly confident sexually. Here they are satisfying such an eclectic mix of men, and yet she and a number of the other women confessed to being quite conservative in their home bedrooms.

LM: In so many cases you describe, the women want this conflicting reaction from the man in their life. They want the man to give them the freedom to do this and not to complain about them working in the brothel, and at the same time they want the man to not feel good about it and want his wife not to work in the brothel.

AA: It is a classic dilemma. There's a lot of autonomy that comes to these women, but at the same time prostitution is such a hard thing for us socially, and that affects these women, too.

LM: Have your attitudes about legal prostitution changed at all as a result of this?

AA: I think they had to. I went in thinking of prostitution, as many of us do, as this objectification—dehumanizing, humiliating for women—but what these women in Nevada showed me is that you can actually sell sex safely, without sexually transmitted diseases, and without violence. You can do it without the women being hurt, unlike what happens on the street. The literature on women and men selling sex on the street says that sixty or seventy percent report experiencing client violence. That just doesn't exist in the brothels, which led me to reassess. I'm a social realist. Prostitution is going to exist. There is a demand that is not going away, and there will be a supply. It begs the question: shouldn't we be protecting these people and enabling them to do what they're going to do safely, rather than punish and criminalize them?

I have been fascinated by Steve Allen since I was a boy, marveling at his versatility as a comedian, talk show host, pianist, composer, and writer. He was an entertainment Renaissance man to the nth degree. I have always thought he was the embodiment of what the television talk show host should be, hip to the cutting edge, musically savvy, facile with language, curious about people, and unafraid of failure.

Most people are familiar with Steve Allen as the multitalented man who created *The Tonight Show* and later hosted more than one thousand episodes of *The Steve Allen Show,* but in his later years, Allen became a highly controversial author. His critiques of American culture were candid, targeting not only people's lack of reasoning ability, but their ignorance on a wide range of important topics. As you will discover in this interview, Allen was also very concerned about what he saw as the coarsening of humor and culture. Allen was always very gracious and complimentary when he came to the KPCC studios; now that he's passed on, I will miss having the chance to talk to him.

Larry Mantle: Let's talk a little bit about the variety of your career. Over the last fifty years you've been a humorist, a writer, a musician, and more. Do you think it's possible for someone to start out today and do the things you have been able to do?

Steve Allen: I think frankly it would be quite difficult, even if we assume the fellow or the woman were fourteen times as talented as I may be. It would be difficult. To this day I run into situations where people suddenly reveal that only about eight minutes earlier did they learn that I write books, or if they are interested in books, they learn that I've written thousands of songs. There's no reason why the world should know all about me, that's no big deal, but people do have trouble fitting you into a niche if they don't know specifically what you are.

LM: What are some of the other changes that you've seen in your five decades in show business?

SA: I think the primary change is that show business generally, and certainly comedy, has gotten pretty darn dirty. When I say that, I don't say it the way Mother Teresa might, or Jerry Falwell. I'm just one of the boys morally, as I perceive myself. But a lot of just regular guys are now really sick of the degree to which garbage talk not only is permitted—I guess there's a Constitutional issue here—but is encouraged in the marketplace. A year or two ago when Andrew Dice Clay was hot, he was able to fill the enormous room called Madison Square Garden. Probably that night, no other of the great comedians, the ones who are many times funnier than Mr. Clay, could have done that. The realization it leads to is that there's a big market for garbage and ugliness and viciousness.

LM: Interestingly, Andrew Dice Clay's career has really been on the wane since that peak.

SA: Well, Howard Stern is going through that same sort of pattern right now. I think that anything one might say critical of Howard he really wouldn't object to, because he's trying to shock. Sometimes if you say something and people are offended, the offender is literally surprised. What? You objected to that? I didn't mean any harm. I love Polish people, or whatever the subject might have been. And they're speaking the truth. They didn't mean to do harm. But he means to do harm. He means to talk rudely and vulgarly, and nevertheless that's what made him big. He was never big before until he resorted to total filth. So what that says about the American people is a little scary.

LM: What do you think fuels the trend toward the shock comedy that we have today? Do you think it's an anger and hostility that people are experiencing, and that connects up with the crudity?

SA: Yes. That is one little mosaic chip of the large and ugly and disturbing picture. Our society is not only in trouble, we're in a state of serious disarray, and there are apparently no exceptions. There are exceptional individuals I'm sure, but there are no institutions which are not tarnished by the general sleaze and ugliness and violence to which we are now daily subjected, not only from the news media and the entertainment media, but from life. Of course, life has always been difficult. The human predicament is notoriously uncertain and dangerous. You find that in the most ancient literatures, and you can see it in the daily news. So it's not the fault of television that life suddenly got tough; it always has been. But the difference is one of degree and one of response to tragedy and war and sickness and so forth. There have always been social problems, but now people seem to be responding with an anger, a nihilism, a negativity.

LM: There seems to be a tremendous amount of anger, and I wonder if that speaks to information overload, being constantly exposed to the savagery of humanity. Have we become so helpless that one of the ways we lash out is through comedy, which has always been a vehicle for dealing with this kind of pain?

SA: There's a lot of choosing up sides, and a good deal of hostility. The other side of that particular coin is a lack of sensitivity. I write several jokes a day. It isn't difficult to do material of that sort, but now there's a big market for it. So you have these two problems side by side. One is the violence problem; the other is the sexual irresponsibility problem. But now it's all in your face, as we say. I don't know whether today's stars or superstars are any more depraved than those of thirty or fifty years ago. But in the old days it was all kept under wraps. I honestly do think that things are worse now. I think that there are more people misbehaving now, especially when they have very little excuse. They're making nine million a year, so they don't have the excuse that totally poor people do whose daughters are sick and they need medicine so they break into a room and steal it or some money. The poor have always had an excuse for their economic crimes. But now you have men who are being paid literally twenty and thirty million dollars a year, and still they go to jail because they tried to get another twenty million. How the hell rich do you have to get before you get satisfied?

LM: It's absolutely staggering. Late-night television has of course not been the same since the *Tonight Show,* that you originated, began. What are some of your thoughts on late-night television? Who do you think is doing it well?

SA: I honestly don't have any more valuable insights than just some guy who drives a truck and watches TV late at night a lot, because I don't. I'm usually asleep by ten or eleven, and if I am up a bit later I will always make it a point to catch Ted Koppel's show, because for thirty minutes you're a little less dumb than you were before you watched it.

LM: And it's the highest rated of all the late-night shows.

SA: That's the first good news I've heard in a while. Thank goodness that shows like that and *60 Minutes* and *Primetime* and shows that are an admirable, constructive use of television are succeeding. If the good shows were failing and only the garbage was succeeding, that would be intolerable. I don't really watch the late shows very much. I suppose even if all three or four of them were absolutely rotten, one of them would still be in first place. So the fact that one is in first place does not always mean that one is marvelous. Hosting a talk show is the easiest gig probably in the history of the job market, compared to brain surgery and writing a novel. When you're interviewing me here, you have to keep on your toes intellectually more than if you had nine guests tonight. But the people who do have nine or five or six or three guests a night are provided with written questions that are on cards. And you can have them on cue cards if you don't like to be caught looking down at your desk. All you do is see the words, and it says, "Hey, Jim, good to see you again. How's that picture doing?" Now, that requires obviously no talent. So if you look at the history of talk show hosts who have done well as hosts or hostesses, the first thing you notice is that very few of them have had talent. Some have. The big question is, what did the person do for a living before he or she hosted a talk show? In the case of Johnny Carson, he was a professional comedian. That's talent. Jack Paar was a professional comic. I did the same thing; I did comedy before I did talk shows, so that covers us. Merv Griffin and Mike Douglas, who had long twenty-year runs at that, were professional singers. Also, Merv played the piano nicely. But this begins to be a short list, whereas you can think immediately of about thirty-seven people who have hosted those shows and don't have any discernible talent. I use the word "talent" of course in the traditional theatrical sense, not in the loose sense according to which everybody on Earth has talent for making a cherry pie or hitting a home run or whatever.

A listener, commenting on shifting standards for what is offensive, recalls one of Allen's shows from 1964, when a gorilla character ended a scene by "waving an up-thrust middle finger at the audience and you."

SA: Yes. I can assure you that was the stagehand's own idea, or the gorilla's as the case may be, and it had not been cleared beforehand. But you're absolutely right. That was offensive to many people. At the time, the four hundred people in the studio audience laughed a lot because it was funny. By the way, I have never said that if something's dirty it can't be funny. Some of the funniest things in the world are filthy.

LM: And you're the Abbot of the Beverly Hills Friars Club, so it's not as though you're offended by dirty jokes.

SA: Well, believe it or not, I am offended by some of them. It depends. I make distinctions, as we all should. But the caller is making a valid point here; tastes do change. In fact, if you get a thousand people they don't fall into just two or three categories; they're in a thousand separate categories, each with his own opinion and standards of judgment. But there is the general perception, and it's entirely accurate, that things have gone, to speak very clearly, all to hell within the last fifteen years or so, compared to how it was in the Fifties. In the Fifties, we just laughed at Sid Caesar and Jackie Gleason and Ernie Kovacs and Red Skelton, because they were funny. It was really that simple. And there was never a single moment on their shows when one of them said, "Boy, you know, it's been going great for the last two or three years, but couldn't we work in a little vulgarity and a little nudity and a little, you know, really filthy language here to help things out?" The subject never came up. It was not that you wanted to and were censored. The gentlemen themselves never thought of that. But starting with, like the gorilla that night, a little grain of sand here, a grain of sand there, and gradually the dikes have eroded. I realize that's a straight line too, but we can't stop for everything.

LM: It seems to me that the context of how the humor is presented can help content in a lot of different ways. I think of Richard Pryor, who was a real comedic genius in his prime, because he could bring the vulgarity of the street to mainstream America.

SA: Exactly. He was something like the black Lenny Bruce. And I'm putting both men up, not down, in saying that. I was a personal friend and big admirer of Lenny's work. They were not just doing dirt for dirt's sake; they were making a philosophical point, a point of social commentary. There was often great wisdom in what they had to do or say or reveal, and that's totally different from what the Andrew Dice Clays do. There are a lot of people doing him now, if you can believe it, getting the laughs just by saying the words and also adding some shocking content, putting down women or, you know, Catholics or tall people or whatever they might be putting down.

A listener asks if Lenny Bruce was censored by the FCC.

SA: I have no specific recollection, but he was often subject to censorship of one kind or another. He was often intimidated by policemen, and I say that as a pro-cop type myself. The police in New York and Chicago and some other cities—they should've been out in the street protecting women—would sit all night long in a club to trap Lenny into making some reference to religion or politics, and then they would arrest him on some usually stupid charge. So he was subject to that kind of censorship. I booked him on television a few times. He was very rarely hired for TV, for obvious reasons.

LM: One of your many talents is as a musician. You're a pianist and you've written jazz. You have a CD called *Steve Allen Plays Jazz Tonight.* Is it fun to work with young, talented guys who really love jazz?

SA: Young or old, that part doesn't really matter. It's just an honor, because jazz is the only art form America ever created, so it's quite special. Not every example of it. If your cousin plays jazz, maybe he doesn't play it so well, so just jazz all by itself does not get you into heaven. But it's so important culturally, particularly because of the great contributions of black performers over the last seventy-five or eighty years. It's really tragic that some young black teenagers and children, through no fault of their own, don't even know the names Count Basie, Louis Armstrong and Duke Ellington. I've checked this out. There are many fine black instructors who are trying to teach them about that, because it's really important. It's not just a guy who had a hot season once and sold a couple of records. We're talking about true artists. They must not be forgotten.

LM: Especially when it's so often said that black culture goes unappreciated in America. Here is clearly an area where black culture has not only been influential, but it has predominated.

SA: It's a pity if some fourteen-year-old kid, again through no fault of his own, is into, as we say, rap, but doesn't know from Fletcher Henderson.

A listener asks Allen if he can predict how long Howard Stern will last.

SA: Gosh, I don't know. I wish Howard personally nothing but good health. I don't dislike him personally, I just dislike what he's doing. And I think if you put the question to the American people, probably seventy-four percent of them, a really round number, would dislike what he's doing. If you could control the audience for vulgarity, there could be a separate niche for it, as there is for printed pornography. There is even a psychological argument that some people seem to need pornography, maybe they can't make it without that. So I'm not getting into that particular issue, but the real harm comes not when two fifty-seven-year-old men tell each other dirty jokes while they're out fishing. It's when they sit in front of a television camera and tell those same vulgar stories and seven-year-old children are watching. That's the point at which it becomes a social issue. You need some censorship. You already have it; it's called "law." We have laws of libel and slander. You are not permitted to just say anything under any circumstances.

A listener asks if the shows Allen did for PBS will ever be available on video.

SA: They are available on video now. They're a little hard to locate, but they are available. And so are audio tracks of all twenty-four of those one-hour *Meeting of Minds* shows. More good news is that the scripts, along with some analytical commentary of those shows, are available in book form. There is an interactive TV game that has been developed called *Meeting of Minds,* so that will go on forever. I wish I could say the same about myself.

LM: Speaking of which, you look terrific. Do you want to keep on working as long as your health keeps going strong?

SA: Comedians as a class don't retire, because there's no reason to. In fact, creative people generally don't retire. There's sometimes the illusion that they have, but that's usually because of the sad fact that nobody's hiring them anymore. Those actors who sold physical beauty, men or women who were just so dazzlingly attractive that they were magical on the screen, the day unfortunately comes when Mother Nature does that nasty thing to them and their beauty is gone. Sometimes they never work again if all they were giving you was beauty.

LM: Well, typically it seems to me actors get better with age.

SA: As a matter of fact there are cases, not many, of men who were really not very good at acting early in their careers and got not only good, but quite good. Clint Eastwood and John Wayne—two true superstars and deservedly so—I think they would say themselves, were they to be consulted, that they weren't doing a very good job as actors in their early films. But the talent was in there just waiting to blossom, waiting to be experienced and developed, and it came out. And then there are those who are always good, the Robert De Niros and the Al Pacinos and the Marlon Brandos, and they seem to get better as the years roll by. Comedians, since it doesn't matter what they look like, as long as they get laughs, can go on forever.

LM: Composing seems to be one area where it's very tough to keep a long career. For some reason people have a period where they say musically what they have to say, and then it's very hard to keep coming up with new things.

SA: It's not so hard for them to keep coming up with new things, although I'm a poor judge because I wrote four hundred songs in one day. I'm a freak in that regard. Don't use me as a measuring stick. But it has been the case with many of our greatest composers that they had two or three hot years, gave us ten or twelve or fourteen marvelous songs as good as anybody ever has written, but nothing much since. We won't mention names because some of them are good friends, but I think these guys are still capable of writing as well as they did ten or fifteen or twenty years ago, but the market changes now. If Jerome Kern, who I think was the best American composer—and Gershwin thought so, too—came along today as a twenty-one-year-old and wrote the same kind of music he did originally, I think he would have a very difficult time getting anyone to record his work. There is no market today for "All the Things You Are" or "The Song Is You."

LM: Is it frustrating for you when you say something that goes over the head of your audience? I remember an incident at a Playboy Jazz Festival, where there was the haze of marijuana over the bowl, and you said something like, "Well, this isn't a rock concert, but it certainly smells like a rock concert." The audience didn't understand it and they started booing.

SA: Well, either they got it, or they just didn't think I should be joking about their religion.

LM: But it's got to be tough when that happens.

SA: Well, in that case you have twenty thousand people in the audience, and even if 912 of them object, you still have the others with you. So that was no problem. But there are cases where an audience just doesn't get a joke. It's not their fault if they never heard of John Nance Garner before and I do four minutes on him. They're not going to laugh because they don't know whom I'm talking about. This is by the way mentioned in the other book of mine you were talking about a while back called *Dumbth*, about the decreasing intelligence in the American mindset. I've discussed this with Bill Maher and a number of other young comics. Guys who say, "Well, let's see, what's in the news today?" and then do nine jokes about today's news, such as Jay Leno does, and Johnny did before him, and Bob Hope did before that, and Will Rogers did before that. They actually depend on the fact that a certain large percentage of any given audience knows what they're talking about. And if you don't know what the term NAFTA means, or you don't know something about Janet Reno because it was only in the afternoon's papers and you were standing in line to get in at that time, you won't understand the joke, which means you won't laugh.

LM: And if what literacy means in our age today is popular culture alone—not politics, not social issues, not history—then it means comedians are going to be forced to either deal with popular culture or day-to-day life that everybody experiences, but nothing on a conceptual level beyond that.

SA: You don't get much of the Will Rogers type of political commentary. You get some from Will Durst, a comedian, but not a great deal. There never was a great deal. Mort Sahl had that end of the business pretty much to himself.

A listener says he found the Crazy Guggenheim character from The Jackie Gleason Show *offensive, and asks Allen what he thought of him.*

SA: Many people did. A very clever, talented, funny comedian named Frank Fontaine did that as one of his characters. He eventually had to stop it; so many people objected who had sons who were either brain damaged or handicapped by loss of oxygen at birth or other reasons, and who talked very much as did the Crazy Guggenheim character. Finally Frank couldn't do that anymore.

A listener asks if any of Allen's old shows or appearances are available on video.

SA: There are couple of compilations that were brought out about two or three years ago. Sometimes they are broadcast on cable TV. For example, there was one of my old sketches, which come to think of it is in *Make 'Em Laugh,* it's called "The Prickly Heat Telethon." It's a satire on a typical Jerry Lewis-type telethon with the announcer's sidekick and the guy from the delicatessen who provides the sandwiches and wants lots of free plugs for that. It's all the stock characters of telethons and it's a classic sketch, if I do say so myself. It runs about twenty-two minutes. I should also mention that for the last two years on the Comedy Central cable channel, my old Sunday-night show with Louis Nye, Don Knotts, Tom Poston, all that great gang, has been available.

LM: *Meeting of Minds* has probably been as talked about as anything you've done, despite the fact it's only one aspect of all the work you did on television. Were you amazed by the impact that show had?

SA: Not really, although there were certain aspects of the reaction that did come as a surprise. For those who don't know what we're talking about, I'll say that *Meeting of Minds* is just one more talk show, but our guests were not starlets and rock stars. They were such people as Aristotle, Francis Bacon, Darwin, Voltaire, Luther. In other words, important figures from history who had affected everyone on Earth and the fate of the world. So I thought that we would get a lot of criticism because we got into some very fundamental issues. Is there a God? Is evil okay? A lot of basic questions like that. And since we gave all sides a chance for their moment in court, I thought some people wouldn't like that. To my great and pleased surprise, conservatives loved it, liberals loved it, communists loved it, anti-communists loved it, white, black, purple, north, south, every philosophical camp loved that show.

Milton Berle

February 3, 1992

hough "Mr. Television" is no longer with us, I'll never forget the brief time I spent with him on air and off. Given Berle's importance in entertainment history, and his reputation for sometimes being cranky, this was a conversation I was anticipating with both excitement and trepidation.

However, I ended up spending a very funny forty-five minutes with the elderly Berle before we even got into the studio. He was full of hilarious, often profane, stories that made me feel like I was getting my own personal performance of Berle hanging out at the Friar's Club in Beverly Hills.

At one point, I mentioned to him that I enjoyed cigars, and we talked about various brands that were his and my favorites. After talking for a bit, Berle asked where the men's room was. I accompanied him, and needing a pit stop myself, I joined him, side by side at the urinals. In the midst of our conversation, Berle reached into his coat pocket and pulled out one of his favorite cigars. He handed it to me with his compliments and highest recommendation, and left me with an image and memory that I will never forget.

Milton Berle joined me for this interview on the occasion of a local film festival highlighting his many roles in movies in the years before he became a fixture in American homes.

Larry Mantle: This Berle Film Festival must be exciting for you.
Milton Berle: Oh, it's wonderful. Of course, especially because there's a slight charge. No, I'm kidding. Here's how this came about. My very good enemy, pardon me, my very good friend, Paul Werth, who, well, he's been more than a friend. He's actually a total stranger,

that's what he is. No, he's more than a friend. He's a very brilliant writer, producer and director. He came to me and he said, "Milton, young people today only remember you from being a clown and a wise guy, throwing one-liners, doing shtick and physical comedy with powder puffs and seltzer and pies from television. That's all they remember of you. But they don't realize that you have done so many motion pictures prior to even starting on television back in 1948." I did. I made about forty pictures at Twentieth Century Fox and all the big studios around there. I played different parts, different characters. I didn't play Milton playing Milton. So he said, "I think it's about time that we showed some of the good pictures and great parts that you played. I think the audience should see the other side of Milton." Of course, he doesn't mean my backside.

LM: Not the backside.

MB: So I said, "Hey, why not? What could we lose?" But I'll tell you, one of the reasons why he's doing it, and I think it's a wonderful reason, is that all the receipts from this Berle Film Festival will go to the American Lung Association on behalf of my late wife, Ruth Berle, who passed away from cancer in 1989.

LM: We should mention some of the films that are going to be screened: *Always Leave Them Laughing* and *Margin for Error*. Also, *New Faces of 1937*.

MB: *Always Leave Them Laughing* was done in 1949. It was a musical, and it has Virginia Mayo, Bert Lahr, Alan Hale, and Ruth Roman. It was a story that is an important background story, the bottom line. The other one you just mentioned was *Margin for Error,* which was made in 1942. The stars of the picture were Otto Preminger—he also directed—Joan Bennett, and yours truly. It's really a wonderful piece of material that stands up so well today in the Nineties that it could be revived or revised for somebody else. I play a New York Jewish policeman—it's during wartime in '42—who is assigned to guard the Nazi embassy on Park Avenue. Well, the conflict is terrific. Preminger is the consul. And he looks at me, and he speaks like that, and the conflict is terrific. There are laughs but it is really more of a serious role. Those are the first two.

LM: There's also going to be *New Faces of 1937*.

MB: *New Faces of 1937* is really uproarious to me because that was, what, how many years ago?

LM: We're in '92 now, so fifty-five years ago.

MB: In that picture we had Parkyakarkus. You never heard of him. He was a Greek comedian. He is the father of that very wonderful comedian, Albert Brooks.

LM: Really?

MB: Yes. And his mother was in the picture, Parkyakarkus's wife, Thelma Leeds, who is now retired from show business. She is the mother of Albert Brooks. Also in that picture was Harriet Hilliard, who married—

LM: —Ozzie Nelson!

MB: —Ozzie Nelson, and is the mother of Ricky Nelson and the Nelson family.

LM: So what was in the water during the filming of this movie that led to the next generation of stars coming from the cast?

MB: Well, I want to tell ya something. It's remarkable. I don't know if I should say this or not, but this picture, *New Faces of 1937*—it's in black and white, of course, and it's made this many years ago, but the story line is the exact story line that was produced years later for *The Producers*.

LM: Great film. Hilarious film.

MB: Hilarious. I just want to say I had nothing to do with the writing of *New Faces,* but it is the same story.

LM: You started out as a very diminutive five-year-old actor, is that right?

MB: Not as an actor, Larry. I started out as a boy model. I used to model clothes and boys' hats. Remember the Buster Brown shoes with the Buster Brown boy?

LM: Yes.

MB: With the dog. My name is Buster Brown. I live in a shoe. This is my dog, Tige, he lives there, too. That's yours truly.

LM: That was you.

MB: In 1913. I have the picture with the Buster Brown. I was in silent pictures and all that stuff, with Chaplin and Douglas Fairbanks, Sr., and Mary Pickford. So this is not my first year in the business. I've gone through the blood, sweat, and cheers, but mostly blood and sweat. But it was all worth it.

LM: I can't imagine there's anyone else who has a career approaching yours in terms of length who's still working as you are. I don't know when George Burns started.

MB: Well, George Burns started in 1910, and I started three years later.

LM: Okay.

MB: George is now ninety-six. God bless him. I was at his party the other night. He was there, but he didn't know it. I'm kidding, George, I'm kidding. There's that terrible joke that's going around. Somebody said to George, "George, I hear that when George Burns orders three-minute eggs, they make him put up front money." Terrible. But he's healthy, boy, I want to tell you. Can I tell you something about Burns?

LM: Yeah.

MB: You know, I smoke cigars often, off and on. I never smoked a cigarette in my life. I never had a drink of liquor in my life. I don't know what beer tastes like. I don't eat red meat. I never did. But here's the switch: George Burns has done everything, I mean everything, from his youth. Do you know that George smokes twenty cigars a day?

LM: Wow.

MB: He drinks two martinis a day and two brandies a day. Do you want to tell me that's not the genes? It's the genes. And he just keeps going on. In fact, he's booked at Caesar's Palace when he's one hundred. So God bless him.

A listener asks Berle who his inspirations were when he was young.

MB: I didn't always tend to go to comedy. I started out as a straight kid actor doing straight parts in silent pictures. I never started throwing lines and wisecracks and one-liners until I was about fourteen. Now that sounds ridiculous, but I started when I was five, so it was years later. I did put people on the pedestal whom I wanted to be like. They were vaudeville stars and Broadway stars, such as the late and great—maybe everybody doesn't remember him—Ted Healy, who had the Three Stooges with him. He was flippant; he was aggressive;

he was ad lib; he threw lines. We had great comedians like Lou Holtz and Eddie Cantor and Jolson. In that era we always put people we wanted to be on the pedestal.

A listener asks what there was between Berle and Joyce Mathews that compelled them to marry and divorce each other twice. He says he read that they fought, and that Berle was a night person, while Mathews wasn't.

MB: That's right. The thing that propelled me to marry Joyce Mathews in the first place was because we hit it off very well, and she was one of the sweetest, and still is one of the sweetest and most charming women I've ever met. She was only a girl at the time. She was the most beautiful-looking blonde that I ever saw in my life. She was Miss Florida, and I think at one time was going to become Miss America. But that wasn't the reason. It wasn't just the beauty. It was her easiness, her sweetness, her sensitivity. We really hit it off great. Then we couldn't have any children—she couldn't, and we adopted a little baby by the name of Vickie. She's forty-six now, and she's married. And she has children, my grandchildren. The reason that I married Joyce the second time was what this musical comedy that's going to be on Broadway is all about. It's about my mother and myself. It's a silver cord story, where I couldn't break that cord with my mother. Everything was, "Milton and me."
LM: The "Me" is your mother?
MB: Yes. Unfortunately, I love my mother desperately, but she wanted me for herself. She didn't care if I slept with somebody or went out with a chick, but don't get married. That happened throughout my whole career. What a little boy learns, he never forgets. My mother did push me as a stage mother, but that isn't the basis of this story. The basis is marriage-divorce, divorce-marriage. She wanted me for herself. And, God love her, may she rest in peace, she was a great woman, but you have to break the ties once in a while, right?

A listener asks about Harold Lloyd, and whether Berle thinks tastes in humor have changed over time.

MB: Harold was a very, very close friend of mine. We used to have lunch in the later years, at Nate 'n' Al's delicatessen in Beverly Hills. I was a big fan of his, and I think that he was a big fan of mine. I learned a lot from Harold Lloyd by watching his pictures, his reactions and his takes. We worked nothing like each other, because he played that all-American schnook, and I played the all-American flippant wise-ass. Nothing is new that's old. Nothing is old that's new. Everything has been done before. There's just switches. If you look back in the annals of comedy, you'll know that even before Chaplin, who was the greatest, it was done in a different style. Today with our new young breed—and I'm for them, I'm rooting for them—they don't know that what they're doing is not new. Who's doing it is what makes it new, their attitude. I don't see any difference in comedy, especially physical comedy, because the pie in the face will last after I'm gone and you're gone, or the open hole where the kid falls in it, or slips on a banana. That was proved twenty-five, thirty-five years ago in the picture that I made, *It's a Mad, Mad, Mad, Mad World*.

LM: When the *Texaco Star Theater* ruled the television airwaves, theaters, restaurants, so many different businesses found their clientele dramatically down the night when it would come on. That must have been an incredible feeling, to know that you're in this brand-new medium of television, and that so much of the country's shutting down to watch you.

MB: I was taken by surprise. I didn't know it was going to be that strongly accepted. I didn't know what television was going to be like. No one knew. I never knew they were going to put a man on the moon and hit a golf ball off it, or put satellites in space. I did it as a risk, but I had millions of people in front of me, or hundreds of thousands, and I didn't know it. One thing I did have in my favor, which I don't think anyone else had, was that I faced a live audience in my career in vaudeville. I flopped and I did good, and I didn't do good and got laughs, and I didn't get laughs. But I faced a live audience. All the shows that I did from '48 to '54 were all live, and you couldn't change it if you goofed. You made a blunder or a blooper, or you didn't get a laugh, and a joke died. Baby, it died. Then you'd have to go in another direction and get out of it. If anybody made a mistake, you couldn't take it over. So it was interesting to me that after two weeks of the Texaco show, it became just like a big whirlpool. It just boomed and boomed, and from thousands it went to millions of people after they bought sets.

LM: You were a television salesman's best friend.

MB: Well, that's the great Joe E. Lewis line. "Well, when Milton Berle was on, he sold millions of sets. That's one million and two, because I sold my set. My uncle sold his set."

A listener asks Berle what changes he would make if he were a network executive.

MB: Oh, boy. That's too tough. You'd need a telethon for me to tell you. I can't answer that question.

LM: Could you mention maybe a couple of things about TV that—

MB: Nope. I will not leave myself open. If I do, I'll write a book, and it'll fill about two thousand pages.

LM: Would you consult with a network executive if he or she came to you?

MB: I'd be very, very glad to do it for them if they got a pen and a check. I think there are a lot of things that can be improved, a lot of things wrong.

LM: Do you have any favorite shows that you like now?

MB: I don't watch television. I really don't.

LM: Mr. Television doesn't watch television?

MB: No, I don't watch comedy shows. I maybe watch the *Golden Girls* or something like that. Or I watched Carroll O'Connor in *All in the Family,* but that's past. I watch news, and I watch *60 Minutes* and *20/20.*

LM: That's where the comedy material comes from.

MB: That's the great joke that I still use once in a while, that I don't do political jokes because they usually get elected.

A listener asks about one of Berle's old Christmas radio shows from 1947.

MB: That was with Arnold Stang and Frank Gallop, my straight man. That was a very clever show. You know who wrote that show, may he rest in peace? His name was Nat Hiken. He was one of the great writers; he died too young. He died when he was fifty-four. He wrote *Car 54, Where Are You?*, and he also wrote *The Jackie Gleason Show*, and wrote for Fred Allen. That Christmas show was the one about, "Hear ye, hear ye, there's a meeting in town tonight." I remember that very well.

LM: How can you? That was 1947. How do you have such a clear memory?

MB: If you want to come to my files and my archives, I'll show you, because I got six-and-a-half million jokes in the computer on any subject you want. And I have every script that I've ever done.

LM: Really?

MB: Another person in comedy was Jack Albertson; he was my straight man. He was a darling man. I remember one scene that Nat Hiken wrote. He was selling me Christmas cards in July. That's the brain that Hiken had. Albertson was a doll. We lost him. We had a lot of wonderful people on that show. We had a few guest stars once in a while. Those shows are all syndicated now. So they may pop up once in a while.

A listener asks whether Berle found any difference between radio and television in terms of the stress factor.

MB: Oh, yeah, the stress factor was much stronger on television, because you fought a time clock, and you did everything live. And when you were doing radio, you read off the sheet, and everything was fantasy to the mind of the person listening. They could fantasize. Like the Jack Benny line, "Your money or your life." That's the standard joke, right? They could fantasize. It was much easier in radio, the stress was different. The stress in television was to be prepared every weekend. I didn't do twenty-two shows a year on television; I did thirty-nine shows a year.

A listener recalls the episode of I Love Lucy *in which Berle did a female impersonation, and asks how he came to do so much of that over the years.*

MB: When I was on television with my own show back in the late

Forties, I did stumble on it. We came out here in the Fifties to do the show from Burbank. My mother and I were passing Frederick's at Hollywood and Vine. I said, "Gee, I've worn every different costume for an opening: here comes Milton dressed like an organ grinder; here he comes dressed like a sailor; here he is a tramp." I saw this exotic stuff with the garters, and I said, "Oh, I can't wear that." But I went in and purchased it. And my mother said, "I got an idea." I said, "If it's the idea I'm thinking of, I got the same idea." She went in and purchased a dress from Frederick's, and I came out in drag. That was the first time I wore a dress. In Frederick's, on Hollywood Boulevard. I gave them that dress; they have it in the back.

LM: I've seen it there in the museum they've got.

MB: That's the first dress I wore on television. And I don't know how to tell you this, but I enjoyed it. No, I'm kidding.

LM: You're going to be the guest star on an episode of *Fresh Prince of Bel Air*. What made you decide to do *Fresh Prince*?

MB: Strangely enough, and it may sound a little hokey, but it's true: I am a fan of the modern-day style of rapping and rock and roll and all that stuff. I'm a friend of M.C. Hammer, and I know this one, I know that one. I know Madonna, not as well as Warren. Or Sean Penn. I'm kidding, Madonna. I happened to receive a phone call from Quincy Jones, who owns the production company that produces *Bel Air*. He said, "Milton, I don't know if you would like to, but there's a script that we just wrote with you in mind as a guest star." I don't make too many guest appearances on sitcoms. I did *Lucy* and a few others and *Love Boat,* which was on a hundred fifty years. I said, "Well, send me the script, Quincy." So he sent me the script and I thought, "Oh, it's a good idea." The characters are the opposites of each other. It's a generation gap story. And here's this young black kid who's twenty years old against an 83-year-old Caucasian who hooks up with him in the hospital. We share the same room. The rapport starts, and it does work. It becomes funny, and yet it becomes very, very solid when it comes to the relationship we start with each other. In fact, they might want to make it a recurring role.

LM: You're open to doing that?

MB: Well, I'm very, very busy, especially making love, because I just got married.

LM: I know you got married, yes. So you have to keep up with that, of course.

MB: I think it's very important that you should be very comfortable with your frau or your girlfriend or your boyfriend, whoever it may be. I mean, there's something else besides show business, ha-ha. You know, Burns always talks about that. He says, "I chase women, but when I grab them I forget what for."

A listener asks Berle what kinds of cigars he smokes.

MB: I got a line here, but you can't do it on the air. I'll drop it off here with Larry and he'll read you the joke on that. I smoke very good ones. Unfortunately, you can't get Cuban cigars, because there's an embargo. I smoke good cigars from Davidoff, which just opened here in Beverly Hills. There are a lot of good cigars around. They're not Cuban tobacco; they come from Colombia or Nicaragua, or the Dominican Republic.

A listener asks Berle if he ever sang with a big band.

MB: No, but I wrote a lot of songs that were sung and played by the Big Bands. There's a cut on a Barbara Streisand album of a song that I wrote back in 1931. It's a parody. It's called, "Sam, You Made the Pants Too Long." [He sings] "You made the coat and vest fit the best. You made the lining strong. But Sam, you made the pants too long." I wrote a lot of the songs for Don Cornell back in the Fifties. And I wrote [he sings], "Lucky, Lucky, Lucky Me." "I'm a lucky son of a gun." And I wrote [he sings], "I Want No Other One, Dear." A lot of big songs.

LM: Song writing has really been more of a hobby for you than anything, hasn't it?

MB: Oh, I don't think so.

LM: No?

MB: No. You take that back.

LM: I take that back. I'm sorry.

MB: No, it was very, very fruitful. I belong to ASCAP and I still get residuals and everything like that.

LM: I just wonder where you find the time to do songwriting on top of everything else.

MB: Oh, I find time for everything.

LM: This hour has gone much too quickly.

MB: It's all over? Well, Mr. Mantle, being a good friend of your namesake, Mickey, how did you get the name "Mantle?"

LM: No relation.

MB: No relation?

LM: My parents gave it to me. That's it.

MB: Well—

LM: We're out of time. But thanks so much.

MB: We're out of time. God bless you.

Peter Bogdanovich

May 3, 2002

Over the first twenty years of *AirTalk* I've interviewed many top directors and stars, some of them true students of the medium's history, others anything but. But I think Peter Bogdanovich is in a class by himself when it comes to knowledge of film history. As a young man, he befriended, and spent significant time with, many of the greatest film directors in history. He's written two superb books full of conversations he conducted with legendary directors and actors.

Bogdanovich belongs among the elite of American film directors for such movies as *The Last Picture Show, Paper Moon, They All Laughed, Mask,* and *What's Up, Doc?* He has been a three-time guest on *AirTalk,* but I chose to include this interview because his movie *The Cat's Meow* was just opening, and it's particularly fitting subject matter for Bogdanovich. The film is set in 1924 Hollywood, and takes us aboard William Randolph Hearst's yacht for a sail that includes Hearst's mistress Marion Davies, Charlie Chaplin, gossip columnist Louella Parsons, and studio system creator and producer Thomas Ince. Ince didn't survive the trip, and there's been much speculation over the years as to how he lost his life. *The Cat's Meow* offers one possible scenario.

Larry Mantle: *The Cat's Meow* seems like a perfect film for you to have made, given your love of early Hollywood. You've done books dealing with your friendship with Orson Welles and your conversations with him and with other noted directors over the years in Hollywood. You clearly have a love of this history.

Peter Bogdanovich: I got to know a lot of the people who created the foundation for the movies and I loved their movies, but I also got to know them as people. Not just Orson but Alfred Hitchcock and Howard Hawks and a lot of legendary names, and a lot of the stars, whether it was Cary Grant or John Wayne. So beyond having an affection and serious regard for the work, I also had a connection—a personal connection—with a lot of these legendary names. It feels like another lifetime, because when I met them they were all of them getting on in years and I was a kid, and so many of them have passed away. So there's a certain nostalgia, if that's the word, or a certain ache of remembrance, that connects with all this. *The Cat's Meow* is set in the Twenties, but it's not really about the movies because it doesn't have to do with shooting a movie. It all takes place on a yacht for a weekend.

LM: And it's about an unsolved Hollywood mystery.

PB: Yes, an unsolved Hollywood mystery.

LM: In those conversations that you had with some of the early film directors, I'm curious if you heard from them laments about the Hollywood of their later days, and whether you hear from directors now who look back at the Seventies and see that as a real golden era and bemoan what's happened to cinema in the past thirty years?

PB: It's so ironic, because when I was starting out we were bemoaning what was happening then. I remember saying to Orson Welles in the early Seventies, "Sad about what's happened to Hollywood; it seems to have all fallen apart." And Orson said, "Well, what do you want? The Renaissance only lasted fifty years, you know." There was a kind of golden age of movies, and my own dating of that is 1912 to 1962.

LM: That's your Renaissance?

PB: That's my fifty years of the golden age. Then there was a dark age from about '62 'til about '68.

LM: The Doris Day years?

PB: Except for Warren Beatty's and Arthur Penn's *Bonnie & Clyde* I thought nothing much happened of any interest at all in movies until John Cassavetes released a picture called *Faces* in '68. I had a picture in '68, as did a few other directors who were just breaking through.

LM: It was the Boris Karloff film you did in '68.

PB: *Targets,* yeah, which nobody saw, but it had a cult following, and then in '69 was *Easy Rider,* in '70 was *Five Easy Pieces,* '71 was *The Last Picture Show,* and so on. Then '72 was *The Godfather,* and that was the big re-birth of the new Hollywood. I was less sanguine about it because they were all just a bunch of contemporaries of mine and I was saying, "Why can't John Ford direct another movie?"

LM: It raises the issue of, when you're in it, the people don't know it's a golden age. It's only in looking back that you can make that determination, as I suspect was also true for Ford or for Hitchcock. I'm sure they were so busy making movies when they were working, they weren't considering, "Oh, these are classics," or, "This is a golden era."

PB: I think you're right, and I think there was a lot of complaining going on in the golden age. Not everything was copasetic; I mean, the studios often were horrible. There were a lot of bad movies made. There was an awful lot of garbage created. There were good movies that were destroyed. There were directors who couldn't work at all. But nevertheless, you have to judge by the work, and the foundation of moving pictures as an art form and as entertainment happened in those fifty years. Everything that's followed is building on that or destroying it. I know directors who worked in the silent era who moved into talkies in 1929 and were saying, the end of movies was 1928, the last year of silent pictures, because that was the real art. Of course, they're not wrong. The real art of movies was based on moving pictures, a way of telling stories visually that had never happened before. There was no connection to theater once it really got going because there was no talk. Theater, after all, is talk, so it was an unusual, unique universal language. Everybody could understand what Charlie Chaplin was doing or Doug Fairbanks or Mary Pickford. They communicated their emotions—everything was silent. It was an extraordinary period. Sound changed it.

LM: It made it difficult to use that same kind of visual brilliance, because to underscore it with talk is to hit whatever the point is with a hammer so hard that it seems to undermine the visuals, if you know what I mean.

PB: I do know exactly what you mean. What's interesting is, if you look at the films made in the early Thirties, from '29 on to say '33, '34 (by which time they learned what to do with dialog), the directors who did the best work were the great silent directors who figured out how to do sound pictures. There were a few of them like Lubitsch, Lang, Hawks. Even as we progress up to '62, the most memorable moments in talking pictures always were visual. People say, "Remember that moment when?" And it's always an image. It's not a line of dialog usually. People don't remember dialog as well—I mean, there are a few lines.

LM: Yeah, *All About Eve,* movies where the dialog does stick.

PB: There are a few lines that come out, but basically what you do is you remember images—it's kind of like a dream.

LM: The influence of the French New Wave is often cited in 1970s Hollywood films, that period where you were talking about the rebirth of film after this period in the Sixties when it was moribund. I think that's very accurate, but I also think one of the big factors is the impact of psychology and psychiatry, that you had a kind of openness to self-examination in American culture that really had not been much a part of our heritage. We were workers more than intro-spective about ourselves, and I think when you look at films like *Five Easy Pieces* or *The Last Picture Show,* that the influence of that kind of self-examination is very evident.

PB: That's interesting, Larry. To be honest, I hadn't thought of it that way, but it's interesting. I didn't get into psychiatry or therapy myself until the Eighties. I needed it.

LM: I think it was part of the Zeitgeist, if you will. It was there whether you were in therapy or not.

PB: I think you're right. I think it's true. I think the first person who actually brought it into movies was Hitchcock with *Spellbound.* That seemed to be the first movie that dealt with psychiatry on any level. It was made fun of in its day, but it's an interesting movie. He does it even more in a picture that nobody liked called *Marnie,* but I don't know what I can say about that. It's a very interesting observa-tion and I think it's true, but there was a self-awareness and a self-con-sciousness to movies as well that came in the late Sixties. After all, the earliest American filmmakers didn't grow up wanting to be filmmak-ers, because there was no medium. So a guy like Jack Ford, he thought he'd be a sailor. Fritz Lang thought he was going to be an architect. Otto Preminger was a lawyer, so was Leo McCarey. They didn't grow up saying, "Gee, I want to be a movie director," and that's a very important point because the other lives that these directors had informed the work. Howard Hawks built racing cars and airplanes before he ever directed a movie, and you can see that intelligence, that knowledge about people who do that sort of thing. You see it in his pictures. It gives it a richness. The problem with a lot of us guys who came in, we were probably psychoanalyzing ourselves and the whole thing. It was part of the modern way of thinking, but we were self-conscious. We didn't bring a whole other life to it. Raoul Walsh, my God, he was riding, and he was in ships and he was a sailor and a cowboy and this kind of adventurous spirit that Raoul communicates in his movies.

LM: Bill Wellman and a lot of these guys.

PB: Yes, oh, God, yes. Wellman was a part of Lafayette Escadrille. So as we've gotten further away from the Seventies, the last thirty years, I think it's gotten worse, so you see movies by kids who clearly want to make movies and have seen some movies, but there isn't a lot of great film culture in our country.

LM: It seems to me that in journalism the rise of journalism schools has been a real mixed bag. On the one hand it gives journalists the tools of the trade, and shares the basic ethics of how you go about the process. But it also seems to have eliminated a lot of the people who came to it with other life experiences before it became professionalized, so to speak. I'm wondering if film is at all similar? The rise of film schools means many more directors have had much more technical training about making movies, but has that come at a price?

PB: I think so, because the technical aspects of making movies are not as difficult to learn. I don't know that it's been a great thing, the film schools. I'm probably the last film director who didn't go to film school, because many of my contemporaries did. I put myself through my own film school.

LM: You came from the film-nut camp of becoming a director.

PB: Well, no, actually. I started out as an actor when I was fifteen, and then when I was nineteen was moving to directing—I'm talking about theater—in New York. I was directing off-Broadway and then upstate New York and was acting and did some live television and so on as an actor and started to study movies as a potential. I was interested in movies, but just to learn about them. As I said, I put myself through my own kind of university by talking to the masters, by talking to all these fellows who were around, all these great directors who were still alive, perfectly happy to talk to me, happy that somebody'd seen their movies and liked them. I was talking to them for three reasons. One was so that I could learn something from them, not second-hand or third-hand, but first-hand. These are the fellows who made it, so it's not somebody interpreting it for me, it's him telling me why he did it that way. That was amazing—these extraordinary sort of master classes that I had privately with Hitchcock or Hawks or any of them. Sometimes it's hard to believe that it really happened to me. That was one thing. The other thing was, I wanted to popularize these people. Some of them were popular but I wanted to critically popularize them. I also wanted to preserve their memories. So there were a bunch of reasons why I did it, and that was my university course. One of the problems with film classes is that they're not taught by filmmakers, they're taught by critics or scholars or aficionados who've done a lot of research. So it becomes a little drier and not as exciting. Also, the emphasis is sometimes wrong. I remember a funny story: I was living in Los Angeles. I live in New York now, but I was living in Los Angeles in the Eighties or Nineties and my daughter had a date with some guy who was going to UCLA. So he was sitting in the kitchen and I came in and I said, "So, you're going to film school?" He said, "Yeah." I said, "What are you studying?" He said, "This semester we're studying Coppola, Peckinpah, Scorsese." I said, "Wait, wait, wait, what about Griffith? What about Hawks? What about Lubitsch?" "Oh, no. We don't study them." I said, "That's terrible. That's like jumping into history, skipping the first few thousand years and picking up somewhere around 1930." He looked a little abashed and said, "Well, next semester we're studying you!" That's no help.

LM: Going back to your second film, which won you all the great acclaim, *The Last Picture Show*. I'm curious: in looking at that film, which is a part of this whole new generation of Hollywood films, how does it relate in your mind to the earlier Hollywood movies? To me it seems so modern in its sensibilities. It is a film that I can't imagine having been made in the 1930s or 1940s.

PB: Oh no, it couldn't have been made, but that's interesting. I remember John Wayne telling me over the phone, "Geez, Peter, I saw your picture. I can't run that at home, I mean, I don't know what my wife would do. It's a good picture but I—" Because it was shocking. There was nudity, there was some swearing, but it was just the approach, the sexuality that we dealt with, hands going under skirts and things like that and people taking off their bras—that never was done in a movie. I can't say I thought of it this way at the time, but since you've asked me . . . What I think worked was the tension between the fact that it was told in a rather straightforward narrative style that was typical of well-made films, particularly American films. I don't even know quite how to describe this narrative approach, but it becomes part of you if you've looked at as many films as I have. I didn't try to show off with the camera. There was no jumping up and down to notice my technique. The technique was understated and in the classic style, and yet the material, what we were dealing with, was very surprising and modern and wasn't old fashioned at all, so there was a certain tension between the two that I think was piquant.

LM: I agree; the movie also had a lot of open space but a claustro-phobia in a town whose very survival is in question. And there was something to me about the pacing of it and the willingness to let scenes happen in some cases that are very slow, that made the film rife with so much more significance and so much more depth. That to me was very contrary to the kind of pacing that one sees in earlier films, where it sometimes seems as if there's a fear that the audience is going to abandon the movie if it goes too slow.

PB: That's true, and particularly today people don't take their time. Everything's just bang, bang, bang, but you know, if you look at a picture like John Ford's *The Grapes of Wrath,* it has a slower pace. It isn't really slow but it takes its time. It's leisurely, but I think it's very involving and really grabs your attention.

LM: And it makes the violence then stand out all the more when things do happen.

PB: Yeah, somebody complimented *The Last Picture Show* and said that I did a very unusual thing, I made boredom interesting.

LM: When you were in the process of making that movie, you did-n't have a lot of experience as a filmmaker. You'd done one feature to that point. Did you have a sense when you were making it that this was a great movie, this was something very special?

PB: Truthfully, Larry, I never had that sense until people started saying that it was great. I was just doing the best job I could. I'd approach every scene a certain way. I thought it was right for the picture. I was hoping to make a very good movie. I knew the performances were going to be good. I didn't look at dailies much because we didn't have much time, nor did we have very good projection down there where we were working. I also had a tremendous amount of personal problems while I was shooting it. We spent ten weeks shooting and during that time I fell in love with Cybill Shepherd, she fell in love with me, my marriage fell apart as a result because my first wife was there working on the picture, and my father had a stroke and died all during that time. So it was a tumultuous kind of personal life and I was quite distracted by some of that and at the same time trying to make a good picture. So the answer is no, I wasn't aware that it was going to be a great film. I'm thrilled that people liked it so much and called it a great picture.

LM: It is a great picture. It's a classic film.

PB: The truth is, Larry, I always thought the cut was a little short, the one that came out. In fact, and people don't know this, but the producers had said please get it down to under two hours. When it was around two hours and six minutes I said, "We're in danger now of taking too much out." They said, "Well, cut it, Peter." So I got it down to an hour and fifty-nine minutes and it opened that way, 119 minutes.

LM: Is there a director's cut of it?

PB: What happened was the picture came out and we got very, very great reviews but there were one or two reviews that said something like, "The only problem is we don't get to know about these kids' background. Where is the father? Where is the mother?" Well, there was a scene that explained that and I'd showed it to the producers. I said, "See, dammit, we shouldn't have cut that damned scene. I told you we shouldn't cut it." I said, "Let's put it back," and six months into the run, the picture was still playing, we actually put a minute back into the picture without any announcement, we just did it. Then years went by and I always felt that it was a little too tight, and that there were some things left out. When laser disk was around I actually put seven minutes back, and then when DVD came out a couple of years ago, Columbia said, "Is there something you want to do to this two hours and seven minutes?" I said, "Yeah, I want to take a couple of minutes out that I put in."

LM: Always the director, constantly fine-tuning it.

PB: Well, they're calling it the definitive director's cut and I don't know what else to do to it.

LM: Until you change your mind.

PB: No, I think it's finished, but the current version on DVD is the best version. So I never thought it was quite as perfect as everybody was telling me.

LM: Turning to *The Cat's Meow,* you are making a film here that has a fascinating story, because as I understand it, it was in a conversation you had with Orson Welles when he first mentioned this incident on which the movie is based.

PB: Yeah, thirty-three years ago we were talking about *Citizen Kane,* and he was trying to impress upon me the difference between Charles Foster Kane and William Randolph Hearst. Contrary to popular legend, *Citizen Kane* was not entirely based on William Randolph Hearst. It wasn't supposed to be Hearst. It was supposed to be a composite character based on two or three different press lords. One of them was a Russian press lord, another one was Hearst, and another one was named McCormick, who built the Chicago Opera House for his girlfriend, who was a "singer." That part of Kane is all based on McCormick, and Orson was trying to explain to me how different Kane was from Hearst. He said, "You know about what happened on the yacht?" I said, "No, I don't know anything about the yacht." And he told me what happened. Well, I was shocked. "My God," I said, "What a story. Does anybody know this?" He said, "Oh, yes. A little bit here and there but, you know, it's not exactly been publicized." I didn't think much of it, except that it was amazing. We didn't use it in the book. Years later, I'm on an ocean voyage, significantly, kind of an extended film festival.

LM: Those floating film festivals where people go and they have critics and filmmakers and writers on the ship.

PB: Yes, it was on the *Queen Elizabeth,* and this was set up by

Telluride. On the ship were Chuck Jones and Ken Burns and Roger Ebert. I was having lunch with Roger alone, just our wives with us one afternoon while he was deconstructing *Citizen Kane* for the passengers and I told him this anecdote, again as a way of showing the difference between Kane and Hearst. Well, Roger was just about as amazed as I was and said, "Gee, it sounds like it'd make a good movie." I said, "Well, it hadn't occurred to me." Anyway, I got home from that ocean voyage and on my desk was this script called *California Curse*. I leafed through it nervously, kind of amazed, and there were all these characters, Ince, Hearst, Chaplin. And I thought, "My God, maybe it's that story." Well, it was. It was exactly the story that Orson had told me.

LM: You clearly still enjoy making films a great deal. You've been making them for many years. What do you feel you have left to say in film?

PB: Oh, my goodness. I don't know. I have a few movies that I want to make. Robert Graves is my favorite writer. Although he was a novelist and a biographer and a historian, he considered himself a poet, and in a way he was best known as a poet. He said once that before he ever writes a poem he asks himself, "Is this poem necessary?" Now, all it takes to write a poem is a piece of paper and a pencil so, boy, is that a good question to ask when you're going to spend a lot of money and spend quite a few days with a lot of actors: is this picture necessary? I have a few necessary pictures that I'd like to make.

hen documentary filmmaker Ken Burns announced he was going to give jazz the same treatment he had given the Civil War and baseball, jazz fans like me were both thrilled and concerned. This conflicted response related to how jazz fans define it as a musical art form, and what they see as the most important parts of its history. Burns had a tough challenge in satisfying fans, but always made clear that this series wasn't for us, it was for those who had little familiarity with the music.

In fact, I ended up enthralled with Burns's history of jazz, even though I had a few quibbles and disappointments over omissions. Burns has clearly had a big impact on the documentary genre, proving that audiences will tune in for a lengthy, multi-part series on important material, provided it's compellingly presented.

We are now in a golden era of documentary, or reality, films. From political to true-life storytelling, we have never seen this level of interest in nonfiction cinema. It is a welcome development.

Larry Mantle: You've been honored for your *Civil War* and *Baseball* documentary series for PBS. Your story of American jazz is the third in this series. Can you share the process you use in creating these documentaries? Is there a structure you follow?

Ken Burns: There is and there isn't. The great genius of America is improvisation. It's in the Constitution, whose greatest test was the Civil War; it's in our national pastime, baseball, and it's obviously at the heart of the only art form Americans have invented, jazz. We found in the course of making documentary films over the last twenty-five years that it's the same thing here. The less we impose our preconceptions and our beliefs on the material, the better we are. So *Jazz* is, at seventeen-and-a-half hours, the culmination of a six-year effort that was born as we finished *Baseball*. We saw *Baseball* as a way to understand what we had become after that searing transcendent moment of *The Civil War*. *Jazz* is the completion of a trilogy that we hadn't planned on making, but seemed clear that we had to pursue. It was, in fact, in an interview for *Baseball* that the writer Gerald Early said that when they study our American civilization two thousand years from now, Americans will be known for only three things: the Constitution, baseball and jazz music. So we began work on this epic just collecting information with an eye toward not imposing our preconceptions and just learning from the material. That really takes time, and this has been for me the most complicated but also the most satisfying production I've ever worked on.

LM: Interestingly, race is a central point in all three documentaries.

KB: That's absolutely right. I don't think you can do any sort of serious study or be concerned about the history of the United States without bumping into race at some point. It's there; it's the monumental hypocrisy of our founding when Thomas Jefferson wrote, "We hold these truths to be self-evident that all men are created equal." He owned two hundred human beings and never saw fit in his lifetime to free them. He set in motion this extraordinary American republic filled with all its possibilities, but with this giant asterisk, an asterisk that had to be removed at least in law by the Civil War, an asterisk that was applied to our national pastime until Jackie Robinson came up. We can see this fault line of race creating very tragic and impatient gestures and events within our history. But we can also see a glorious, sort of ironic, almost poetically just story in jazz. That's the only art form that Americans have created. It was created mostly in a community of individuals who have historically a memory of being un-free in a supposedly free land. That's an amazing, amazing kind of contradiction, and it has set in motion a very glorious manifestation of this question of race that's always at the heart of American life.

LM: It seems today that the Latin influence on jazz, particularly Afro-Cuban music, is creating some of the greatest inroads into new forms of the art, just as the Black American experience was formative to jazz in earlier decades.

KB: I think that's true. But I think it's very important to stress from the get-go that jazz is not black music, and jazz is not African music. Jazz is American music born out of the circumstances of the ability to improvise. And who has to improvise more than African Americans who were given as a result of the Civil War only their freedom and nothing else? So what you have is a set of artistic and musical solutions. It has a kind of Biblical poetic justice behind it. It's like Cinderella. The person you keep down and keep from the ball turns out to be the belle of the ball. That happens throughout human history. But it is in America that this music happened, and that's the very important thing. That's why it is an art form. It can be shared with everyone else. Everyone else can play it. We can't extend the racial metaphor so much that we see it as a racial gift. It is not. It's an American gift.

LM: Jazz is so much like religion for so many people that you've been criticized for using Wynton Marsalis prominently as an advisor.

KB: The last time I checked we live in a democratic country. When you're making a broad survey of something, you want to be influenced by lots of different people. Besides, many other of our advisors are diametrically, philosophically opposed to Wynton, and one of those critics actually appears on camera more than Wynton. So I just assume that people have some funny views about him. He's a terrific help in the film, and that's it. There's no philosophy. I think your listeners will be pleased to know that we didn't make it for the jazzerati. We made it for everyone. When you tell a story, even one that's ten episodes long, you have to make choices. You have to pick several symbolic and emblematic stories and tell them well, rather than try to tell all the stories and end up with a narrative drive equal to the reading of the Los Angeles telephone book. This is not an encyclopedia. We will necessarily leave lots of people out and, in a few cases, a few important people out.

But we didn't do it carelessly or without attention to trying to tell a broad national narrative about what happened in this music. Jazz used to be seventy percent of the music industry. Now it's down to single digits. One of the reasons it's down to single digits is that those apparently charged with its care, the jazz critics and writers, have also become extremely guarded, and have given the impression to the rest of us that you need to have some sort of advanced degree, some sort of esoteric knowledge, to understand and appreciate jazz. This effete kind of snobbery has separated jazz from the mainstream population. Everywhere I go around the country I meet people who say, "Well, I'm not really into jazz." Then you show them a clip from the film or an episode of the film and they're now wildly enthusiastic, and it's, "Oh, I didn't realize I could approach it."

Because we have to tell a good story to make a good documentary, we have celebrated some wonderfully peripheral artists, in terms of their popularity, because their stories are so compelling and they help bring in a new appreciation for that music. We've got wonderful sections on Ornette Coleman, who even within the jazz community is a source of great controversy, and Cecil Taylor, who is to many listeners on the outer orbit of Pluto. But we've made his story compelling, and I've learned to understand and appreciate what's great about his music by understanding where he's coming from. Most jazz writing and jazz criticism is about the contemporary period.

I'm involved in a history in which I've fought to go back and gather up the threads of where this music has been. This film has much bigger fish to fry than the music and the individuals, as remarkable as they are, who made it. This is an opportunity to look at the country and see where we've been over the last hundred years and where we might be going. They are the same forces that animate *The Civil War*. God forbid if that film had been all military history, military movements, and military strategy. No one would have watched it. But it was an emotional archeology dealing with the soul of the country. That's what *Baseball* was, too. People would say to me, "Oh I really loved *The Civil War* but I'm not into *Baseball*. My son or my husband is." I'd say, "I'm making it for you because this is a story that all of us can understand." It's not whether you have the prior knowledge of jazz. It's whether you have the prior curiosity of who we are as a people.

LM: Is it the view of the documentary *Jazz* that New Orleans and the multicultural life there is the cradle of this music?

KB: Without a doubt, and we've basically gotten no argument. New Orleans was the most cosmopolitan city in America in the nineteeth century. It had all sorts of people there and all sorts of musical influences went into creating jazz. You had the complex African percussive polyrhythms that the slaves brought from Africa. You had the infectious pulse of the Caribbean music that would come into New Orleans. You had slave songs and work songs and the call and response of the gospel church. You had Scotch-Irish hymns and songs. You had French and Italian arias. You had a fondness in New Orleans for not only brass instruments but parades of any kind, including Mardi Gras and funeral parades. You had the introduction of ragtime, which gave a kind of propulsive, syncopated beat to the music. And then you had what we call the "roux in the gumbo," the Blues, this utterly American form which is, in many ways, the underground aquifer that has fed all the streams of American music, including, most notably, jazz. It's a very simple form that is incumbent upon the player not just to be good at playing it, but to be able to communicate something about how he or she feels in the moment. It's all of these musical ingredients, plus the social circumstances of slavery and Jim Crow and emancipation and reconstruction, that coalesce around the turn of the century into a music that became jazz. It's very much a gumbo in the spirit of that, and because it was born in New Orleans, the home of the gumbo, we felt it was very appropriate to call it that.

LM: Very fitting. It seems as though the arc of jazz reaches its peak in the Swing era. Who are some of the major artists in that period?

KB: We look at some of the earliest guys in jazz, like Buddy Bolden and Jelly Roll Morton and Sidney Bechet and Freddie Keppard, and the great seminally influential folks, like Duke Ellington. But our great hero is Louis Armstrong, who's the most important person, not just in jazz, but in American music in the twentieth century. He rearranged the molecules of music in America, the way Einstein changed everyone's view of physics, the way Freud changed everyone's view of medicine, the way the Wright Brothers changed everyone's view of travel. Armstrong is that influential. In his wake come lots of great people. We deal with Bix Beiderbecke and Benny Goodman and Artie Shaw and Chick Webb and Fletcher Henderson and Count Basie and Coleman Hawkins, Billie Holiday and Ella Fitzgerald. When I began the documentary, my image of Armstrong was of a guy with a big smile and a white handkerchief who was a transformer of popular songs. Almost instantly I began to understand that even though the jazz world is highly contentious, everyone was in agreement about the centrality of Louis Armstrong's contribution to American life. We have to understand that the twentieth century was the most transforming century in human history. Things happened. The Wright Brothers flew and Einstein had the theory of relativity. Jazz is equivalent to those, and Louis Armstrong is the man who single-handedly transformed jazz into a soloist's art, inventing the concept of swing, the playing before and after a note. His influence is so great that the Swing era was originally called, not Big Band Swing, but "Orchestrated Armstrong." Duke Ellington heard Armstrong playing in the Twenties and said, "I want Armstrong on every instrument." Even today musicians are struggling with his legacy, whether they are aware of it or not. He also transformed the way everyone sang, applying the same sort of thing that he had done with his trumpet and cornet to how people vocalize. He introduced scatting. He changed the whole concept of popular singing. Everyone, including Frank Sinatra and Bing Crosby said, "Armstrong was the beginning and the end of music in America." Billie Holiday, Mildred Bailey, Jon Hendricks, people of all stripes, in all types of singing styles, are in some ways influenced by Armstrong. And the great thing about him is that he is such an amazing human being. Everyone we interviewed for the film—Wynton Marsalis, older musicians who played with him, family friends and hangers-on, as well as distinguished writers, critics and historians—would all tell us how great he was. Then their eyes would fill with tears and they'd say, "He was a gift from God, an angel." You'd expect that from a friend or maybe from a musician who played with him. But you wouldn't expect it from sober-minded critics and historians. If this film has communicated anything, it is this notion of Louis Armstrong as a seminal figure, not just in music, but in American history.

LM: Why did you choose to stretch out your documentaries on the

Civil War, baseball and jazz into many parts over many hours?

KB: I found in those subjects opportunities to really get into broad sweeping epic stories of America and found, in their retelling, a way to understand where we are now. When you say the word "history" to most people, their eyes roll as if it's like castor oil—something that's good for you but hardly good-tasting. But to me, history is just the questions the present asks of the past. So I think there must be something that happens now as a result of our investigation of the past. There must be some medicine that our questions of the past provide us. That's what I look for, the kind of healing power of story and narrative in American history. The world we live in is so chaotic and so random. Humans have superimposed religion or science or art over our inability to deal with it. History isn't just about dry dates and facts and events. It's a kind of emotional archeology of not only where we've been but who we are now in a strange, complex way. I think that good history telling always changes me and makes living a little bit better. Just the way a great symphony or a piece of jazz music or a painting or a sculpture sometimes just changes how you are.

LM: Bebop is one of the most controversial areas of jazz. What do you think of the argument that bebop is great music to play but not great music to listen to, and that it's more for musicians than fans?

KB: I disagree. First of all I don't know how great it is to play because I'm not a musician. I know how hard it is to play. I've been focusing on bebop over the last six years. I know it's fantastic music to listen to. People got away from jazz, which had its zenith during the swing craze in the late Thirties and early Forties, because they thought it wasn't danceable. In fact, all the other forms of popular music that have crowded jazz out of the way, like R&B and soul and rock and even hip hop and rap, all have their birth in jazz music. What happened is that someone like Louis Jordan, who was a swing big band player, took the simplest, most crowd-pleasing aspects of swing music and helped create R&B, which was a way of providing, at least initially, for an African American audience, a form of dance expression. And the popular music sort of went away. But something doesn't have to be popular to be important and influential. My goodness, the Constitution's the greatest four pieces ever written in human history and I guarantee that

99.99 percent of the listeners still haven't read the whole thing since high school. Bebop is an amazingly important music. It is very much rooted in swing. It swings in the concept that Louis Armstrong understood. It is not this sort of spontaneous beatnik music that the beat poets tried to appropriate. The very few people who are able to play it well, such as Parker and Gillespie and Thelonious Monk, are some of the greatest musicians and greatest artists in American history. The analogy would be to painting, the way abstract expressionism came in after the second world war and a lot of people just thought, "This is scrambled eggs; I don't get it." We've tried to make this musical abstract expressionism available and accessible. The real proof of the pudding for me is that I still listen to bebop even though the series is over.

A listener says his fourteen-year-old son is in a jazz program in school and he, his friends and their parents are excited about Jazz.

KB: We're particularly excited because we read that kids aren't interested in jazz and then we see what the response has been. In every town I've been in to promote this show, there seems to be a high school with a jazz band. These kids are playing really well. At the very end of the film, we visit a high school in New York City where there was a young kid from the Ukraine named Michael playing the saxophone. He was playing it so well, swinging so wonderfully, that you looked into his future and saw that all was well, not only with him, but with us. The American republic is in good hands if we are producing people who can swing like that.

A listener asks how Burns decided to do his documentary on the suffragist movement, and whether he wants to do more on the history of American women.

KB: Absolutely. It's an amazing and neglected part of our history. These women changed the lives of a majority of American citizens, and they usually rate no more than a footnote or a paragraph or a caption and a photograph in most textbooks. I'm particularly drawn to Elizabeth Cady Stanton and Susan B. Anthony. They single-handedly codified not only what would be this seminal movement that would take half of our country out of the dark ages legally and polit-ically. They also set the example for a host of political movements and agitations that would take place in the twentieth century. Not just in India, but the American civil rights movement and other labor movements borrowed heavily from the tactics and the strategies and more important the patience and the forbearance of these remarkable Americans, these women who were the forefront of the suffragist movement. I found it was American history running on all cylinders. It wasn't the sense that this was some boring obligatory story that you had to tell, but in fact as riveting a narrative as anything I've come across.

LM: How do you reconcile the conflicting accounts you get about people and events that you gather as you're making a film?

KB: I think when the narrator speaks we want to be pretty damned sure that we're telling what is historically accepted at that moment. Even our understanding of the facts changes. Five years ago, you would never in a film about Jefferson state categorically one way or the other that he did or he didn't sleep with Sally Hemmings. Yet, as it turns out, DNA evidence has proved in the last couple of years that he, in fact, did. But you can in a film on Thomas Jefferson have one person say, "No, he didn't. He wasn't that type of person." And you can have another person say, "Yes, he did and, in fact, as an African American, I am his great-great-great-great-great-great grandson." So you are allowed within the context of documentary to engage lots of conflicting points of view. In fact, most of us see things from our par-ticularly subjective point of view, and history is an attempt to sort through the variety of subjective perspectives and come up, at least for the moment, with some commonly accepted or acceptable idea of how things really happened. But as you know, times will change and new evidence will emerge and things will be turned on their head. So one never makes the final word in history. One is really just saying, "This is the first word, let's begin a conversation, let's explore, let's continue to ask questions." And that's the best thing about history, that it's always changing and always evolving.

ichael Caine is one of the most prolific and highly regarded actors in cinema. In his seventies at the time of our interview, he was still keeping up a pace of at least two movies a year. His work can be stunning, as in the terrific 2002 adaptation of Graham Greene's *The Quiet American*. Caine received a best actor Oscar nomination for his starring turn as journalist Thomas Fowler.

Larry Mantle: Audiences currently have the opportunity to see one of the great performances of your career: the role of Thomas Fowler in *The Quiet American*. Share with us your passion for this film, because I've read that this is, of all the great performances you've done, one of those that is really dearest to your heart.

Michael Caine: It is, because it's several things. I was in the Far East as a young soldier in Korea with the Americans when the British army went in there. When the Vietnam War started, I was very surprised that the British didn't go in with them. And it wasn't until later that I read *The Quiet American,* and I sort of put two and three together and made six. I knew that Graham Greene had been in British military intelligence in the second world war. And he was in Vietnam at that time and I felt sure that British intelligence, when they were trying to make a decision whether to go into Vietnam with the Americans, had talked to him. And if you read *The Quiet American,* or see the movie, you will know that he had said, "No, and under no circumstances." And then I met Graham Greene. I did a picture called *The Honorary Consul,* and I met him through that. And I figured that Thomas Fowler, the character in *The Quiet American,* would be autobiographical, because Thomas Fowler is a *London Times* correspondent living in Saigon, with a very beautiful young Vietnamese mistress, which is exactly what Graham Greene was. I've been building steadily over the years towards playing this part, becoming a much more experienced actor, a much more experienced human being. The timing seemed absolutely right when I was offered this film. And it's the kind of film that I like to do, which is a film that is completely different from any film I've done before. The character is completely different from me, but is written by someone who understands the character completely and can write deeply about it. The combination, with Phillip Noyce directing and Chris Doyle, the cameraman, and Christopher Hampton, the writer, and Brendan Fraser as a co-star, I just couldn't believe my luck. I thought Christmas had come early that year.

LM: You've had such a wide range of roles in both comedies and dramas, to say this is completely different for you, that's really saying something.

MC: Yes, it is. I mean, I'm no Graham Greene. He was from a different class from me, a different education from me, a different generation from me, a different outlook from me. Here was a character who had a young mistress. I've been married to the same woman for thirty years. So I'm completely different from this guy, even voice and accent. I had to assume a different accent for the role.

LM: The film was shot both in Vietnam and in Australia. Share with us what it was like to spend considerable time in Vietnam to do the film.

MC: The Vietnamese were very, very cooperative with the making of this film. I understand that they're cooperative with everybody who goes in there. From a personal point of view, every conception I had about Vietnam was wrong. I figured it would be a place that was destroyed by war and, of course, it wasn't, because the Americans never bombed the cities. I imagined it would be ugly. It's a beautiful place, with great places to go to visit. I didn't get the time. I would have loved to have done a tour, gone all over, but I was working so hard. The most important thing for me was that the Vietnamese didn't know who I was, but as far as they were concerned, I would be an American.

I never, ever experienced one single moment of animosity from any Vietnamese and I worked with four, five, six hundred of them. Every day, all day long, for six weeks, I was with Vietnamese actors; never a sentence, never a scintilla of anti-Americanism. Everybody was so pleased to see you, so happy that you came there. They were delighted. I sat next to a professor from Hanoi University at some dinner and I was mentioning this fact. And he said, "Well, that's for two reasons." He said, "One, the Americans never bombed the cities. And two, they didn't come here to occupy us." He said, "Everyone came to occupy us. The Americans, all they wanted to do was give us a government. We didn't want them to go home as quickly as possible." So Vietnam, for me, was extraordinary, in my misconceptions. The other misconception I had was that the living, for us, would be rough. But, of course, we lived the same life as a tourist, and it's absolutely luxurious and incredible. And the people are so wonderful. Plus, of course, we had wonderful Vietnamese actors and actresses in the film. Do Thi Hai Yen, who plays my mistress, and Mai Hoa, who plays her sister and Quang Hai, who plays General Thé. They were all fabulous people.

LM: And as you say a beautiful country, which really comes through. The film is beautiful looking and beautifully shot. Also, Brendan Fraser gives a great performance as the American in the film, Alden Pyle.

MC: Yes.

LM: He obviously has had a much shorter career to this point than you. Did you talk a great deal with him before filming particular scenes about how to approach them, since you two spent so much time together on screen?

MC: No. As an actor, if you're on a set, which is your home, you go all around, looking to open doors and shut doors and turn on lights, because, to go into your own flat and try and open the door the wrong way outward, instead of in, or vice versa, you know what I mean? So you familiarize yourself with the set. In this case, I had never met this character in the movie. So we never, ever discussed anything. We let everything come as a surprise to us, because we knew nothing about each other. I mean, Brendan and I are obviously very good friends, but the characters had never met, so we never anticipated anything.

LM: The character of Alden Pyle that Brendan Fraser plays seems to be very much a metaphor for the United States as a country and its approach to Vietnam. And as a result, it calls for a very nuanced performance. This is not an American-bashing film. It's one that raises a number of very important issues. It certainly damns American naïveté, but at the same time, I think it is a very well-rounded look at American involvement with Vietnam. Did you see your particular performance as at all metaphorical, or more of the embodiment of Graham Greene in his persona?

MC: As Alden Pyle, Brendan was the epitome of American good intentions, but also complete innocence, which, of course, has disappeared now. Americans have good intentions, but they're no longer innocent, you know? That's what happened from the Vietnamese war. It's so obvious with him. And then, with me, I represent, I think, the climbing empires, like Britain and France. And then, there's the young nation, which is the new Vietnam, which is represented by Do Thi Hai Yen, who played Phuong in the picture. I think we were all metaphors for our countries, in a way. I think what Greene was saying was, with a man like Pyle, what a lot of damage a well-intentioned innocent can do.

LM: As you are approaching your seventieth birthday with an incredible number of films behind you, are you enjoying acting as much now as you ever have?

MC: I am enjoying myself now more than I ever have in my lifetime, and more than I ever believed that I could. And the reason for that is that I no longer have to work for a living. I only do exactly what I want to do. I used to be an amateur actor, which means that I acted for nothing because I loved it. And so here I am, having spent a lifetime earning a living, doing something I would have done for nothing and having the best time of my life right now, with this sort of renaissance of my career. I mean, at the age of seventy, I'm getting better and bigger parts than I've ever gotten in my life.

LM: Do you feel that you're growing as an actor? One of the things that seems so great about acting is that you can just keep getting better at it.

MC: You get better every time. There's never perfection in any actor's life. There's no such thing as perfection. You can always improve, always. That's what I try to do. And the way I try to do it is to disappear in the roles, rather than to make a stronger appearance as myself. That's what I've been doing, trying to disappear.

LM: As you look back, say, forty years ago at some of your earliest film roles, what are your feelings about that young man and his performances then?

MC: Well, the performances were based on my personality, which is what's called a "Movie Star," right? Now I'm a movie actor, and I'm trying to make my personality and my persona disappear. It's a terrible risk, because you just leave the people with the character and hope that the character is interesting enough. I figured Thomas Fowler was interesting enough to stand on his own, without any help from me. So I tried to disappear right into it, so at the end of the film, you didn't say, "What a wonderful performance by Michael Caine." You just say, "What an interesting person Thomas Fowler was to watch for two hours."

LM: And is that what you're primarily looking for in the roles offered you now, that opportunity to disappear?

MC: To disappear. Exactly. Yes.

LM: How does that occur? Is that something that has been a natural evolution in your performances?

MC: I think it's a natural evolution from age. There came a time in my career when I would get a script—this was the first inkling I had that I was getting on a bit—and I sent the script back, saying the part was too small. And the producer sent it back to me with a letter saying, "You've read the wrong part. It's not the lover, it's the father we wanted you for." So I knew things were starting to go away, you know? And also, the basic difference between a Movie Star and a movie actor is that when you get a script, a Movie Star says, "How can I change this script to suit me and my personality, and what I do, to be a Michael Caine Movie Star?" And then they go away and change the script to suit me. If you're Michael Caine, movie actor, you say, "How can I change me to suit the script, to keep the script exactly the same?" So that's the difference.

LM: Who are the actors you most enjoy watching?

MC: Nowadays, I love DeNiro, Pacino, Hoffman, all those guys. And I like a lot of young actors. I like Brad Pitt very much, and Johnny Depp. Joaquin Phoenix, I've worked with Stephen Dorff, Tobey Maguire, Karen Carlson. There's a mass of young talent out there now, which there wasn't before.

LM: Do you think that acting has gotten better or gotten worse as time has gone on?

MC: Oh, by far, far, far better. The American cinema has produced some extraordinary actors. You used to have great film stars. Now you've got great film stars and great actors. I can't think in the Thirties the actors that you would've compared with DeNiro, Pacino or Hoffman.

LM: You've worked with so many great directors. Are you able to distill, even given the wide variation of directors you've worked with, from Woody Allen to Phillip Noyce, what they have in common?

MC: None of the great directors shout. A lot of directors shout and bull. My version of a great director is a director who leaves you alone until he spots you veering off the straight and narrow path and can put you back on it with the fewest possible words. And that goes for directors as different as Woody Allen and John Huston. They're both exactly the same in that way. And also, directors who cut in their heads, rather than what I call "make the picture over the actor's dead body," inasmuch as you spend hours and hours doing a master, you know.

LM: So if a good director is one who, at least initially, leaves you more to your own devices, how does that work? As you're relating to other actors who've done their preparation for a role, how much of this comes organically from bouncing off of other actors in the moment as you perform it, versus your taking it with you to the set?

MC: You start to do it with the other actor. If there's anything wrong it's immediately obvious. You just know. And that's when the director will come in. And again, a great director is very quiet about what he does. He will take whichever actor it is aside and talk to him. They don't make you look a fool in front of the others.

LM: How much of acting can be taught, versus how much is inborn?

MC: I don't think you can teach acting, but you can give a sort of guide as to what route to take. It's like driving lessons. You give the people the car. You teach them how to drive, but you can't teach them to be good drivers. So acting is something you can either do or you can't, unfortunately, and you can't be taught it. But you can be taught how to be a better actor, or you can be taught a lot of technical tricks in movies. There are many.

LM: If you are born with that gift for acting and then, like yourself, you develop it over a period of time, is there any trade-off that's involved? Is there something that comes with that gift that perhaps is a deficit in another area?

MC: One of the things, when you're an actor, is that when people are talking to you, if they're insincere, which means they're acting, you spot it immediately. It's rather uncomfortable, you know? You get tremendous insight into people, plus, of course, you've spent your entire life studying people, watching them. You're like an emotional Peeping Tom.

LM: I assume you do spend time with other actors, and often actors can be among the less sincere people. How do you deal with that, with your acquaintances, or with people that you come in contact with in this business?

MC: Well, you leave them alone, but it's amazing how many actors are very nice people. The more successful they are, the nicer they are.

LM: Really?

MC: Yes. A lot of the nastier traits of actors come out in failure.

LM: So they get nicer as they get more secure, as they get more positive feedback?

MC: To become an actor in the first place is a sign of insecurity. So as you become more and more successful, you become more secure, and you're much nicer. All the tantrums that you hear about on sets that so-and-so wouldn't come out of the dressing room, it's got nothing to do with the dress being wrong, the suit being wrong, the dressing room is not right, or the motor home's too small. That's all to do with not being able to do the scene when they come out, or fear that they may not be able to do the scene when they come out. It doesn't necessarily mean they can't. It's just that it's their own insecurity.

LM: Given that you're so clearly a born actor, it's hard to imagine you doing anything else, but if you'd not found your way into acting, what do you think you would have done?

MC: I would've been an architect. I love architecture. I love buildings. I love designing things. Every time I buy a new house—which isn't very often, I must say—I buy what they call in America a "doer-upper," so that I can design stuff. The last house I bought was in England. It was a two-hundred-year-old barn, and I put my house inside. I had the best time ever. It was like being a real architect. It's fantasyland.

LM: And clearly you're enjoying your work so much. And I would guess, given your good health and the fact you're enjoying it, you have no plans to retire?

MC: No, none at all. I believe motion pictures retire you. They may retire you after the first movie or the third movie or the 103rd movie, in my case. But there just comes a time when you're not getting the scripts. You're not working with the right people. And you go, "Well, I'll give up here now. That's it. That will do me."

LM: Do you feel, at this point, that you're not only looking for roles that you can really inhabit, but that you're looking for films that have something to say?

MC: Yes, I do. Yes. I don't want to be Western Union, with the message, you know, if you want a message, send Western Union. But shall we say I like to do a film with some substance. I don't mind doing something which is complete fluff, like *Miss Congeniality* or *Austin Powers*. I enjoy that now and then. I like to get some fun out of it, too.

LM: And you're doing that for the fun of it, not for the paycheck alone? You really enjoy doing the comedies, too?

MC: Oh, yes. I love doing the comedies. I'd love to find another *Dirty Rotten Scoundrels*.

Since his presidency, Jimmy Carter has had a high profile working to advance peace, human rights, and health worldwide through the Carter Center and as the author of numerous books. I spoke with the former president immediately after publication of his childhood memoir of race relations in the Jim Crow South, *An Hour Before Daylight: Memories of a Rural Boyhood.*

Larry Mantle: What is the influence of your black friends and older black men and women on your life?

Jimmy Carter: I started writing this book to share a personal family memoir with my grandchildren, to let them know how old people lived back in the Depression years and back when racial segregation was the law of the land. I think that the reason it's interesting is that people nowadays don't have any idea about how we lived from the end of the Civil War until the Civil Rights Movement was successful. The Supreme Court ruled that the law of the land was segregation, separate but equal. And obviously we were not equal, in that blacks had no way to vote or to serve on a jury or to go to a decent school. And we were also not separate. As a matter of fact, on the farm where I grew up, I didn't have any white neighbors. All my playmates were African American boys. We fought with each other, wrestled with each other, played together, worked together in the field, went fishing together. That was my life. My mother was a registered nurse who was quite often on duty all day and night. My father was busy. So I spent many nights in the home of my next-door neighbors, Rachel and Jack Clark, an African American couple. I slept on a pallet on the floor stuffed with corn shucks, and in wintertime Rachel would let me move my pallet over near the fireplace. We ate together, worked together and so forth. That time of America's history is really not very well known or understood.

LM: You also tell a wonderful anecdote about taking the train with your best friend to go to the movies. On the train, you'd sit in separate sections, and at the theater he'd sit up in the balcony and you'd sit on the main floor. And you were both so excited to be going to the movies that these laws, as bizarre as they seem to us now, were just accepted as fact.

JC: That's true, and it wasn't just the Jim Crow South, because this was a prevalent circumstance in many states. We really didn't pay much attention to the separation. There were not any white liberals. There were not any black activists who were insisting then publicly that the Supreme Court change its ruling. That effort didn't come until fifteen years after I left the farm. And A.D. Davis, my closest friend, we'd go to Americus every now and then. We would put a little flag on the railroad track; the train would stop. We'd get on it; pay our fare. He sat in the colored section. I sat in the white section. We'd get to the county seat, we'd both get off the train, find each other, walk down the street maybe hand in hand since we were intimate friends, get to the movie theater. He would go to the third floor where you could just barely see the screen. I would go to the mezzanine, nice section, and then afterwards we'd go back home in the same segregated manner. This was a part of our lives that was not challenged. We had a lot of interesting and funny experiences together back in those ancient days. I think that this is part of our nation's history for about a hundred years that many people don't even know existed.

LM: You argue that while we would not want to go back to those days, in many ways we live more segregated lives today.

JC: That's true. Because of the changed Supreme Court ruling and the Congress passing voting rights laws, our minority citizens under the law have equal rights. They're still not treated equal yet, but legally they are. But we have gone back to a much more segregated society than any that I knew when I was growing up. For instance, the Carter Center had a program in Atlanta a few years ago with about 500,000 poor people. We visited all the high schools in Atlanta. Some of the high schools, say in Southwest Atlanta down near the airport, have 850 to 900 students in the high school, not a single white student. That's because of geographical arrangements for housing and cultural choices. It's not mandatory, but still we have grown much more segregated racially.

LM: Your father, James Earl Carter, Sr., rejected the racist groups of the time. But he also was very careful to observe the segregated culture of the South. How did that affect you as a boy, in particular seeing that your mother, Lillian, had her own way of dealing with black southerners?

JC: There were really no white people that I knew, or black people either, who challenged segregation. Nobody questioned it then. My daddy was a segregationist as was everyone else that I knew in those days. Mother was different in that she was a registered nurse and she was part of the medical profession. In our isolated community called Archery, she was, in effect, the doctor. So the poverty-stricken people who lived in a broad range of our home—white and black—would come to mother for medical care. When a midwife would have trouble delivering a baby or when somebody had an unidentified, undiagnosed disease, mother would go and nurse them. There was not any money to pay her, so quite often they paid her a dozen eggs a week for a year or something like that. This was a time, too, during the Depression, when millions of northerners moved to the south because their factories closed or because the assembly lines were mechanized and they lost their jobs. We had two hundred or three hundred hobos who walked in front of our house or rode the train in front of our house every day. Unemployment was prevalent. The next step up in the economic circle was day labor, at least getting some kind of employment. The wage was one dollar per day. The next high step was sharecropping, where you actually had your own home, your own garden, your own mules, your own plows. But the average per capita income for a sharecropping family for an entire year was just seventy-five dollars. How can we even conceive today of a person living an entire year for food, clothing, shelter, everything, for just seventy-five dollars? That's the way we lived. I think it was that pervading poverty that pulled together people, regardless of race.

LM: You write of why the land means so much for southerners, particularly in the historic context of what was known as the War Between the States in the south.

JC: At the end of the Civil War—the War Between the States as we called it in the south—there was no discussion of slavery having been a reason for the war. Then for a long time the so-called carpetbaggers came down to the south and dominated everything that my grandparents knew, economics, politics, and everything else. Anyone who had fought along with Robert E. Lee couldn't vote, for instance, and the wealth was wiped out. A lot of the wealth, as a matter of fact, was in ownership of land, the ownership of slaves if a person did have slaves, and money. The money was Confederate money, which became absolutely worthless. The slaves were freed. So the only thing that had any permanent value was the land. So I think that was the reason why, in the culture that I knew as a child, even many years after the Civil War, land was looked upon as the precious possession to be preserved and protected. That permeated the consciousness of the society. Sharecropping, which I describe in some detail in the book, evolved after the slaves were freed. The landowner still owned the land. The former slaves and white people too, who didn't own land, were looking for something to do. So it was a natural coming together of landowners and people who wanted to work the land. So there was a mutually acceptable negotiation, so that when the crop was harvested you got this much and I got this much, and that's where sharecropping originated. It was a very logical way to arrange the economic system of the rural south. And it was very good. But nowadays, of course, sharecropping has a very bad image because people lived in such poverty. But I think it's a very intriguing look at the nation's history, in a highly personalized way.

LM: How did your rural background, and particularly the years of hard work on the farm, inform your public life later? What do you think it gave you that other elected officials didn't have?

JC: There was no challenge to my daddy's authority; he was my hero and he was also my boss. We worked starting an hour before daylight when the big bell in the farm area was rung by Jack Clark, our next-door neighbor. We would get up out of our beds and take a lantern, catch the mule assigned for us for the day, or the two mules, hook them to a wagon or plow and we would stand at the end of the row until it got daylight so we could plow without plowing up the cotton or peanuts or corn or plants. An hour before daylight is the way we started our day, and we didn't stop until sundown. The average wage for a good, healthy dedicated man was one dollar, and for his wife was seventy-five cents for the entire day. That was how I grew up. We didn't have electricity. We didn't have running water. We didn't have indoor plumbing. As a kind of a fortunate family, we had an outdoor privy. A lot of our neighbors didn't have outdoor privies. They used the bushes and so forth. So we were privileged in a way, compared to our neighbors.

My life was so deeply submerged in the black culture. When I finished with the text of the book, I tried to analyze who, other than my mother and father, were the five people who shaped my life. Only two of them were white. I tried to describe in the book how the three black adults with whom I grew up actually determined my moral values, my ethical values, the priorities of my life, my awareness of the outer world. I also saw the ravages of racial segregation and how human rights or civil rights should be the law of the land, and I tried to enhance that when I was president. I also saw the ravages of abject poverty. There was no money, and people lived in as penurious a fashion as any third world country does now. We survived and we respected each other and were brought together by that poverty.

But there was an excitement and a challenge and an adventure that also attached itself to my life. I was an entrepreneur when I was five years old. I would pull up peanuts in the field, pick them off, boil them, walk two and a half miles to Plains, sell a dollar's worth of peanuts, and then walk back home. I was like a fly on the wall in the town of Plains, which had a population then of five hundred. The adults wouldn't pay any attention to me, so their lives, their dirty jokes, their filthy language, their experience with prostitutes the previous night, were discussed without restraint in my presence. So I think I had a broad-based awareness of the world as a child in Plains that might equal that of a child growing up in an urban area.

LM: What was it like for you when you went into the Navy?

JC: Even during the time of Franklin Roosevelt, racial segregation was absolutely permitted or mandated in the Army, the Navy and the Air Force. It was not until Truman became president that he issued an executive order prohibiting racial segregation in the Army and on ships. And it was about that time, when I was on a submarine, that I saw the beneficial effects and the fairness of President Truman's decision. That was really the first indication back in the late Forties that the laws of our country would change. It was not until Lyndon Johnson became president that the Voting Rights Act and other laws were passed, but Harry Truman was the one who took the initiative on what you might call now civil rights.

LM: I didn't realize until reading your book that you've lost all of your siblings and your father to pancreatic cancer.

JC: Scientists have studied our family. There have been a lot of scientific experiments done on me and on my blood type and that sort of thing. They've tried to understand why my father and my brother and both my sisters died with that disease. The difference is that I never have smoked cigarettes. All of them did smoke. And I think that's the difference between dying with cancer and living a longer life. My daddy was addicted to cigarettes when he was in the first world war; the cigarette manufacturers gave them away free to get people addicted to them. When I was about twelve years old, the only thing he ever asked me to promise was that I never would smoke until I was twenty-one years old. And I kept my promise. When I was twenty-one I was a midshipman in the Naval Academy. I bought one pack of cigarettes, took one puff, didn't like it. I've never smoked another cigarette and maybe that's what saved me from dying early with cancer.

LM: You describe yourself as a dutiful son and an entrepreneurial one. But you describe your siblings, particularly Gloria and Billy, as real characters, real personalities. And certainly we're all familiar with your mother, Lillian. How do you see your "good boy" upbringing relating to the eccentricities within your family?

JC: It was kind of embarrassing to me to describe their idiosyncrasies. One of the best stories that illustrates this point was when I was running for president and the little town of Plains, Georgia, was full of national correspondents. They questioned my brother Billy, and they said, "Billy, you're one of the peculiar members of the family." And he said, "No, just think a minute. My mother went off to India in the Peace Corps when she was seventy years old. My oldest sister, Gloria, spent half her time on a Harley-Davidson motorcycle and she's in her early sixties, and my sister Ruth is an evangelistic pastor. She is a holy roller preacher," he said. "And my brother thinks he's going to be president of the United States." He said, "Which one of our family members do you think is normal?" So we did have a very interesting family. My grandfather was killed in a fight with a neighbor. My great-grandfather was killed in a fight with a neighbor. My great great-grandfather killed a man in northeast Georgia and moved down to my area, although he was found innocent of any crime, to get away from the embarrassment of that violent death. I describe briefly in the book some of the interesting things that happened to some of my relatives and my ancestors. But I think all of that complicated environment is really what shaped me ultimately to go to the White House.

LM: Tell us about Plains, Georgia. You returned there after your military career in the Navy, and you returned again after your presidency. What it is about this town that draws you? Any time you have had a choice, that is where you've chosen to make your home.

JC: We're unique among all the first families in that Rosalyn and I came from the same small town. In fact, when I was four years old, Rosalyn was one year old and we lived in adjacent houses. Then we moved out to the farm. There's always been an attraction of Plains and the community to me. Both when I resigned from the Navy and when I finished my tour as governor, I moved back to Plains. When I finished as president I came back to Plains. One of the attractions is the land itself. It's really a great factor in my life to walk in the same fields in which my grandfather and my father worked and walked. To see the same house where my daddy and all of us grew up together, to visit the store, the blacksmith shop, the barn, all unchanged completely in the last hundred years. We have the same farmland that's been in our family since 1833. The families are basically unchanged. The churches are still a major element of our life. It's just a haven for us. I work at the Carter Center and we have programs in sixty-five nations. With the Internet, with e-mail, with telephones and so forth I don't feel a handicap on the days I'm in Plains compared to the other days in the week when I have to go to Atlanta. And you notice, just inadvertently I said, "have to go." I'm always eager to get back to Plains. So there's a great attraction just for this little, small community that hardly ever changes. If you take a picture of Plains now in the year 2001 and compare it with a picture of Plains taken in the year 1900, you couldn't see any difference. It's still the same as it was.

s a teenager growing up in Hollywood, I would encounter all different types of people on my way to and from school. There were runaways, religious wackos, prostitutes, cross-dressers, and others considered on the fringe of society. Even a country as open to diversity as this one finds it hard to accept sexual, gender, and religious rebels. I appreciated many of these misfits, because despite their struggles, they had found a place where they could be themselves.

It was with that appreciation of extremists in mind that I looked forward to interviewing the cross-dressing actor Divine. Born Harris Glenn Milstead, Divine had achieved cult fame for his starring roles in a series of movies directed by his friend and maker of filmic trash, John Waters.

It was in 1971, starring in the disgusting and amateurish (and I mean that as a compliment) *Pink Flamingos* that Divine became a cult icon. The actor appeared in several other Waters films, getting particularly strong reviews for *Polyester* and *Hairspray*. Divine acted for other directors as well, and ultimately made guest appearances on television.

I spoke with Divine just sixteen months before he died in his sleep at the age of forty-two. The Harris Glenn Milstead who appeared at the KPCC studios didn't look much like the repulsive, foul-mouthed, depraved character he had created earlier in his career. Instead, a very nice, soft-spoken actor joined me for an hour.

Larry Mantle: Let's start off talking about what has distinguished you in the acting profession: you have performed in films as a woman.

Divine: That was not out of choice. It's just something that happened. It was one of the first parts I got and it stuck, the image of the Divine character, even though every part that I played in every movie has been a different character with a different name. Everyone seems to lump them together and call them Divine, because that's my name. I got typecast, but I've always considered myself a character actor. I always have been looking for the other parts, the male parts. But they were never offered. When you're a young actor out of work and someone offers you some parts and some good money, you take them, whether it's being a man, woman or dog. That's how I ended up playing all the female parts for so long.

LM: You were closely associated with John Waters's films. Was your first film role in one of his films?

Divine: John and I were neighbors and grew up together in Baltimore, Maryland, in the suburbs south of Lutherville. On Sunday afternoons a whole group of friends, about twelve people, would get together. John would write scripts for us during the week and we would film them. It was just for our enjoyment. There were no discotheques or things like that in the Sixties, so that's what we did for fun. Then they just sort of caught on with the college crowd from the University of Maryland and Georgetown University. Both schools had filmmaking courses and they thought it was great that they could show their students how you could actually make a huge feature film for five hundred dollars.

LM: And how you could make a very unusual statement in the film as well.

Divine: Really.

LM: Was *Mondo Trasho* the first one that was released?

Divine: Before that there was one called *Eat Your Makeup* that was about two people who kidnapped high-fashion models and fed them only makeup and made them model themselves to death on the runway in front of their best friends. It was an obscure film to say the least, but actually very good. I was Divine in that film. So I worked my way up through the ranks.

LM: And then?

Divine: I upstaged everybody to the point where they finally had to give me the lead.

LM: You do command the screen when you are on; there is no competing with you.

Divine: I think that has cost me a lot of other parts. I was talking to my agent today and she said, "They wanted you but then they didn't want you, because they realized that you command the whole screen and it upstages other actors." I don't know. It's my way of acting. I'm a ham, from a ham school of acting. The bigger the better.

LM: Was *Pink Flamingos* your breakthrough to the average American's attention?

Divine: Yeah, and quickly. We made it in 1969 and it was our first feature-length, color film, costing all of twelve thousand dollars. It was our first big budget film, and no one would show it. John took it all over New York and sent copies to Los Angeles and to different distributors who had played *Mondo Trasho* and *Multiple Maniacs*.

LM: *Multiple Maniacs,* that's the film where your character was raped by a lobster, right?

Divine: Yes, Lobsterora. A fifteen-foot broiled lobster. It was bright red. I turned into a monster after being raped by him. I had rabies and foamed at the mouth. I ran through the city streets and then the National Guard shot me down like Godzilla. So you have to see these movies to really enjoy them and believe them. They're difficult to describe.

LM: What is fascinating is how John Waters took the most bizarre premise and brought it to the screen and executed it so effectively. They're absolutely hilarious films.

Divine: I think John's brilliant. I have to say that; no, I don't. I can say anything I want to. But I've been a dear friend of his for many years, and he's one of my very favorite writers and filmmakers. Of course, I always know I'm going to enjoy the film when I go to see it, because I'm in it.

LM: So with *Pink Flamingos,* you finally got some attention. People started showing it.

Divine: It took two years, then finally a theater in New York said, all right, they would do it. They would show it once and if fifty people came, they would show it again. John and his friends went out and posted bills and passed out handbills. The movie was sold out to fifteen hundred people the first night, and of course the movie owners loved that because they made more money. They booked it immediately for the next week. They put it on at midnight because they didn't know what else to do with it. It became the first midnight cult movie. It became a very, very popular thing to do in New York. The movie ran there for a few years, and it still plays. That's the thing: about all of John's movies that we've done together still play everywhere. They've never just sat on the shelf. They're always out. They're being distributed. They are still very popular and still hold up.

LM: In most of the films your costar was Edith Massey. She also added a lot to the films. She's no longer with us, though.

Divine: No. She passed away about eight months ago. She had cancer. I always said working with her was like me being the Joan Crawford and she was the Shirley Temple of the studio. She was the little sweetheart who couldn't do anything wrong, and I was the big bad bitch. People, of course, loved to believe that we didn't get along, but people liked to believe all those things, because on the screen we were very often against one another. But actually we got along very well. That's the great thing about working with John, about working with a repertory company, which he had set up there. You know their wants and needs and their likes and dislikes. All that is very important when you're stuck together for about two months, or sometimes a year. One of the magical things about why John's films work so well is all that's already out of the way. You don't have to do that again.

LM: Yeah, there's not an introductory period. You just get in, and you do it because you know how everyone is going to react.

Divine: With other movies that I've done, like this new Alan Rudolph movie, I was thrilled to get it, and it was something that I looked forward to for many years, but still, the first day I walked on the set I was scared to work with Kris Kristofferson and Genevieve Bujold and people I've seen in movies. These are big movie stars. Of course I've always been very impressed by all of that, so I was a wreck.

LM: And yet your role certainly garnered you more than your share of outstanding reviews.

Divine: Oh, I was flipped out and completely shocked, because I was so worried about the character being very feminine, and I didn't want him to be. I'm so used to playing a woman that I was afraid that some of that was going to slip through. You know, with just a look or something. It was very difficult to make the movie. It was much harder to be a man than to be a woman.

LM: What were some of the major differences you noticed working in a so-called mainstream film like *Trouble in Mind*, compared with working on the lower budget John Waters films?

Divine: Well, they were like a luxury to work on. Also *Lust in the Dust*. It's the way that you are personally treated, not by the director or anyone, but just having your own trailer, for instance, and having your workday set up for you in advance. With a small budget movie like John's, you more or less have to get in there and get it done every day, because there is only so much money to work with.

LM: I've been a big fan of Alan Rudolph's movies. How was it working under his direction?

Divine: He's great. I've been very lucky with directors. John and I grew up with him and I know him inside and out. And Paul Bartel was wonderful to work with. But Alan was most gracious and an actor's director, I think you would say. He wanted to hear everything that you had to say about the part, and what your feelings were. He would discuss all that with you in depth on his own time, and would give you a few ideas of what you might be able to work with. He would try it your way, and was willing for you to change lines and things, as long as you got the point across. That's what I mean that he's an actor's director. Other directors want to stick right to the script, and that's fine too. That's your job as the actor to do it the way they want you to do it. I thought Alan was a very sensitive person, a very sensitive man.

LM: You have played a lot of real heavy roles where you've been vicious, nasty, ruthless. Is it more fun to play a character like that?

Divine: Yes. I think that's one of the reasons I watch *Dynasty*, because of Joan Collins. It's fabulous to see somebody sink their teeth into someone else like that and just be a hideous person, because those people are out there. There really are people like that, and anyone who thinks there's not is crazy. It's more fun to play that. Anyone could play a little wimp or a nice person. That was the great thing about playing Hilly Blue, because I didn't want him to be boisterous, just mean and nasty. He didn't have to raise his voice, and you still know what we have to deal with. There are different ways of showing anger. I wanted to make him a quiet angry man.

LM: Now that you've had a character in a mainstream film, are you looking for more?

Divine: That was always my idea. I just got sidetracked in other people's minds for a while, playing more or less one type of character. Of course in *Polyester* we changed it quite a bit; I played the underdog.

LM: Dawn Davenport was definitely a distressed woman.

Divine: It was the first time I ever got good reviews. I had to be distressed to get good reviews. That was fun; I love a challenge. For me to play a completely different type of character is a challenge. With something new and different, you really want to put everything you've got into it just to prove to yourself that you can do it. So I hope there are a lot more of those out there.

LM: Has the female character Divine become an enterprise unto itself? Do you have any sorts of endorsement or advertising or things like that?

Divine: Over the years I have, and we're going to Japan where I think I'm going to pick up a few endorsements and commercials. So I'm excited about that. I also have my own record company now in London called Moore Music, and am producing my own songs. I've done singing for about five years all over Europe and the rest of the world. I have gold and platinum records and have done very well, so we're putting a new one out on our label.

LM: You have also had a nightclub act, a stage show, haven't you?

Divine: Yes. A stage show and nightclub act. I play a lot of large discos all over the world and a lot of clubs. A stand-up act, comedy and singing.

LM: Does your character have a stronger identity or response from the gay community than from mainstream America?

Divine: No. I think less and less all the time, actually.

LM: Really?

Divine: In the very beginning, it was like that. I think that's very true with a lot of new acts and with a lot of new things that come along. I'm not going to say just gay people, because that's insane. But a large majority of gay people would be the ones who go out and really pull something out, and say, "This is fabulous; you've got to see this or do this." It starts to build after that, and then naturally everyone eventually gets in there. So in the beginning, yes. But over the years, not that they're not still fans, but I find myself becoming more accepted in straight clubs or mixed clubs, not just the gay clubs. I would say ninety percent to ten percent, straight clubs to gay clubs, is what I play now.

LM: You got exceptional notices for *Polyester*. I recall reading reviews that said you brought a tremendous sensitivity to the role. One said that this is the film that proves Divine is an outstanding actor.

Divine: In the *New York Times*—I couldn't believe it. I was sitting there waiting to read the *Times* just to be cut to smithereens, and the mainstream critic, Vincent Canby, said that the best female performance of the year was given by a male named Divine, and listed Glenda Jackson and all of these big stars. I was like a peacock that week.

LM: Why haven't we seen you more often on the screen? Is it because of the typecasting as a woman?

Divine: It's what started the career, but it's what's held me back. It's really a love-hate sort of thing. I love it, but I hate it. Of course, it seems very hard for most Americans to accept the whole drag thing, the man in the dress. But in Europe and other parts of the world, it's nothing. It's always been that way; women weren't allowed on the stage or anything. I don't have to fight all of that. It's taken me twenty-something years in America to get to this point. I should have gotten a lot further along. I went to some of the studio heads in Hollywood a month ago; they were more than willing to see me. They sat there and told me what a fabulous actor I was, but TV was too square for me. I said, "You mean I'm too far out for television." I'm sitting there in a three-piece suit or something, and all they seem to visualize is this big bitchy blonde in a tight sequined dress.

LM: How difficult is it for you when people can't separate you from your screen persona?

Divine: Many people think that the big bitchy blonde is going to walk through the door in a red sequined dress, and beat some people up and puke on the floor and jump all around and break things and leave the office. So I think it takes about fifteen minutes to get over that initial shock. "Who is this fat man in a three-piece suit sitting here," you know. And because I'm really quite shy and calm, I think they're disappointed. In a way they're so in shock they don't know how to deal with it.

LM: What do you think John Waters finds so intriguing about your work?

Divine: I can act like a crackpot, but I'm not. I can be completely insane but I'm not. That's what he wants. He really wants acting, because to work with a really insane person, someone who is out of control, you can maybe get what you want in the end, but it's going to take a long time and a lot of hard work to get it. I can walk on the stage or on the screen and be a complete lunatic, and when they say "Cut," I can turn it off and be like I am right now with you. I know there are a lot of actors who carry it all home with them and sit up until four in the morning being whatever part it was that they were being, and finally they end up committing suicide, because they go nuts. But I've never had that problem, and that's one of the main things he told me, because he knows me so well he can write for me so well.

LM: Was it at all difficult for you to do these offbeat films, to go to the extreme with your character, to do things people might find extremely crude—all the while knowing that it's being recorded for posterity on film?

Divine: I must plead that I was completely naïve. I just thought John was crazy. I didn't give them a second thought. Crazy not in a bad way, but in a funny way. A few of the things I never took seriously for one minute. What did I care, because when you are fifteen and sixteen and seventeen years old, what do you care? You don't really worry about too much at that age except having a good time, and that's mainly what we were doing. No one had any idea, especially in Baltimore, that these movies would become popular. Whoever heard of that? Movies were made in New York and Hollywood.

LM: So you weren't even thinking that the average person would end up seeing the film, so what was there to worry about?

Divine: It was like home movies for us, so there was nothing to worry about, nothing to care about, nothing to think about. It was just acting out John's fantasies and the things that he wrote for us during the week. We just thought it was a lot of fun. There was a lot of boredom involved, and that took away from it. We all loved film. We went to every movie. So it was great fun for us to do it, pretending that we were movie stars and he was the director. It just so happens that it's ending up that way. That is the direction we all dreamed of going in, but never dreamed that it would be possible. The Cinderella story.

LM: At what age did you start working together?

Divine: We started working together when we were sixteen, because we're all about the same age, except Edith. We found her a few years later.

LM: And the other people, like Mink Stole?

Divine: Mink, she's the most hideous one on the set, one of my oldest and dearest friends, but she is really the bitch. She's without a doubt the most difficult one to work with, but at the same time the best one, I think.

LM: Really?

Divine: Unbelievable actress. Fabulous actress.

LM: And there were others who were a part of that inner circle?

Divine: There was Mary Vivian Pearce who played Cotton, my sidekick in *Pink Flamingos*. She was a really good friend of all of ours, but did it just to make John happy, and wasn't really into it. And then John found Edith, who had an unbelievable past. It was quite sad actually, but she died a very happy woman because she was truly a movie star when she died. She had fans in her room with her to the very end. She was very, very popular with the moviegoers and with the fan club; people wrote hundred of letters and she wrote every one of them back.

LM: Speaking of Edith Massey, a lot of people are curious as to whether what they are seeing on the screen, the character, was similar to what she was really like.

Divine: Yes. That was her. That was her exactly.

LM: That kind of innocence.

Divine: And at times you wanted to strangle her.

LM: Naïveté.

Divine: Very, very much. She died at fifty-two or fifty-four years old, so she wasn't that old. But like I said, she came from a very poor and a hardworking background. She worked in a lot of bars with strippers and hookers and had been in and out of jail and things like that, not for anything wrong, but for standing up for us, for her boyfriend. I remember one day in *Polyester*, we're running across the front lawn and the reporters were after us, and she has on a riding outfit. And I said, "Come on, we're going to run across the lawn," and she said, "Oh no, no. I can't run." And I said, "Listen, you're going to run." And I grabbed her hand and I think her little feet were flapping in the wind. We got in the car, and she's crying hysterically. I said, "You can stop crying now, we're in the car and the scene is over." And she said, "I'm not crying from the scene, I'm crying because you made me run."

LM: There were some critics who wrote that she was being exploited. Were you taking her innocence?

Divine: Of course, of course.

LM: But we're really laughing at her. That's demeaning.

Divine: It doesn't matter. It doesn't matter if they were laughing at her, as long as they buy the tickets. That's what it's all about isn't it? I mean, that's show business. It is exploitation. Yes, he exploited her for being a fat, crazy woman, but people loved her for being a fat, crazy woman—or they hated her. He exploited me for being the big, fat hideous bitch who's really a man. So, I mean, that is all exploitation.

LM: At least with your image, you have a choice about doing the Divine character.

Divine: I did it because I loved to do it. I remember in the late Sixties when we would go to Los Angeles or San Francisco, and there would be street festivals and summer fairs. I would be all done up in my costume and would walk down the middle of the street while John and friends would be passing out leaflets on the side of the street saying, "Come see this movie tonight starring this person." I'd stop people in their tracks in the middle of the day with a gold cocktail dress on and eyebrows up to my forehead. We're talking about exploitation. But I was the one who put myself right out there. I was willing to be exploited. I wanted to be exploited. It was a very important part of show business.

LM: Tell me a little bit more about your background. Did you have any professional training before you started acting, or was this a natural talent that you just cultivated by performing?

Divine: I guess it's just a natural talent. I never had any profession-al training. I was going to start working with some teacher, and my manager and my agent suggested not to do that.

LM: Don't stop—don't ruin yourself.

Divine: Exactly. They said, "Don't take something that is working for you, that is a natural talent, and mess it up." They said they thought perhaps the next time I get a role, I could work with some-one who might be the best person to work with for that kind of role.

LM: Are there any elements to the Divine character that are a part of your personality? You seem so mild-mannered, and the Divine character is so abusive, so foul-mouthed. It seems as though she would have to be a part of you.

Divine: You've never seen me at home. I'm hopefully not like that. I would have been in a mental institution or prison somewhere. I think I'm completely different. Whenever I'm not, I have very good people around me to tell me to tone it down, or don't start believing your own publicity. I like people to be nice to me and I like people to be calm. I don't like to be shouted at. I don't like to be talked down to, and I don't like to do that to anyone else. I'm really a firm believ-er in karma and getting back what you give out and all of that. I think it does work that way.

LM: I would think it might have been easy for you to adopt the attributes of your character once you gained recognition and acclaim for her. Is it a conscious decision that you are going to stay who you are and not become your character?

Divine: That did worry me at first, because when I first came on the scene in New York City in 1971 with the opening of *Pink Flamingos,* all of a sudden Warhol was giving parties for us, and every photogra-pher in New York wanted to take my picture. I was thrilled, natural-ly. All of a sudden it was a whole different world, and I was famous, so to speak. People knew who I was when I walked down the street. People asked for autographs. People wanted to take their picture with me. I thought, "Oh, this is great." But then I met people like Candy Darling, who is dead now, too—a Warhol star—Holly Woodlawn and Jackie Curtis. These three were all men who lived and worked in drag all the time, and were quite famous, mostly in New York. But I thought, "Do I want to get up every morning and shave and put on a pound of base makeup and eyeliner and lashes and a pair of heels and walk around like that all day, when actually I'm a three-hundred-pound man?" I didn't find that appealing and it really did bother me, because it wasn't me that was popular, it was that character Divine that was. That big bitchy woman was popular, so I did have to fight that. At first, I didn't know what to do. For the first publicity campaign that we did in New York City, I was in drag every day and went around like that every day for two weeks. That's when I made up my mind, when I went home with blisters between each toe and just horrible rashes from shaving and everything. "No. This is not what I'm going to do. I don't want to be called a female impersonator. I don't want to be called an impressionist." I didn't want to be called any of those things. I thought the only way to do that was to be a man, and that those were my work clothes and costumes for my part.

LM: I think the thing that really sets you apart is that you have such a great acting talent that you don't have to rely on being that character.

Divine: Well, thank you. I wanted to be famous all over the world, to be an international star. And we've done that, we've managed to get me all over the world.

LM: Have they discovered Divine in the Soviet Union?

Divine: They do play the records there. They are popular, actually. They quite like the whole drag thing in Russia.

LM: What kind of music do you perform?

Divine: Mostly it's disco, and then it was called high-energy dance. But I just did a new record, which will be out in London called "Little Baby." It's more of a rap type of song, and it has a message.

LM: Do you do this in the character of Divine, or do you do it as yourself?

Divine: I do it as a character of Divine, and a character that we've made up just for these shows, because I talk in-between and tell jokes that go anywhere from funny to just downright filthy, depending on the crowd. If you go to Vegas or any of these places and see comedians there, that's what people want to see when they are out drinking. It's something they can't see on television and something out of the ordinary, so I'm much more at ease when I have the costume on. I can be a much more outgoing person than I can like this. So I have incorporated the character of Divine into the act.

LM: It sounds like you're comfortable with the Divine character, and it has given you recognition all over. And yet, it has been a prison that's been hard to get out of, making it difficult to find straight roles. Does this frustrate you?

Divine: Yes, at times it has been very bad, to the point where I was seriously going to quit and do who-knows-what because I felt like I was beating my head against the wall. Every once in a while I still go through that. You go to see someone in a studio about a film or something, and you are sitting there in a suit and tie and they're telling you how funny you are, but then they tell you they can't use you, because they're only making comedies that week. I think, "Well, what am I having, a recurrent trip or something? Do I hear this person correctly? Am I crazy?" In one case, the movies they were making were with Dan Ackroyd, another one was with Jim Belushi, and the other one was with Chevy Chase. And I said, "You can't find me a part in any of those three movies, male or female?" And I guess because the image of the Divine character is so strong, they really cannot see beyond that. It's going to take more than just the one movie with Alan Rudolph to really help—not erase the character completely, but move it over a little bit, so I can do something else.

LM: But what a great calling card: a film that got critical acclaim. Your performance was so strong.

Divine: That's a good thing to build on, so you can't ever give up. I've been in the business twenty-four years, and I'm still building the foundation, while others have come and gone and been big stars and now are retired or forgotten already. I've seen them come and go; it's unbelievable.

George Foreman

January 15, 2003

I am not aware of any prominent person who has made as dramatic a change in temperament as George Foreman. From angry young boxer to beloved ex-pugilist elder statesman, Foreman has become a highly articulate fan and critic of his sport. When you are in his presence, his energy level and enthusiasm are palpable. It is no wonder he made a fortune selling his home grill.

Foreman is a major part of boxing history, taking the heavyweight title by knocking out Joe Frazier in 1973, suffering a knockout loss to Muhammad Ali in the famous "Rumble in the Jungle" in Zaire in 1974, then coming back after a ten-year retirement to regain the heavyweight championship by knocking out a much younger Michael Moorer in 1994. As a fan of boxing, it was a particular delight for me to interview Foreman. Though he hadn't fought in several years, my memory of the forty-five-year-old Foreman's come-from-behind victory over Moorer was still fresh in my mind.

Larry Mantle: You have reinvented yourself in many different ways. You write very candidly about this in terms of your personality, your profession and your family. I'm wondering how that change of mind occurred; was there a moment when you decided that you were going to revolutionize who you were?

George Foreman: Oh, no doubt about it. I had my grand experience in 1977, when I didn't even believe in religion, but it took a great part of my life at that point and I went on to be an evangelist. In the ten years that I was out of boxing I never even made a fist, no shadow boxing, nothing. I had to learn how to re-create myself, but

I found out the greatest asset you can have is life. Three years after I'd gone from boxing I'd cut all my hair off, no mustache, no one noticed me from the old boxing days, but people were kind to me. I thought you had to be rich and famous to have people be nice to you, that's why I had fancy cars and all of that. All these things changed me. If I had been heavyweight champ of the world and had known that people were so kind, I would've been a different person. I got a second chance to be the heavyweight champ of the world, to go back into boxing, and it made me a better person because of what I saw people had.

LM: You're one of those rare people who, when people talk about you they describe two very different folks. There was the young man early in your career, the gold medal in the heavyweight division at the 1968 Olympics, the heavyweight champion beating the dominant heavyweight of the time, Joe Frazier—tremendous success. But when you hear people talk about you at that point it doesn't sound like you were a very nice guy.

GF: Not at all.

LM: Now when they talk about George Foreman, it's as if they're describing a teddy bear.

GF: When I won the Olympics in 1968 it was the happiest time of my whole life as an athlete, and afterwards I paraded around the room with a small American flag. I was just a happy nineteen-year-old boy. I wanted the whole world to know where I was from. At the same time there had been the raising of the clenched fists in the Olympics, so when I got back home people said, "Why would you raise the flag? Why would you do that?" There were a lot of people angry at me. These were the days when America was not that popular, especially domestically, and the people didn't appreciate patriotism. Mine wasn't so much patriotism as it was that I wanted them to know where I was from. I had been rescued from the gutter by a Job Corps program—I got a second chance to get an education. I got a general education diploma, vocational education, and for me it was, "Hey look, look what I've done." So when people started to chip at me I became angry about it. I'm not going to have you come up to me and ask me what did I do that for. Why not do it? Also, I had met

Sonny Liston, my original role model. Dick Sadler was the trainer and manager of both of us in those days. Liston was mean. When people would walk up to him and ask him for an autograph he would take an hour to do it, and then when he was done he'd tell someone else, "Get out of the way." And I thought, "Boy that's the way you've got to be to be heavyweight champ of the world—catch them if they run from you and kill them. And if they come to you, just hold them and kill them." That became my personality. As a matter of fact, I perfected it even more so than Sonny Liston.

LM: Wow, that's saying something. He was a pretty surly guy.

GF: Yeah, and believe me, I was worse than Sonny Liston. That was the way I wanted to be because I thought that was the way you had to be. But I found out later that Sonny Liston was running people off who were asking for autographs because he didn't know how to read or write. He was actually making a portrait of his name; it would just take too much time and he'd run them off, and they would have no idea that he didn't know how to write. So I was taking on characteristics of people I didn't understand. I had to find out why he was doing that, and then it changed my life.

LM: So often we try to figure out what is going to make a difference for a young person who's in trouble, whether there's a problem with the law or they're alienated from their family. I think maybe there's something they can learn from your background, because you describe being a young mugger, a kid who was in trouble with the law until the Job Corps program turned you around. What was it in the program that enabled you to see there was another way?

GF: I was running from the cops one night. I'd been out mugging guys, and the police got behind me. They were going to get me. I was bigger, so I was slower. I had to crawl underneath a house to hide, and I thought they were going to send those big dogs. They were going to sniff me out, and on television I'd always seen when the crooks were being pursued they'd go into the water and the dogs couldn't smell them and they'd get away. So I covered myself—there was a burst sewage pipe—I covered myself from head to toe so the dogs wouldn't smell me, and I heard one of my cousins telling me, "You're never going to be anything, no one from this family will ever become anything." I didn't want to be a criminal. I had no idea I was a thief. From that point on, I never stole again. I just had to do something with my life. I heard Jimmy Brown, the great football player, do a commercial for the Job Corps. He said if you're looking for a second chance, join the Job Corps, and I did. That's where I started to read books, things like that. I read my first whole book at about sixteen years old. That started to make a big change. In the evening I was lonesome for the family; I took up boxing as an avocation and became pretty good at it. A year after I had my first boxing match I was an Olympic gold medalist, but like I said I picked up the Sonny Liston habits and that made things a little brutal for me. But the big change happened in 1977, when I had a religious experience.

LM: Which seems odder to you as you look back on the development of your life, that you would end up as the two-time heavyweight champion of the world, or you'd end up becoming a beloved icon selling a grill?

GF: It's not like I'm happy about how many grills I sell. I'm happy about how people approach me in airports: "George, I love your grill. Man, look how much weight I lost." It makes something out of you. I'm known more for the grill now than boxing. Kids walk up to me and their parents say, "That's George Foreman. He used to be heavyweight champ of the world." And the kids will say, "That's the cooking man." They don't even know me as the boxer.

LM: How did the George Foreman Grill come about?

GF: It's strange, my attorney, Henry Holmes, was approached by one of his friends who said, "George is always making other people famous. He's doing all these commercials for Doritos and hot dogs. Why doesn't he come up with his own product?" He told me about it and I said, "Well, sure. How much money are you going to give me?" He said, "No, no, no. We can't give you any money. We're going to give you this grill. No one wants it. You go out and market it yourself. We'll even put your name on it." They gave me most of the partnership. It was my grill, so I started talking about it, using it successfully to lose weight and to stay in shape. I was 315 pounds and I needed meat for the punching power, and fish and chicken and all those things, so getting the fat off was an ordeal. We did an infomercial. People talked about it. Word of mouth got to spreading and today we've sold over forty million of those things. It's all because someone joked, "Why don't you get your own product?" Salton, the electrical appliance makers, they made it a beautiful piece of furniture, a lot more now than what it originally was.

LM: You never have to work again because of all the money that's come from the Foreman Grill, and you made a good living from boxing as well. Why do you continue to do the boxing commentary, to be such a high-profile figure? What do you get out of it, when clearly from a business standpoint you don't have to do it?

GF: It's because of my wife. When I was trying to be heavyweight champ of the world my wife treated me so nice. As soon as she convinced me to retire it wasn't even a couple of months before she was saying, "You better take out the trash. What do you think you are, spoiled? Wash your own plate." I said, "Okay. I got to get a job." So I got many jobs, but she insisted that I continue to work with HBO. She said it gives the fighters a voice, and when I'm out there talking for them I can explain some things that they're going through and it'll make people appreciate them even when they lose. I tell the whole story inside out, that's why I'm still with HBO, over ten years now. And I got out with Meineke, the discount muffler people. I'm still working with them because they gave me the first three-year contract. Other people would sign me up to do a commercial and afterwards, no matter how much money was involved, they said, "Thank you." But Meineke took a chance. They said we're going to do a long-term deal, and I've been with them for ten years now, too. When people start doing things like that for you, you stay with them until they say, "Well, we've had enough."

LM: You have ten children, five of them sons with the name George Edward Foreman, and you've gotten a lot of attention for that. Why did you choose the same name for all five of the boys?

GF: Well, people say, "George Foreman is already making preparation for memory loss." If you're going to be a good boxer you better make preparation for memory loss. I didn't find out about my biological father until later in life, and I had already lost the heavyweight title. One of my sisters told me, "You know daddy isn't your daddy." I said, "What do you mean?" She explained it to me, and I found this fellow, and it just tore at me. You think you have certain roots and you find out you don't. Don't feel bad; go plant something. I decided I was going to give all these boys something they would always have in common: a name. Five of them are named George Edward Foreman, along with myself, so there are six of us. That's the main reason to give them that name, to plant some roots.

LM: So they're always going to know where they came from, but how do you distinguish them?

GF: When I was a young boy there were seven of us, and when my mother would get upset with me and start calling my name, I could ease out of the door. I said, "This will never happen to me." I just say "George!" and they all come, and I can sort it out once they get there. Speaking of my mother, she called me the night I won the heavyweight title back, and for the first time she said, "Son, I think you got it this time. I think if you get in there and do what you can do, you can win it." I was forty-five, and I felt like a little boy. My mother was never concerned about my boxing, but here she was telling me, "I think you got it this time." Can you believe that? My dear mother's passed on now, but I got a lot of my wisdom from her, and all of the lessons that she's given me I pass on to my kids.

LM: That Michael Moorer fight in 1994, in which you won back the title, I think is a wonderful lesson for people. I saw the entire fight live and, as I recall, you were in a really tough fight and it was very unclear that you were going to win. You could just have easily lost it, but late in the fight there was that punch. It looked more like a jab, and you just nailed him on the cheek with it, and it was as though you'd grabbed a hammer from out of the corner and hit him with it. To me there's a great lesson in how you hung on at this advanced age and had the power to finish him off to retake the title. What was that like for you?

GF: In hindsight, I am happy that the fight did go ten rounds, because most people said, "George, if he has any chance, he's going to have to be early with his punch." But the fight went on, and I was able to get stronger and stronger and land the harder punches later on, and it was a message to everyone. The age forty or fifty is not a death sentence for an athlete. If I can go back and become heavyweight champ of the world, anyone can go back to college, or start a new profession. In Texas especially, when I went back into boxing they were laying people off from all businesses. I wanted them to know, you were the asset. They lost you. The company needs you. Go make another company. That's what I was trying to do, show the whole world that it doesn't matter what you're up against, just get up and start another dream.

LM: Where did that strength come from, though? I didn't get the impression you were hitting anywhere near that hard late in that fight. At that point I have to admit I thought you'd probably lost, and then this punch seemingly came out of the blue. Where did that come from?

GF: Well, he was young, at least twenty years younger than me, and I'm out there boxing, and it's more like Muhammad Ali did with the rope-a-dope, to hide from a big puncher like me. But he was so sold and indoctrinated on the point that George Foreman is old, he can't move, that he just stayed right in the range. So I'd just tap him every now and then, not move him back, so he would be right in the range. Finally I was able to go from the left side, left side, and then I switched to the right side, and I got him, but it was all tactical, believe me.

LM: We have to talk about your relationship with Muhammad Ali, which I know is a source of a lot of troubling emotions for you. You lost the "Rumble in the Jungle," the fight in Zaire, after you had won the heavyweight championship from Joe Frazier. Muhammad Ali belittled you, he ridiculed you as a black man, and he courted not only the fans in Zaire, but American fans as well, in opposition to you. It was obviously a very painful experience for you.

GF: Good point. It was I who decided to take the fight to Africa, and for good reasons. You know, those were the days of doing the Afro this and Afro that, but when I got to Africa I was treated like I'd just come from Mars, because he had campaigned like he was running for office or something. Not only that, he was loved by a lot of people at that point. And then there was the shock of the fight. I'm beating this guy up in the ring, and then because he was wise and strong he finally beat me, but that didn't hurt as much as the fact that I could hear him in the background: "I told you. I am the greatest. I told you. Nobody can beat me." It took me years to live that down, but to hear the screams of all the people once I was on the canvas, so happy, so elated, how could people be so happy for a man to lose? That made me bitter and I started to hate Muhammad Ali even more, to a great length, more so than when I fought him. I hated the man and I wanted to get the heavyweight championship of the world back, and more importantly I wanted to beat him and show him that he couldn't beat me, that something had to be wrong. I would wake up in bed at night, sweating. I'm on the canvas, I'm listening to the count, and I can't beat the count again, and this hate just drove me. I came back to be a No. 1 contender in the world before my last boxing match, to get him. That's how I lived for years until I found my break with God.

LM: Did you also feel that if people knew what Muhammad Ali was really like, and the terrible way that he treated you in Zaire, that they wouldn't love him so much?

GF: Not really. I didn't particularly care too much for what people thought. I was such a bad guy. If people had known the kind of guy that I was, they probably would have hated me even more, would've cheered more greatly when I lost. It was I who had the problem, and Muhammad Ali was just a guy trying to win a boxing match.

LM: But I understand you didn't change your attitude towards Ali until you were being interviewed by the late columnist Alan Malamud of the *L.A. Times.*

GF: I had been making all kinds of excuses for losing, like, "Someone doped me. The ropes were fixed." I wasn't giving this man the credit for beating me fair and square. I think around 1980 Alan Malamud asked me, "George, what really happened in Africa?" And I told him, "Look, I lost. I've got proof. I've got some tape in the house on film. He beat me fair and square." I was healed from that moment on. Not only was I healed, but I found I recaptured the love that I had for Muhammad Ali when I was a young boy. I used to watch him on television doing the shuffle and making jokes and poems. I had to find him and make certain that he understood that he was beloved in my eyes; he's like a brother to me now. I still wouldn't want to take him on a fishing trip in the morning; he takes his medicine and he'll talk to you. He'll make the fish go away, but the guy's a wonderful guy. I've enjoyed the last several years that I've had to be with him and hug him and joke with him. He's kind of ill now, but he's sharp as a tack and he still makes you want to be around him. When you see him you get excited, and your heart starts beating.

LM: Muhammad Ali has paid a price for his career, particularly the latter part, when he took so much punishment. You know many fighters who have paid a mental price because of the punishment they've absorbed. Does it ever make you question the sport that you've devoted your life to?

GF: I tell people all the time kind of jokingly that every boxer has this big protective cup under his trunks where you can't hit him below the belt. If you do, it doesn't hurt him, but then there's nothing on his head, like headgear, so later on you see all these boxers with ten kids and no money. I tell them, "Take the protective cup off, wrap it around their head, then later on you'll see them with some money and brains, maybe no kids." It's all mixed up. They should be protecting the brain. There should be a protective headgear in boxing now. We can afford it. People are civilized enough to appreciate it.

LM: There are a couple of arguments against it, though, one of which is that it makes it less thrilling for the audience because you're not seeing the direct glove punch on the head. The other argument is from the medical standpoint, that having the protection on the head makes it heavier, and that can cause problems in and of itself.

GF: First of all, they feature headgear in the Olympics for safety, and billions watch it. It's a popular sport; all over the world people want to see a boxing match, and headgear doesn't take away from it at all. As far as scientific data that it could add weight, I'd like to have one on, and then you can give me the scientific stuff later on. I know for a fact it helps.

LM: You wouldn't have fought that when you were a boxer?

GF: No, I would've really appreciated it, because I know you wouldn't get so many chances to get scarred up, and you could have longevity; you could stick around for a long time. Boxing needs to be safer. They did shorten the rounds from fifteen to twelve, that helped a lot, and I think they should drop it down to ten.

LM: Even for title fights, down to ten rounds?

GF: For title fights. No one should be in that ring that long. No, no, no. That's a long time to be in a ring when a guy's being hurt. When a guy gets hurt the referee will ask him, "You're knocked down. How do you feel? Do you want to go on?" As though some brave man will say no in front of the world. You've got to tell them no, you can't go on, and sit them down. Make it safe. Get headgear so that we can't get beat up so much.

LM: Beyond headgear, what do you think could provide greater safety? Should referees be quicker to stop fights than they are? I think referees have changed in the past few years and have become quicker to do that.

GF: Some have; they know they'd better be. In Las Vegas, they've done a good job of making certain that the pads on the ring itself, on the floor, are thick, so if a guy hits his head on the canvas it's not so subject to injuries. Then the referees have a doctor to examine these guys in-between rounds. We're doing some good things, but we need to go further. There's going to have to be some educated research on this.

LM: What do you think about women being involved in boxing? One of your daughters boxed, didn't she?

GF: That's right, Frieda. Her name is Frieda George Foreman.

LM: What do you think?

GF: I hated it. When I got the word that my little curly-haired daughter was boxing, I didn't know what to do. I tried everything to get her out of it. In her last boxing match I went out and helped her in her corner. I even trained her, because I didn't want her to get hurt. I was going to teach her some of my old tricks, and I knew then there's no such thing as women boxing. It was just boxing. That lady had heart. I never thought I had a daughter with much heart. She sat down after taking a beating in the first couple of rounds until I thought she'd say, "I got a daddy. He has everything. I don't have to do this." She didn't even look at me. She got up and answered every bell, and it wasn't long before the other lady was running from her. It taught me then that there's no difference when it comes to heart and soul.

That girl made me respect her, and respect women in boxing, too.

LM: Because of this issue of developing heart, does it concern you that there are fewer kids now who are getting involved in boxing? Obviously there are physical risks involved, but boxing enables kids who are directionless to find that place deep within themselves to come back when they think they're out of gas, to keep doing it.

GF: At the George Foreman Youth Center in Houston, we still have a lot of young girls and boys coming down to the gym, and they learn that very lesson that you just mentioned. I've had the bullies come out; I mean, big bullies. I put them in the ring with those big, heavy gloves on, with a small kid who's real skillful. They can't lay a hand on him, and after a while they're tired and those gloves feel like iron and they're looking at me like, please Mr. Foreman, can you get me out of this? I think every kid should have a chance to do it at least once. And there are still a lot of good up-and-coming boxers.

A listener asks Foreman about his religious conversion.

GF: I was in the dressing room after a boxing match, and I had a vision I was dead. I saw everything I'd ever worked for like ashes, crumbled behind me. I didn't know what to do. I sat in this dark, empty, sad place. I still believed there is a God; I just didn't believe in religion. I just couldn't do it. I don't know why. I was wealthy and everybody I'd seen in religion was poor. So I'm on that dressing room table, and I saw blood on my hand and on my forehead, and I hadn't been cut from the boxing match. I started screaming, "Jesus Christ is coming alive in me." Of course they grabbed me and strapped me down and took me to intensive care. There was nothing wrong with me, but I told that story to Dr. Robert Schuller.

LM: Of the Crystal Cathedral.

GF: I told him what happened. He said, "George, I'm a psychologist and I'm a reverend, and I believe you." That was the break I needed. I still hid from it. I didn't want anybody to know; we made fun of religious people, you know. And that changed my life. I was shocked. I couldn't even make a fist for ten years. I didn't know what to do with my life. I didn't know, but I started preaching, of course. I was ordained in 1978 at the Church of the Lord Jesus Christ, and I started preaching. I'd go into prisons and hospitals, but I didn't want to be involved with athletics, because I'd seen so many dumb athletes who didn't know there was a world in need. But the kids weren't coming to church, so my brother Roy and I started the George Foreman Youth Center. We were going to provide role models, show kids that everybody wasn't stealing hubcaps and all of that. They didn't want me to come and preach to them. I never brought out a Bible. I never gave them a sermon. They just wanted people to pay some attention to them, and I did that. To this day I still go into the gym and watch them. That's all they want from me, and that's what made me understand that the best thing that you can do is to give of yourself.

LM: And that's your ministry as you see it today?

GF: I still do. As far as the youth center, I still preach in the church. I still have services on Wednesdays, Saturdays, and Sundays, where I'm still the main speaker.

LM: Even with your travel schedule.

GF: I do.

LM: That's got to be tough.

GF: I usually come back from those boxing matches with my eyes all swollen, and preaching the sermon on give a little, take a little. The youth center is such a treasure in my life. That's what drove me back into boxing, to get money for the youth center. I was broke.

LM: That was before the grill?

GF: There you are.

LM: In the mid- to late Seventies you were actually a street-corner preacher for a while, too. What happened when people saw you on the street?

GF: After I left boxing there were so many preachers waiting their turn at the church that I would attend. A young kid told me, "You know, George, you can really preach. You can just go on the corners and talk. Nobody knows who you are." I cut all my hair off, and there wasn't a mustache, and I'd stand there all day and no one would pay any attention to me, but I would deliver the best sermons in the world. Then I would get people to stop, and I realized if you could say something to make a person on their way to somewhere important stop for a second, you could really sell. That's where I learned my technique as far as selling—on the street corners.

LM: Did that also help you with your television presentations on HBO? Was that in a sense an audition for what you would do later?

GF: I sometimes think so, because I'm always talking now. My wife is telling me, "Okay, it's time to go to bed." I'm always talking. I love to talk.

LM: Well, you also have to be calm when people are talking in your earpiece and yelling all around you.

GF: The whole world is going on outside and you've got to stay calm and stay cool and not let anything bother you.

LM: Your wife has obviously been a big influence in your life. You've been married a number of different times; which number is your wife?

GF: I've been married five times, and the fifth I've found to be the charm.

LM: How long have you been married to her?

GF: We're closing on our twentieth year; it's a charm. I don't know how I ever made it. It was my fault, the other marriages. They were nice girls. I was married to women who really treated me nice. I gave cars and homes and jewelry, but I just didn't know how to give of myself.

LM: Is it difficult for you, though, because everybody out there in the world wants your time, wants your attention? Does that make it difficult for you to have enough left for your wife and your kids?

GF: I do. You'd be surprised. With this brain that we have and this spirit we have, you can't even count the things that we can do, and the amount of people we can embrace, and the amount of books that we can read. I've got so much to give.

Anne Garrels

September 9, 2004

nne Garrels wrote a bestselling book, *Naked in Baghdad,* about her experiences as one of only a couple of dozen American journalists to stay in Baghdad during the invasion of Iraq. It was yet another journalistic coup for the highly regarded NPR roving foreign correspondent. I first spoke with Garrels about the war shortly after her return to the U.S. from Baghdad. For this interview, Garrels talked about her recent reporting sojourn to Iraq.

Larry Mantle: What has Iraq been like since your book, *Naked in Baghdad,* was originally published?

Anne Garrels: The situation is much worse in Iraq than it was a year ago. It is much more dangerous for everyone: Iraqis, American troops, and certainly for journalists.

LM: Does it seem a bit ironic to you that while your book details some very scary moments, you're saying it's even more frightening to be there now than then?

AG: Oh, absolutely. I was given far too much praise for having stayed during the war. I made a very calculated decision then. I'd seen the bombing in '91 and '98 and I knew basically how accurate it was. But so accurate from the air and so messy on the ground is all I can say. And the U.S. was clearly ill-prepared for what it saw afterwards, even though Iraqis predicted so clearly what we have seen in the aftermath.

LM: Given the very scary situation in Iraq today, how far did you roam around Baghdad on your most recent trip?

AG: I was there basically from the end of June through July, into the beginning of August [2004], and I traveled freely in Baghdad. I say freely, but let me put it this way: I get in the car inside the courtyard of the house where we live. I no longer walk to the dry cleaners or the laundry. I don't wander the streets as I used to just chatting to people. I get in the car; I go to my destination; I do the interviews and then I come back or go on to the next interview. I don't just meander any longer. Sadr City, an area of Baghdad, has become very dangerous to go to. I did go there, but with great caution. I traveled to Najaf repeatedly and to villages in the area. That was before the fighting, but it was, once again, quite dangerous. There were certain areas along the road where I basically would lie down in the car so that I was invisible. I think it's a little bit easier for me as a woman. I wear a veil and *chador* (a black robe) and I think I draw less attention than male correspondents do. However, my illusions that women were not taken hostage or kidnapped—or if they were, it was the exception— changed the day before yesterday when two Italian women workers for a non-governmental organization were abducted from their house in broad daylight in central Baghdad.

LM: Is that the biggest fear that you and other journalists have, the prospect of being abducted?

AG: Yes, that clearly is, and journalists have been abducted, along with other foreigners, not to mention Iraqis. The other dangers are being embedded for three or four days with the military. It's dangerous because the military now are regularly victims of car bombs and of these insidious roadside bombs that are triggered by a walkie-talkie or a cell phone. Sometimes I can't avoid being with the military. Generally speaking, I try to avoid being around a military convoy. I keep my distance from them because they are targets. I don't drive around in a big SUV because that just screams "Attack me." Those are what contractors working for the U.S. and security people travel around in. Even the TV networks that had been driving around in these cars because they've got camera crews have started using far more low-profile vehicles. And you need to change your vehicle regularly just in case it has been targeted. These are the sorts of things we are thinking about on a daily basis. It's not just for myself; I am also concerned about Iraqi staff who work for me and put their lives at risk every day.

LM: Having to deal with all of these security concerns I would assume has some kind of an impact on your ability to spend as much time reporting as you'd like.

AG: Oh, there's no question. Our ability to travel freely is nonexistent. There are some places, you know, I just can't go. I cannot go to Ramadi or Fallujah, the key areas where the insurgency is operating out of in the heart of the so-called Sunni Triangle. I can go to some areas up there but the roads are very dangerous. It's very capricious. You might go one day and everything will be all right; the next day you go into that area and you are taken. And Fallujah, it's just not even worth the effort of trying because within seconds of getting there, the insurgents basically said, "No journalists can come in." If you go in there, you'll be arrested at best within seconds and quite possibly killed. So, there is no benefit to even trying. Our Iraqis do a lot for us. They can travel to these places but only if they wish to. I won't ask them to do something that they are uncomfortable doing.

A listener asks if the people of Iraq are better off today as a result of the American invasion.

AG: Most Iraqis would say they are not better off today than they were two years ago. The security vacuum is dire. The people feel insecure. There aren't enough jobs; employment has not improved. The electricity situation/infrastructure situation has not improved and is indeed worse than it was before the war. So, what is freedom? I remember when Paul Bremer, who was head of the occupation administration, sort of chastised Iraqis in the early days for not appreciating what the U.S. had done, saying, "You now have the freedom to travel. You have the freedom to do what you want." And Iraqis that I subsequently interviewed scoffed and said, "Yeah, who has got the money to travel? You can't get a visa to any country. We don't have passports." (Although they do have passports now.) And, "We're afraid to let our children go out on the streets," because in addition to the insurgents, there has just been a huge crime wave with kidnappings for ransom, rape, you name it.

LM: So you think if there were to be some kind of a referendum, where you could offer Iraqis either the opportunity to go back to the pre-war time or to stay where they are today, you think that they would turn back the mythical clock if they could?

AG: Not entirely. With Iraqis, it's always on the one hand, on the other hand. They don't want to go back to living under Saddam. But they thought that things would get better faster with the United States. Perhaps they had inflated expectations about what the U.S. could or would do. The U.S., in turn, has been unable to do as much as it thought it would do because it was so ill-prepared for the looting in the immediate aftermath, and for the widening insurgency later.

LM: And is there much hope about the election which is said to be coming up in January 2005?

AG: I'm not sure that there will be an election. The security, once again, is the key issue. There are several areas of Iraq right now, Ramadi, Fallujah, Samarra, Ba'qubah, mainly Sunni areas, north and west of Baghdad, where the insurgents basically are in control—and where it's unclear how the U.S. military will wrest control back. The United Nations, which is responsible for preparing for these elections, has been unable to keep up its schedule. The prime minister has said that they are, in fact, way behind schedule because they can't move about the country because they don't have enough security. And other countries, far from joining the coalition, are, in fact, withdrawing and cutting back their commitment, and new countries are not coming forward to help protect the United Nations staff.

A listener wonders about US troops' morale, saying, "They were told they freed the Iraqi people, and then on the other hand they see the chaos every day. That's got to wear on them."

AG: It does. They see exactly what you have just described and many of them are frustrated. Either they say, "Hey listen, we came to fight and now we've been pulled back and we are sitting on the outskirts and we're not fighting," or, "We came to help and we can't help because the security is such that we can't do lots of projects that we'd like to do to help the Iraqi people." So it's very frustrating for them. Increasingly I am hearing soldiers who are saying, "I feel like we are fish in a barrel." Where soldiers feel they can fulfill their mission, they feel more satisfied. But when they feel stymied, it's a problem, and platoon sergeants have said to me, "It's a big problem trying to keep them sufficiently occupied in some cases because they are just not able to do their mission." It's a real mixed bag. The military is made up of lots of different people. The military is in fact taking the lead on economic development, or it would like to. Part of the problem very early on was a lot of the money that Congress made available was not disbursed. When I was there, even as late as July, only about a half billion of the eighteen billion that Congress authorized had been made available to the Iraqis. And the military is increasingly saying, "We have got to provide jobs." They had lots of projects in various places that they wanted to push forward, although it's become so much more dangerous in the last two months I don't even know if they can do them now. But they said they just didn't have the money to do them. I know that Ambassador Negroponte has been really pushing to get that money released and made more available. But instead of doing big, big, big projects that take too much time, they are trying to do smaller ones that get a lot of Iraqis engaged fast and that do make an immediate impact on the community, whether it's cleaning up sewage or trash or you name it. The other thing is security. The U.S. had said that they would have two hundred thousand trained and armed Iraqi security personnel on the streets by now. They've got under half that, and one could question just how well trained they are. The Iraqis clearly are not ready to take a major role in their own security at this point.

A listener asks about Garrels's driver and translator, Amir, who is a character in the book.

AG: He really stood by me during the war, and was a major reason why I stayed during the war. He's desperate. He is working for some Japanese journalists. We still see each other all the time. He resents the American occupation. He often says to me, "Don't hate me for saying this, but I just think you've done a terrible job. It's like you have thrown a rock at the mirror and fractured my country." He sees civil war ahead. I should point out that he is a Sunni. He is very concerned. He wants to be an Iraqi; he wants the country to pull together. But he sees it fracturing. I think this was probably inevitable over time but he blames the United States for this.

LM: And do you think that most of the Iraqis with whom you have spoken want to have an intact Iraq?

AG: I would say yes. However, it's going to be very tricky down the road, especially with the Kurds in the north. They have aspirations to claiming the city of Kirkuk, which has always been a mixed city, although it was predominately Kurdish until Saddam basically bought off or forced out the Kurds over the last twenty years and "Arabized" it, if you will. It's important because it's oil rich. And there is going to be a battle over this city and this region. The Shia want elections and they want them in January. If they can't be held for security reasons, they want to see their newfound power and their proportion of the population—sixty percent—reflected in a new government. But there are differences among Shia over what kind of Islamic state it will be. Everybody is more or less in agreement that it will be some form of Islamic state, but just how moderate, how extreme, is the question. I think the majority of Iraqis want an Iraq that is part of the world. They want an Iraq that is inclusive. But whether that will be allowed as tensions grow, I don't know.

A listener asks Garrels about ordinary Iraqis and their attitudes towards her.

AG: Basically most Iraqis—not the extremists—make a distinction between the U.S. government, which they may like or disagree with, and the American people. They are enormously welcoming. And as much as they may criticize the United States, they would all love to get a green card and come here. So there is always this inherent contradiction. I spent a lot of time in small villages on this last trip. It was in an under-reported part of Iraq, and I was welcomed enormously by these people who have questions about the U.S. role in their country. They're concerned about U.S. intentions. They're suspicious about what the U.S. is really doing. I think the administration has done a really bad public relations job in general, in part because it was so ill-prepared for the aftermath. Nonetheless, I was welcomed, and there was enormous curiosity about America. They now have access to satellite television and they were watching TV. I asked them what their favorite program was nowadays, and the amazing answer was *Oprah*. To a man and woman, they all watch it; life stops at seven o'clock at night. They watch it with Arabic subtitles. I said to them, "Wait a minute, you know *Oprah*?" That particular night, we were watching a program about credit card debt. Now, this is a bunch of people, in remote villages who have never seen a credit card. I said, "Isn't this like watching Martians?" And one man said, "No. This is a human drama, and often on this program these poor people go through terrible things. But there is hope at the end, and we need that hope. We don't have hope and we really like the ones about when people get sick because you have access to doctors who can do something." They watched this program for the human element of it all and they liked the stories about family problems and how we resolve them or don't resolve them. But when *Oprah* got involved with issues of sexuality or homosexuality, they clicked to another channel.

LM: So they appreciate the universal human drama even if the drama revolves around something they don't see or have access to. It also sounds like maybe there is a bit of a wish to be a part of this as well, that there is a kind of fantasy in it.

AG: Of course. It's unclear where this is all going to end up. Iraqis have been living in a police state and under U.N. sanctions and isolation for the last twelve years. They don't know who they are. They don't know where they fit in the world. The Arab world is extremely confused about its own identity. You add to this that Iraqis are moving out of this cocoon that they've been in, and with the insurgency going on, it's a mess.

LM: How much freedom of the press is there in Iraq at this point?

AG: The Iraqi government had suspended Al-Jazeera, the Arabic satellite channel, and they have now extended that ban, although they have not yet made a case in court backing up their charges. So there are some problems. For me, apart from the security problems that limit one's freedom, I am obviously able to work much more freely than I ever was under Saddam.

LM: Do you think there is a way that U.S. troops could or should be pulled out?

AG: Most Iraqis would say at this point that they want the U.S. to go. But then you say to them, "Now?" and they say, "No, God forbid, not now because we are going to eat ourselves alive." Pandora's box has been opened. I think at this point an effort has to be made to beef up Iraqi security forces before U.S. troops can leave. The U.S. dismantled the army, creating hundreds of thousands of unhappy people, and now it has to start from scratch. It's been very, very slow, as the training was inadequate and very slow to start with. Providing weapons, vehicles, flack jackets, that's all just picking up pace now.

I joined the noted architect Frank Gehry for a walk-through of downtown Los Angeles' Walt Disney Concert Hall not long before the hall opened. For many years, those in L.A.'s classical music community had been pushing for a new concert hall designed specifically to showcase the Los Angeles Philharmonic Orchestra. The Dorothy Chandler Pavilion of the Music Center had been the orchestra's home for more than three decades, but it lacked both the acoustics and the intimacy that the Philharmonic and many of its fans wanted.

With the opening of Walt Disney Concert Hall in the fall of 2003, most critics said the orchestra finally had a place to play that was worthy of its talents.

Larry Mantle: Take us back to the genesis of this project.

Frank Gehry: God, do I have to?

LM: What are we talking about here, twelve years ago, something like that?

FG: 'Eighty-eight.

LM: So fifteen years ago. How did you come to be involved with the concert hall project?

FG: They had an architectural competition and people submitted their qualifications. I did not because I just assumed I was considered a bad boy of architecture. I was working with chain link, I was working with the materials I could afford and people could afford, so it got me a bad rap. Then I got a call saying they wanted me to submit. I said, "Why bother? You'll never get me through." Anyway, long story short, I won the competition, and we started work on it. First thing we did was we traveled around—Ernest Fleischman and I—to look at halls.

LM: Ernest Fleischman, who was the managing director of the L.A. Philharmonic for many years.

FG: Right, and the musical spirit behind the design, I think, from the beginning. He's kind of an unsung hero. He took me to Berlin, to Concertgebouw, to Leipzig, to a bunch of them.

LM: You went to these great halls to hear the orchestra in that environment.

FG: Yes, and we met with acousticians; we talked about issues. We loved Berlin Philharmonie very much; it had what they call vineyard seating, where seats are on levels around the orchestra. It creates an intimacy with the orchestra. There are people sitting behind the orchestra. The Concertgebouw in Amsterdam, which is a much older hall, also has seven hundred people sitting behind the orchestra.

LM: So you were trying to wed the best of these halls that you admired.

FG: We were trying to accrue values that were important. What stood out to both of us was that the relationship between the orchestra and the audience was the crucial thing. In theater work I'd done before I came to that conclusion.

LM: Back in '88 or in the couple of years that followed, had you designed any kind of musical performance to that point?

FG: Yes, I did the Merriweather Post Pavilion outdoors; I did the Concord Music Pavilion outdoors; I worked on the Hollywood Bowl from the time Ernest came here.

LM: You did the acoustic redesign on the shell there, didn't you?

FG: Yes, the balls as they call them.

LM: The balls, right. Gehry's balls on display.

FG: Right, that's what Robin Williams called them. I think I had a lot of experience with the orchestra. I got to understand the culture of the orchestra. That was important for an outsider to the music world to understand that if you have a hundred musicians, you have a hundred rugged individualists. And their seat and their place in the orchestra is their domain.

LM: You need to have a place that's comfortable, and yet everyone has his or her territory.

FG: Right, and I watched that over the years at the Bowl. The musicians would befriend the stagehands and get them to push their seat, give them a little more space. Anyway, understanding the culture of the orchestra was a very important thing for me. I've listened to a lot of music over the years and met, through Ernest, a lot of very important conductors and musicians, not the least of whom were Pierre Boulez and Zubin Mehta. All these people would come by while we were designing. I would drag them to the office and make them look at what I was doing and talk to me about it. That was very helpful.

LM: How important is this for you personally? This is your hometown. This is a symphony that you've become close with over the years. You've been involved with this project for so long; it's been a roller coaster ride for you. Does that make this project stand out?

FG: No. Obviously it's nice having it here where I live; when you go out on the town you meet people and it's nice to have them greet me as they do now. So that's very nice. But I don't think of it that way.

LM: Is it like choosing between children?

FG: Yes, we wouldn't be able to choose between children, that's exactly right. You love them all. I'm more interested in the experience of the music. The biggest thrill for me was at the first rehearsal, when Esa-Pekka Salonen stopped the orchestra, turned around and said, "Frank, we'll keep it." I lived on that for—I'm still living on that one.

LM: Can you describe what it was like for you to sit down in this hall when the orchestra gathered for the first time to play there?

FG: I was sitting next to Diane Disney Miller, who was a really important factor in this thing getting done. They started playing and I know enough about the critical issues that I watched the bass players, because I knew that was the moment of truth. The bass response is the most difficult thing to create in a hall. The first bass was standing there and then all of a sudden this big smile came over his face and it rippled through the other bass players and then he saw me. And he gave me a thumbs up. That was thrilling. I turned around to Diane; she had tears of happiness in her eyes. I think I've come to all the rehearsals, and it's thrilling to me to listen to the orchestra begin to adapt itself to the room and start to play with the room. The first few notes were trumpets, brass, and they sounded too bright. Slowly they've started to play down. The people aren't blowing as hard as they were in the Chandler. You can see them relaxing into the building. I love that, I'm just thrilled with that.

LM: Let's talk about the challenge of bringing acoustical integrity to the building, making it sound the way you want it to sound and look the way you want it to look. How do you work with an acoustician, in this case Yasu Toyota, to integrate your vision of what the building's interior should look like and the acoustician's vision of what it should sound like?

FG: Strangely, I know there are horror tales that other architects have with their acousticians. None of that happened here. Yasu and I blended together, became a creative entity together. Being Japanese, he was extremely polite; I used to have to push a little to get him to talk and say things when they were negative.

LM: He didn't want to offend you.

FG: He didn't want to offend me. I listened to everything he asked for and I responded to it with the visual tools I had, and in most of the cases he would say, "That's better than what I expected." Because of our computer stuff we could get into spheroid shapes instead of just using cylindrical shapes, which meant that there was a greater spread of sound. He was overjoyed with that. He believed that the visual impact of the room and the character of the room was very important to the perception of the sound. He thought that what I could bring to it would enhance, rather than detract.

LM: I want to talk about the whole on-again, off-again saga of this. That must have been extremely frustrating for you, to put so much of your heart and energy into this and at various times have fundraising efforts lag. Then all of a sudden after Bilbao, the museum that you completed in Spain, it seemed like there was a whole new flurry of energy here.

FG: That started with Richard Riordan, the former mayor, who I played ice hockey with and would meet on the rink. I checked him a few times, which he'll tell you. I think that he saw the models in my office and said, "We have to do this." He brought in Eli Broad who spearheaded it. There are a lot of partners in it. The complexities and the internecine wars, whatever you've heard, are in the end really trivial. We did pull it off together and it was a partnership. A lot of cities try and they can't. So it is a miracle if you look at all the trivial arguments and stuff that have gone on and still go on, about the most mundane things that could drive you nuts, like how they're going to handle the parking tickets when the patrons leave. I've been in situations like this where they haven't pulled it off, where the wagon got pulled apart by people who went in six different directions at once. You see it a lot in New York, where they're struggling.

LM: So does that make this particularly rich that, after all that's gone on, here it is, a finished work?

FG: And all the people involved are still friends for the most part. Eli Broad and I are still friends.

LM: You have to get him playing hockey with you though.

FG: No, no. He'll beat me up.

LM: . . . As you can probably tell from the traffic moving behind me, we are standing on the front steps of Disney Hall at the corner of Grand and First Street, right across from the Dorothy Chandler Pavilion of the Music Center. Mr. Gehry, talk a bit about the outward appearance of the hall. We've all seen it go up over the past year plus and enjoyed seeing the design of it. How did you come up with the vision for what the hall would look like from the street?

FG: It was designed from the inside out. The interior for music was lead, to these sail-like shapes in wood. I wanted to express the same aesthetic on the outside of the building, so I carried those forms out. The hall itself is a simple box and it's flanked by two wings that have the toilets and the elevators and stairways and they're joined across the front where we're standing with a foyer that connects both those elements. Those simple parts were tweaked slightly to get the curves. So it's not a lot. It looks like more than it is. Then the smaller elements that are less expensive were made a little more flamboyant. So basically it grew out of the interior. I was concerned about context. I was concerned about the Chandler a lot because the Chandler is an icon of the city and whether I liked it or not didn't matter; the people who created it are still around, some of them.

LM: I can guess by your answer how you feel about the pavilion.

FG: Well, I think it looks like pseudo-Lincoln Center, but they like it. It's an important part of the city and a lot of money and a lot of love and care went into it. It doesn't matter what I think. So I tried to make this building relate to it, even though I wasn't going to copy that aesthetic. That's one big shape, one big huge iconic box with some curves on it. I didn't make this that way. I broke this down in scale so it was a different language. It still allowed that big box to have its iconic presence without usurping it. Even though this building is shinier and will get a lot of attention, I don't think it trashes that building. I think it helps. It makes it a sister or brother or whatever you want. The curves of the Chandler coming down Grand toward where we're standing bring you in as you're coming down the street toward Disney Hall into this space. And on Hope Street it does the same thing. The curve brings you into the sculptural shape of the Founders Room. And there are actually places where you stand on the street, on Grand Avenue under the canopy, where you look up and you'll see the curve of Disney—the Walt Disney Concert Hall fits into the curve of the Chandler. People can go looking for it. They'll find it. On the Hope Street side we made a garden that faces the apartments that were there. And that's a good, friendly, neighborly thing to do, even though those people complained a lot about the shiny metal and they're ungrateful sometimes. I heard their land values tripled. People like to complain. The south side is designed as the office block of the Philharmonic and it relates to the future office blocks that I suspect are going to be south of it. Grand Avenue is designed as a pedestrian walk in that you can enter right off the street. The big doors, on days like this, will be open and people will just walk in. There's no security there; it's back inside.

LM: And the gardens are open to the public as well?

FG: The gardens are open to the public, and the gardens are beautiful. They are designed by Melinda Taylor, who's the wife of one of my partners. So it's all nepotism.

LM: Another thing that is so intriguing about the building is that, wherever you stand, much like a mountain, it's a totally different building when you move even a few feet away.

FG: As you stand in it, it frames views of the city. I tried to be inclusive visually with the City Hall. There are beautiful framed shots of City Hall as you walk around and through the building. And the garden is very special. It's got a lot of full-grown trees. It will have bars for intermission. I did a special fountain to the memory of Lillian Disney. She used to collect Delftware and so we made a Delft Rose in the garden that a good artist friend of mine, Thomas Osinski, is building, and he's doing a great job. This is a tribute to Lillian that's been sponsored by her grandchildren.

LM: You undoubtedly are aware of the project undertaken by former District Attorney Gil Garcetti chronicling the ironwork at Disney Hall, and have seen the book that's resulted from it. I'm curious to hear your thoughts about the process of constructing the hall.

FG: I'm very much interested in the process of construction, and we were only able to do this because of the software we've developed that allows us to build these shapes and demystify it. I remember reading in the *L.A. Times* that the steelworkers complained at some point, but I think when Garcetti started taking pictures of them they were all excited and professed a pride in having been part of it. So that's what we find, mostly. When people look at the models and the drawings they say, "You can't do this." Then when they get in and do it there's a "How did I do that?" kind of attitude. I feel the same way, actually. How did I do this? But it is a special relationship with the construction industry. I have to rely on them. This curtain wall, the exterior skin, is done by Permasteelisa, the same company that did the skin of the Guggenheim Museum in Bilbao. I've worked with them a lot and technically this is one of the best curtain walls that I've ever seen; they really did an immaculate job.

LM: Let's talk about the cladding on the structure because it is so beautiful and so striking. What is the material, and how is it adhering to the framework of the building?

FG: The material is stainless steel, which is different than Bilbao. In Bilbao I used titanium. It's adhered with clips. It's not the weatherproofing. There is a vapor barrier behind this metal. So if anybody thinks it's going to leak, it prevents a lot of the water from going in but there is a vapor barrier. The trick is to get the material to lay flat and not be wrinkly. Permasteelisa did a great job. We worked two years with them on perfecting this wall system. We built mock ups. We knew what we were going to get. The surface of it is called "angel hair" but it's not the normal stuff they do. It's an abrasive surface; they abraded the surface and we did about fifty tests until we got a surface that took the light especially for L.A. Los Angeles has so much sunlight, and when it touches this stuff it's magical and you can see it all around.

LM: When the cladding was being added to the building, were you down here regularly looking at it to see how light was reflecting off of it?

FG: I came down, but I wasn't worried about it. We'd built a mockup and I was pretty sure it was going to work. But you can't leave a lot of that to chance because it'd be very disappointing.

LM: And many millions of dollars later you've got a serious problem. Let's talk about the entry with the large staircase that brings you up to the entry level of Disney Concert Hall, how it addresses the corner of Grand and First.

FG: This is made like an amphitheater. I saw people from the courthouse sitting here having brown bag lunches and maybe somebody playing music down there or using it for a lecture. This is the ceremonial entrance for the grand parties and stuff. The street entrances are much freer and more open to the street and more activity. So I try to address both characters that they asked for.

LM: Given that there have been attempts to make Grand Avenue more of a pedestrian-friendly street, what kinds of conversations did you have with city officials about what the plans were for Grand Avenue and how Disney Hall would address the street?

FG: I was involved with two or three go rounds with teams addressing Grand Avenue. The best one was with Arata Isozaki, who designed MOCA, and with Rafael Moneo, who did the cathedral. Working with Laurie Olin, the landscape architect, and Stu Ketchum, who was part of the building committee, we came up with a scheme that we thought was kind of nice. What's being built out here is going in that direction. I suppose it's going to be a long process until it gets done.

LM: . . . Now we are seated in the audience in the heart of the hall itself. It has more than two thousand seats, but one of the things that strikes me is that it feels so much more intimate than one would expect of a two thousand-plus seat hall.

FG: We spent a lot of time trying to make it more intimate. I did a lot of things to do that. I made the hall smaller and squeezed more seats in, rather than make a bigger volume. A lot of things led to that, because of my belief that the relationship between the orchestra and the audience is the crucial issue here architecturally.

LM: That sense of being in such close communion with the orchestra is pretty overwhelming. I can only imagine the power of that orchestra as it viscerally affects the audience sitting so close.

FG: The orchestra also feels the audience, and that's crucial. You talk to these musicians and you talk to actors who use theaters, and they say the relationship that they have with the audience is the big deal. The more intimate that can be, the better the response from the audience and the better the response from the musicians. They play to that. That gives them the energy and the desire to connect. They feel the connection and it enriches their experience and the audience's experience.

LM: You have so many different seating areas here in various tiers. You have about three hundred seats at various levels behind where the orchestra will be sitting. Does each of the spaces have a unique perspective to it?

FG: The intent from the beginning, and this comes from our glorious leader, Ernest Fleischman, was to make all the seats equal. He was into equality. And of course, you can't have everybody sitting in the same place. Friends of mine have asked during the construction, "What are the best seats?" I've brought many of them here and showed them the hall, and they sat in a lot of different places and they said, "Well, all the seats are good." I think that's true even way up by the organ way in the back of the hall toward the Chandler. All of these seats have this intimacy with the orchestra. I would say they're different but they're equally good. And musically they're fantastic. So I don't think there are any bad seats. There are a few sections where the legroom got truncated a bit. So if you're six feet three, you should ask at the box office to keep you out of those sections. There are only three or four lines that are like that.

LM: What about the wood that's in the hall in the ceiling, and that surrounds the organ pipes?

FG: The wood is Douglas fir, plain, ordinary wood except it's the highest, the most expensive part of it. It's the straight grain Douglas fir. It's the closest grain to the grain of the wood used on musical instruments. So if you put a violin or cello next to that grain it matches it pretty closely. That was the intent. I loved the color of it. It darkens with time like a fine wine. It really gets beautiful. I would say it's about halfway to its finale where it'll stop, but it'll get a little darker than this. It'll happen so slowly you won't even notice it.

LM: While you might have reflection of sound off of the wood, I assume you have a certain percentage of absorption in the fabric on the seat cushions.

FG: In every hall that's built, the seats are designed for absorption, so that when there's no audience they can use it for practicing. It has to be a similar acoustic. So everybody does that. I wanted to make these seats special because I don't like going into a hall where all the seats are the same color. It looks like the night after the show until people come in and enliven it. So I thought, why not make these different colors, make it like a flower garden. Lilly Disney was into flowers; I promised her I would make a flower garden. I think it works because it looks great when it's empty, it feels festive, and when people are in it, it's okay too.

LM: The organ is quite spectacular, with what some have described as looking like huge matchsticks at various angles up behind where the orchestra will be performing. The organ is on a raised level behind where the orchestra is seated. Is it true that you were involved in the design of the organ?

FG: This is the first time anybody let us play pick-up sticks like this and change the shape of the organ pipes. We brought all the wooden ones that are normally behind out in front. Then we added the traditional trumpets to give it a flare so it's a centerpiece for the room, which it needed. The room needed that background. When the orchestra's in place, it looks like a crown. It's to die for—for me, anyway. I'm looking up there and I see Manuel Rosales, the man who built the organ, and I'm waving to him to come and play a few notes for us. At first he told me that it was impossible to build an organ like this, and then slowly we became friends and I convinced him that this was possible. Now he's built it, and he loves it. And I see he's now going over to play for you.

Rosales plays the organ.

LM: Wow! I don't think it's possible for radio to quite do justice to the power of that organ. You were telling me that that's only twenty-five percent of the pipes installed?

FG: Yes, he's got another six, eight months work to get it all finished. I think what you heard was louder than it would normally be. He was trying to get a lot of sound for you because he didn't have all the juice behind it. It'll be much more subtle when it's done, when he has more tools to play with.

LM: So the L.A. Philharmonic is going to have to program many more symphonies that use organs as a result of having this available.

FG: Yes, I think they intend to have a program of organ music. And I hear from the grapevine there are a lot of organists around the world who are already coveting this organ. They want to come play.

LM: I can tell your passion for this, how much you love this building.

FG: Another thing that the public will notice is that I have these skylights and windows in the hall so that an afternoon concert will be much different than the afternoon concerts were at the Chandler. At the Chandler you came out into the sunlight and it was like going to a theater in the afternoon, which is not as pleasant. Here, the natural light will make the afternoon concerts, and it already has increased the number of afternoon concerts they intend to have.

LM: The playfulness of the building is another thing. We haven't really talked explicitly about it but the floral feeling from the seats, the matchsticks of the pipe organ, how the pipes are arranged, there is a fun feeling to the building, and it's clear that was very intentional. You didn't want this to be considered stodgy.

FG: It wasn't about fun, but it was about creating an appropriate place for music and making it a place that would be inviting to the younger generations. The stodgy halls have a problem with getting kids in, especially in America. In Europe it's not a problem, but here, it is. I guess maybe our musical education is deficient, but the idea of creating a space that would attract younger people was on their mind.

LM: What do you hope will be the concert hall's effect on the cultural life of Los Angeles?

FG: First thing I hope is they'll build a bus lane on the freeway from the westside to bring us downtown, because it is tough to get here from there and a lot of the patrons are coming from the west side. I think that downtown, in order to function as a real downtown like the model of a nineteenth-century downtown like New York City, requires more housing, more people living down here. As these attractive cultural elements come into place they'll bring people who'll want to live in the vicinity. They'll get people building housing around it. For a long time now, MOCA has been the new baby that has to do the attracting with the old baby, the Music Center. Adding this and the cathedral starts to create a critical mass that might be different.

LM: After all that has gone into a process that began fifteen years ago, it's hard to believe it now is culminating in the opening of Walt Disney Concert Hall just a little bit over a month from now. In some ways it must feel hard to believe it's finally coming to an end.

FG: I hope all people will come here, not just the people who are used to going to concerts. I hope this will be inviting to all kinds of ethnic and economic groups. I know that that's the intention of the orchestra, and I hope that they use it. It's theirs. We've put fifteen years of stuff in it. There's a lot of love put in this place by a lot of people. So come and get it.

Chuck Jones

October 25, 1989

During the time he was animation director at Warner Brothers, Chuck Jones helped create the characters of Bugs Bunny, Daffy Duck, Porky Pig, and Elmer Fudd. Jones personally created such characters as Road Runner, Wile E. Coyote, Marvin Martian, and Pepe Le Pew. Jones made more than three hundred animated films in his career; along the way he won three Academy Awards as a director, and a lifetime achievement Oscar in 1996.

Like everyone else I've met who knew Jones, I was impressed with what a smart and caring person he was. Though Chuck Jones died in 2002, we'll always have his Warner Brothers cartoons.

Larry Mantle: You're working right now on a series of lithographs, is that correct?

Chuck Jones: I was always wondering how Van Gogh or Gauguin or Toulouse-Lautrec would have painted our characters, so I made a painting of a Wile E. Coyote with a missing ear with a bandage around his head, painted in the same style as Van Gogh. Then I did a Duchamp, which is a nude duck descending a staircase, painted in that style.

LM: That's great.

CJ: We have a lot of fun doing those, but what I'm doing is, I'm a contractual advisor to Warner Brothers again. Next year is Bugs Bunny's fiftieth birthday; unfortunately Bugs Bunny was gray to start with so he doesn't get gray with age.

LM: And he's long in the tooth, to start with.

CJ: That's right. And, of course, Daffy was a couple of years older, and as far as I know he uses Grecian Formula. Porky is a little older—

Porky's the oldest one, he's fifty-four.

LM: And the Road Runner, Wile E. Coyote, they're forty years old, is that right?

CJ: Coyote and Road Runner are forty years old, as of the eighteenth of September.

LM: When you were creating these cartoons with your colleagues at Warner Brothers, did you have aspirations that these cartoons would last so many years later and be regarded as classics of the genre?

CJ: No, if we had, we would have made very bad cartoons. I know of no one who ever starts out to do anything for posterity. When I was a little boy, we lived on Sunset Boulevard right across from Hollywood High School, about two blocks from Chaplin's studio. So we were able to go down there and watch him, because Chaplin and everybody else shot most of their pictures outside. The reason they shot them outside was because that's where the light was. They didn't have the best kind of lights. They hadn't been perfected at that time.

LM: This was down on Sunset and La Brea, right?

CJ: Yeah, that's where the studio was. It was surrounded by a wire fence, so you would go down there and watch them work. I think more than anything else I wanted to be a Keystone Kop, because I figured that with my temperament, that was about right. I tried to Keystone Kop my way through childhood; at least my mother said I did. I don't think I was terribly successful, but I do know those people were trying to be funny. They were trying to be not tickled funny, but they were trying to do what they thought was good humor to themselves and to each other. And that's the way we were, a whole bunch of people from all walks of life, from all different parts of the country who happened to come together with one thing in common, and that was a sense of humor. All of our films, even the very last ones, the ones that are on television now, were all made for theatrical release. None of them was made for television. Since we didn't know what the audience was, we certainly didn't make them for children. Because you couldn't assume that, if we made a cartoon and it went out with something like *Little Caesar*, or *I Was a Fugitive in a Chain Gang*, or *Dr. Ehrlich's Magic Bullet*, that the audience was going to be composed of six-year-olds.

LM: Of course.

CJ: But on the other hand, you couldn't attend pictures like that with the supposition that those people were going to be intellectuals. We didn't know what the audience was, so we decided the only thing we could do would be to make pictures for ourselves. Then we could make each other laugh; we hoped that might lead to continuing employment.

LM: Obviously, the main answer to this question is that you had an assemblage of very talented people working on these cartoons, but I wonder what else you think it is that led to this tremendous creative energy and ability at Warner Brothers to do successful cartoon after successful cartoon?

CJ: The one thing that is certain is that the first critic hadn't been born. There was no such thing as Nielsen ratings, or trying to figure out who the audience was, or anything like that. Nobody told us what to do. We also had people to hate; both of the two producers we had all those years. One of them was terribly lazy and one of them was basically mean. Was it Aristotle or Plato—I always like to bring in names like that in an interview just to give culture to the matter— who said that he wanted to be a gadfly on the rump of the universe? And he meant that as an intellectual process to stir the people of the world to do things. But we had this one producer who was a gadfly on our rump, basically because he was very negative. Once in a while he'd have a brilliant outburst; he'd come into the room and say, "Use lots of purple—purple is a funny color," and so I'd say, "Yeah, that's probably true, Eddie." Then I said, "Why don't we use a lot of quarter notes in the music, because quarter notes are very funny." He never heard of a quarter note so he didn't know what it was, and he said, "That's it, boys, put in lots of quarter notes." So from that point on we tried to avoid purple. One time Mike and I were working on a story—Mike Maltese was the great story man who worked with me— and suddenly we looked around, and here was this man standing in the doorway. He was furious. We didn't know what he was furious about and he said, "I don't want any pictures about bullfights— there's nothing funny about a bullfight," and then he turned on his heel and strode away. There was a deathly silence for a moment. Then Mike looked at me and I looked at Mike, and Mike says, "We've been missing something. This man's never been right yet, and if he thinks there's nothing funny about a bullfight, there must be something funny about it." Indeed there was, and *Bully for Bugs,* which we made then, turned out to be a very, very good Bugs Bunny for us.

LM: It's amazing he would come out of left field with a comment just out of the blue about bullfights.

CJ: Yeah, I don't know where he got these things. One time he told Friz Freleng, "There's nothing funny about a camel. I don't want any camels in our pictures," so Friz immediately followed our lead and made *Sahara Hare,* which is a very, very, very funny picture. So he served a purpose in a way, because we always had somebody to fight.

LM: So having this friction really helped the creative process.

CJ: Oh, absolutely. When we worked on a picture neither of our producers ever saw the films, they didn't really know what the heck we were doing. When we did run the picture, Leon Schlesinger would come striding in and walk back to the end of the theater and he'd get into a throne he had there. And then he'd say, "Roll the garbage." That gives you a feeling of appreciation, that he really cared.

A listener asks about what Jones went through at Warner Brothers in the early 1930s.

CJ: I worked for less than twenty-five dollars a week, and Jack and Harry Warner thought we were making Mickey Mouse cartoons. Jack Warner didn't even know where the studio was; this was fifteen years after I started directing. Friz Freleng contends that both Jack and Harry believed that we made Mickey Mouse until 1963 or '64, and when they found out that we didn't, they closed the studio.

LM: What was the official reason?

CJ: They didn't give us one.

LM: Really?

CJ: They just said, "That's all." We figured that every one of those cartoons we made brought Warner Brothers over a million dollars, and there were five hundred of them. We didn't have any residuals, we didn't get any money for having made all those films. But you know, you can be bitter, or you can go ahead and try to make some more, which is what I did.

A listener asks if the director is responsible for the storyline as well as the art work.

CJ: Yes. He worked with the writer but it was axiomatic that the director represented about half of his own story division. He worked with the writer, but when it came down to it, most of the writers didn't draw very well. I would do three hundred to four hundred drawings for each picture. Ultimately there would be five thousand in each cartoon. Also, I would write all the finish dialog and direct it with Mel Blanc, or whoever the actor might be. The director's job at Warner's was unique. You had to do an awful lot of things or else you couldn't keep your job. It wasn't so much out of artistry as it was survival.

LM: I'd like to talk about animation today, which might well be a sore point with you. I wonder if you'd comment on the kind of limited animation that we see typically on Saturday morning on television.

CJ: I can only respond as a viewer, and because I had children, grandchildren and now I have great-grandchildren. I don't appreciate anybody making films that are talking down to children; I never did. I never talk down to children; when I do talk to them I might get something very brilliant out of them. Children are remarkable critters. Within the last ten years, a little boy finally told me what the hell I was doing, because his father introduced me as a man who draws Bugs Bunny. The little boy looked at me and he was furious, and he said, "He does not draw Bugs Bunny, he draws pictures of Bugs Bunny." It was a magnificent "of," because that's exactly the way we felt. We never thought of ourselves as doing drawings; they were snapshots of the characters, because the characters were alive to us. If they weren't alive they couldn't be believable to us, and therefore they couldn't be believable on the screen. I think you have to generate sympathy with a character before you can even make them funny. All great comedians have been that way. There's an enormous difference between a stand-up comedian and a practicing comedian. Ed Wynn probably put it as accurately as anyone can put it when he said, "A comedian is not someone who opens a funny door; he's a person who opens a door funny." If you look at our Road Runner cartoons or many Bugs Bunny shows, you'll find out that if the coyote uses a bow and arrow or any piece of equipment, a lasso or a pole vault or anything like that, it should work. The problem is, he got it from the ACME Company, and there is going to be a glitch somewhere along the line. So those are not funny bows and arrows, hopefully they are funny because of the way they are used.

LM: I wonder if it's your feeling that the cartoons that are aired today don't get into that kind of identification with characters that you had with Warner Brothers.

CJ: We had to learn to move characters or the same character under different circumstances. If Daffy is triumphant he'll move differently, he'll walk differently, or he'll stand differently. There's a lot of difference between Bugs Bunny running when he's being chased and running when he's doing the chasing. The animator has to learn so many things about behavior and the physical movements, so that you'll decide whether you care about a character or not. Now, on Saturday morning if you want to know the difference, take The *Bugs Bunny Show* and turn the sound off and watch our cartoons. You can still tell what's going on. But I defy you to turn the sound off with most of the Saturday morning stuff and tell what is happening, because everybody moves the same and they're distinguished only by their voices and by their basic appearance. I call it illustrated radio.

LM: That is a great point; I hadn't thought about that.

CJ: When I'm at an airport, when they put the movie on the airplane I usually watch it for about five or ten minutes without putting the earphones on. If it's a good picture you'll know very well what's happening with it, and then if you get really interested in it, then you put your earphones on. But if it hasn't proved itself in the first ten minutes, it's not a good picture.

LM: What were your thoughts on *Roger Rabbit*?

CJ: I didn't care much for it, because I didn't care much for Roger. I thought it was technically brilliant, but when you think about it, it seems to me there are two things that go into any kind of creative work. One is the love that you have for what you are doing, and the other is the work you put into it. My belief is that the work shouldn't show in the finished product. In other words, I don't care how hard he worked in order to do, say, the singing frog that I did in *One Froggy Evening*. A lot of people liked that cartoon. That was one of the most difficult things I ever did. *What's Opera, Doc?* was another difficult thing, but hopefully it didn't show. It should look easy, because the audience doesn't have to participate in that; it's like a brain surgeon forcing you to watch what he's doing. It isn't fair. He should do it well and he should do it without your being aware of what he's doing.

LM: In talking about characters in your book, you mention that it needs to be a reflection of something inside yourself, that you draw on something in you to develop the character. I wonder if we can talk a little bit about that, about where the characters come from.

CJ: They must come from you. The relationship between the animation director and animator is exactly the same relationship there is between a live-action director and his actors. You can't go outside yourself. Because then you're only dealing with outside appearances, and what you look like is different from who you are. Laurence Olivier is a rather heroic example of all this. Think of the roles he played, and he played them all without changing his voice. It's curious because the same thing was true of Mel Blanc. It's been said that Mel had a thousand voices and they were all the same. They were; it's the intonation, it's the rhythm, and it's the timing that makes any voice work. Bugs moves differently than Daffy, and Daffy moves differently than Coyote, and so on. If you're animating a horse it runs differently than a dog does, and a mouse runs differently than an elephant. And if you want the believable, that's what you'll do.

LM: Speaking of Mel Blanc, how important were those voices to making the cartoons work?

CJ: Mel was a brilliant actor, and we always developed the character; we never started with the voice. Let's say I was doing Pepe Le Pew; I wanted a character that was a particular kind of a character, but I didn't know what he looked like. So when I was writing down what he would do and his environment and so on, then I began to cast him in the live action. You would go through a casting book that had pictures of all kinds, like, this guy might work or he looks about right. But in my case, I started drawing. The first Coyotes and Road Runners and the first Bugs Bunnys didn't look anything like they look now.

LM: Really?

CJ: It took several pictures to find out what they looked like and how they stood. In fact, in the early pictures Bugs had very short legs and stood in a bent posture with his legs crooked at the knee. Then we realized that he was kind of elegant in terms of the way he stood. He would stand with all his weight on one leg and very delicately nibble at a carrot, not chaw at it. So he did change.

LM: So it evolved over a period of time?

CJ: I know Olivier would agree with this: the character that you are playing is either somebody you realize you are, as in his case *The Entertainer* was a good example, but he said he was most familiar and most at ease with that character because he always thought he was going to fail. That's the way I feel about Daffy Duck and Coyote and Elmer and the rest of them, because, like the entire history of comedians, most are wimps or losers, even up to Woody Allen and Richard Pryor and people like that, great comedians. But once in a while you get a character who is a kind of hero, like Burt Reynolds in some of his films, or Clark Gable in *It Happened One Night*. Bugs Bunny is that way. That's the kind of person you'd like to be. So what you do is pull up all the characters and all the characteristics that you admire. If you took Rex Harrison playing Professor Higgins in *My Fair Lady*, and mixed him thoroughly with Errol Flynn playing D'Artagnan in *The Three Musketeers*, and then add a dollop of Dorothy Parker and stuff that into a rabbit skin, you get Bugs Bunny.

LM: And Mel Blanc is really the icing on that cake, to have him take that already created character and give him a voice.

CJ: The animation director would very carefully work out the rhythm of what he wanted to say because we had to time our picture completely. None of our pictures was edited in any way, they were all pre-edited by the director, and timed by the director using mark sheets. We would account for every step; if there are three steps to a second, that means one every eight frames. When Bugs walked—he tended to stroll because he was under control—he would step every twelve frames, which is twice a second, a slower kind of walk.

LM: So it's very precise then.

CJ: Yes, very precise indeed. For him to dance, I had to learn how to waltz, and to know the difference between a waltz and a two-step. Very few men know that, but I had to learn it because in some places

I had waltz and in some places I had two-steps. And the difference is between step-close-step and step-step-close. It doesn't sound like much, but it's all the difference as to where the beat comes. Something else I want to mention: there are two things that I think are necessary when you're in a directorial position. One is that you must give everything that you have; you owe any audience everything that you have. The second thing is to surround yourself with talent. Every one of the people who worked with me was talented. Mel Blanc was a brilliant voice man, and I probably had the best designer in the world, Maurice Noble, who brought success to pictures like *Duck Dodgers in the 24½th Century*, and who invented the gantry crane and the ten-story outer space missile ten years before anybody ever built one. And there was Mike Maltese, who worked with him for so many years, a brilliant man, and many, many animators who worked with me.

LM: A real team effort, putting these together.

CJ: Yes, although each one of the directors had absolute control over the material that went into his pictures. Originally that was Tex Avery and Bob Clampett and Frank Tashlin, but from 1948 through 1964 every film that was done at Warner Brothers was directed by Friz Freleng, Bob McKimson or me.

LM: And you and Friz are the ones who are left who can talk about those wonderful years. What is Friz Freleng doing these days?

CJ: He's still very much alive, and Yosemite Sam still lives within him. It's interesting that a man can have Yosemite Sam and Tweety Bird within him, isn't it?

A listener comments that he never considered Wile E. Coyote or Elmer Fudd as villains.

CJ: Elmer always said, "I'm a vegatilian." He said he just hunted for the sport of it.

LM: I think this is a really good point; you can't assign good or evil to them because they are full-blown characters. They are complex in the same way people are complex.

CJ: That's right, and Louis Brown wrote in a book, "There are no judges, there are only men judging; there are no tramps, only people tramping." You may remember a series of cartoons I made about a sheep dog and a wolf—it was actually the coyote playing another part. But they lived together—they lived in bungalows adjoining one another. They'd go to work, and they'd punch in a time clock.

LM: I love it.

CJ: Then the sheep dog would start guiding sheep, and the wolf would try to steal them. So it was like all the rest of us: when we go to work, we're one thing, but otherwise we're all very similar. When the man who conducts the New York Philharmonic goes home at night he has hangnails and sneezes and has trouble with his wife, just like the rest of us. So that made it a lot easier for me, to realize that Daffy and Bugs and all these characters are just people who are playing particular kinds of parts.

LM: Certain cartoons seem to have a message. Is *Duck Dodgers* the one that makes an anti-war statement?

CJ: Yes, my wife thinks it's a very powerful anti-war statement, because at the end these two guys are fighting over a little piece of earth about as big as a football. I never started out with a message, because I'm just not sure that I'm capable of doing anything like that, but if you have something to say, you'll probably say it.

A listener asks about how to find old serigraphs of Warner Brothers cartoons.

CJ: They're not serigraphs. There are a few production cels that were left over from about 1968. In 1967 Warner Brothers was under another management—not the present management or the original Warner Brothers—and they needed space to store the records for their publicity department, so they went in there with bulldozers and took all the cels and drawings and everything that we had done for thirty years and burned them.

LM: Oh, no.

CJ: So there's almost nothing left from the millions and millions and millions of cels. When you think about it, there were thirty years, and thirty cartoons each year, and each cartoon had five thousand drawings and five thousand cels. When you start multiplying those things and think how much people care about them, you realize that was a pretty dumb thing to do. Anyway, since that time I made a few short subjects for Warner Brothers. Some of those productions cels still exist, but about twelve years ago my daughter said, if people wanted cels, why couldn't I recreate some of the cels from my own films? So that's what I started doing. Then she started releasing them as etchings, they're hand-inked and painted like an etching. There will be maybe a run of three hundred to five hundred numbered. They're in a few galleries. Here's a strange thing: when Disney opened Disneyland they gave them away as a little gift. The second year, they thought they'd make a little dough on them, so they started selling them for a dollar. Then a few years later they gave them away with original backgrounds for five dollars, and one of those was sold recently at Christie's at auction for twenty-five thousand dollars. Another one, an old black-and-white Mickey Mouse cel, sold for $152,000 at Christie's. That was one of the old celluloids, rather than acetates.

A listener asks if some scenes in some animated features have been shot first with live actors, and then animated.

CJ: They tried that on *Snow White,* where they actually traced some of the action. But they discovered that some of these really intricate things, particularly fabrics and stuff like that, made it very difficult and awkward for an animator to use. What they discovered was they could shoot the action, and then blow it up onto twelve-inch by sixteen-inch sheets of paper, and then the animator would use that as a guide. He didn't actually use the drawings, and he didn't trace them, because he had to dramatize the movement. So yes, they did use it for study mainly, but it was extremely difficult.

A listener asks about a series of cartoons Jones did about a character named "Inky" and a mynah bird.

CJ: There is such a bird, but he doesn't move like that. The music that he moves to is the overture to "Fingal's Cave" by Mendelssohn, and so he would phup, phup phu phup, and that little hop. I'm like Ulysses S. Grant, I only know two tunes, one is "Yankee Doodle Dandy" and the other one isn't. So carrying a tune is not really my thing, but anyway, it was a very mysterious thing. I really didn't know what the hell I was doing with that series. But there was one interesting thing about it. The first one was done in 1941, and Manny Farber, who teaches at the University of California at San Diego, was a film critic then for the *New Republic,* and he said it was the first time that anybody ever put a black boy on the screen that didn't use stereotypes like eating chicken or eating watermelon or playing dice or something like that. He was just an ordinary little black boy. It's difficult to remember that up until probably the Fifties, no black could play any part on the screen except that of a maid or butler or somebody who was scared or something of the kind. When you're young its hard to believe this was so, but it was so. In the early *Tom and Jerrys,* the maid was afraid of mice, and whenever Jerry would run in he'd squeak. He'd purposely scare her and she'd jump up and she'd say, "Get movin', feet," and then she'd jump up on a stool and a pair of dice or a razor blade would fall out of her clothing.

LM: It was a whole different era.

CJ: Yeah, it was a different era, so later on when I worked at MGM I took those cartoons and remade a lot of that material, because, my God, it was grotesque.

LM: There has been a minority, but a vocal minority, that has taken issue with what they claim is the violence in television cartoons. The Warner Brothers cartoons have also been targeted for that, and I wonder how you feel about having your work attacked in that way.

CJ: I have never been able to understand it, because we never did anything that wasn't done by Chaplin, Hunter, Keaton or the Keystone Kops. The main thing, though, is that anybody under forty-five who watched television has grown up on our films, and so if the United States is a country of psychotics then obviously I must take the blame for it, because they watched Coyote and Bugs.

T he ability of Steve Martin to evolve in his work over time, and to use so many different vehicles for his humor, makes him stand out even among the other giants of American comedy. Combining slapstick with the cerebral, Martin first established himself as a television writer and star, before writing, directing, and starring in feature films. He's also a playwright and novelist. Unlike many other comedians, he has never been stylistically confined nor stuck in the era of his greatest commercial success.

I talked with Martin just after his novel, *The Pleasure of My Company,* was published.

Larry Mantle: You have transitioned through a variety of different ways of expressing your comedic muse. What's led to these transitions?

Steve Martin: To me, it's just a continuum—writing for television. I was always doing stand-up. Stand-up is essentially writing on your feet or it's spoken word and written word. And writing skits for television leads to writing plays and writing plays leads to screenplays and it's just all part of the same thing to me.

LM: Was there a certain point where you felt as though there was a better way of presenting what it is you have to say? Did you start writing novels because you felt that format would be the best way to communicate what you had to say?

SM: An overlooked philosophy we've kind of forgotten is from Marshall McLuhan: "the medium is the message." I'll paraphrase it in an amateur way: to me it always meant that the medium you are talking through actually changes what you're saying. I have found that it's not that I have something to say and then I find the best medium to say it. I just approach a medium and see what it dictates. So in other words, writing a book is very different from writing a play. And I find that whatever the medium is actually changes what it is you "have to say." Whatever that means.

LM: You are seen as a very cerebral writer and comedian who doesn't shy away from the physical. When you're writing, though, for the page, you don't have that same kind of physical advantage because you don't have the visual element beyond what you are able to create with your words. So do you feel like you are going even deeper into the non-physical part of your humor?

SM: I think that writing sentences is a lot like doing radio. Because it's almost like a cartoon can make a character do anything, and you can have his head blow off. And in a way with writing, you can create such extreme visual images or even touching visual images that you can't if you were doing it live. For example, I am doing a movie of the book *Shopgirl,* which was very much about tone and mood that was expressed somehow in the writing. I'm not quite sure what it is; it's kind of a lonely, isolated character. And now that we're doing the movie we found that there wasn't much dialog in the book at all; it was mostly interior. So bringing it to film meant I had to write a lot of dialog and try to figure out how to say things. You know, you can't just say, "Gee, I'm lonely," in a movie. I found that the director, Anand Tucker, who did *Hilary and Jackie,* found a way to bring the tone to the movie without having to say it. So now the tone, which used to be in the language, in the words, in the spareness of the words, will now be visual.

LM: That's so much the challenge of adapting a book. But often people are disappointed if they are fans of a book when they see the filmed version of it, because it's hard for a film to have a universal appeal to everybody who experienced reading it.

SM: I think you are right. But it all depends on the nature of a book, too. If a book has a lot of plot, that's almost easier to bring to screen. If it has a lot of tone then you could actually make a more artistic movie and still express the same emotions that were in the book. That was the challenge in writing the screenplay. At first when

I finished the book, I thought, "There is no movie in this book." Then after several years went by, scenes started to appear in my head and I started to think, "What actually is the plot of *Shopgirl*?" because I know that's how movies move and I realized there was one.

LM: But you hadn't considered it before.

SM: Right. It wasn't the essential part of the book. So then the question became, "How can I present the plot and maintain the tone?"

LM: One of the real challenges for funny people is staying relevant as the Zeitgeist changes in this constantly evolving world. Going back to the humor of, say, *The Smothers Brothers Comedy Hour,* your earliest public presentation of your work, all the way up through *Picasso at the Lapin Agile* and the books that have followed, there is something that is very consistent and at the same time you are commenting on a world that's very different from the late-1960s world of the Smothers Brothers. I wonder if you can elaborate on it and describe what you see as the through line of your view of the world?

SM: That's a complicated question. I'll pick it apart the way I heard it. One is: how do you stay fresh?

LM: But keep a consistent voice, so to speak.

SM: I think the consistent voice comes from being a consistent person, being the same entity. I've observed people in my own life who, as they grow older, stop at a certain era. They dress like that era and they have their hair cut like that era and that somehow it must symbolize that that's also where their thinking stops. And I, God forbid I would ever try to be hip. There's a time when you're naturally hip. For me it was the late Seventies, I was hot and it was an effortless kind of thing. But the idea of trying to stay in the forefront of entertainment or something would just kill you and you would ultimately be defeated. So you can only carve out your own niche by being—sorry to use this cliché—true to yourself and reacting to the world and staying interested in the world, by actually subscribing to a newspaper. It's as simple as that.

LM: So a lot of it is staying engaged. I guess what we see then in other performers is that they get stuck in a time perhaps because it's so exciting for them to be in that hot period.

SM: I don't know the psychological reason, I don't know if it's that or something else or fear to go forward, I don't know. But I wasn't even talking about entertainers. I was just talking about people I know. Then other people stay fresh and stay engaged, and I have also noticed that as my friends and people I know age, either their worst qualities start to crystallize and become dominant or their best qualities do. They kind of go one way or another. It's like a complicated person who might be cynical and judgmental yet kind, can grow older and become completely cynical or completely kind.

LM: As you look at conflicts in your personality, which way do you think you have gone as you've aged?

SM: Oh, I am much more accepting. It's kind of a cliché to say, you know. A friend of mine was sitting next to a psychiatrist on a plane—this is a true story—and he was talking to the psychiatrist and he realized the psychiatrist was deaf or very hard of hearing. So he said, "You know, you are a psychiatrist and you're hard of hearing. What do you do? How do you treat your patients?" He said, "I've heard it all before." And that's sort of what we do as we get older and are confronted with new situations; there is some ring of having heard it before.

LM: After all the success you've had, do you still get the same level of charge that you did earlier in your career when you broke through with something new?

SM: Yes, I do. But it's not so much that it's something new, it's just something that you've done and made. I must say I get less of a charge, that kind of emotional charge, from movies than I used to because movies have been really my entire entertainment life. It's like having a long relationship where you win some and you lose some and there's excitement and then there's disappointment. Pretty soon you almost have to get a little more blasé about it or you'll be on an intense emotional roller coaster.

LM: But that's not necessarily the case with writing at this point.

SM: No, no. Writing is also a very personal experience. Moviemaking is a very collaborative experience. So in moviemaking, when you have a success or failure, there's a lot of people to share all that with. With writing, there's no one to blame but yourself.

LM: In my experience it seems many comedic writers are naturally on the shy side and also prefer working by themselves. Yet film is a very collaborative process. Temperamentally which are you more: the loner comedian type, or someone who likes working in the larger group format?

SM: It depends on the nature of the project. I really like the social aspect of making movies. I love to hang around with comedians. I love dinner parties with lively people. And yet I remember years on the road where you're just alone from morning until night, and it's a kind of a fog that comes over you except when you're on stage.

LM: Is writing at all like that?

SM: No, because writing is alive with the characters and you have a phone and you have your dog and there's a lot of activity that goes on. When I write I generally won't write longer than two or three hours. So it's a small part of the day.

LM: Steve, let's talk about *Pleasure of My Company*. Share a little bit with us about this neurotic man who lives in a Santa Monica apartment building and has a life that I guess according to some would be average, for others, quite eccentric.

SM: Right. It's about a young man in his early thirties living in Santa Monica who has isolated himself through, say, neurotic expression, neurotic tendencies. I don't want to say obsessive compulsiveness, although you could. For example, he can't cross the street at the curb; it's too forbidding. He must find two scooped out driveways that are opposing each other because it makes sense to him. And he always must have 1125 watts lit in his apartment. So if he turns out a light in the bedroom he must turn on a light in the living room. But that's really only a part of his problem. His real problem is that he has found ways to keep people out of his life. Even though he engages in the world he goes to the Rite Aid, he goes shopping—but it's really the story of how he subconsciously reaches out and how people consciously reach into him in spite of all these problems. It's really a story about how life essentially seizes you if you open yourself up a bit.

LM: Do you see somewhat of a thematic connection with *Shopgirl* to people trying to connect in the world, trying to find their place by moving out of where they are to find a place of greater connection or fulfillment?

SM: Right. But also I should say that this book is actually funny.

Shopgirl was much more poignant than it was funny, although there were funny scenes. I wrote this book with the intent of being funny.

LM: And when you're writing humorous scenes or funny lines versus something that's going to carry more poignancy, are you in a different state of mind?

SM: Well, no. *Roxanne* is a good example of that. The character himself is inherently poignant, so you never really have to play it up. In *Shopgirl* the character herself is inherently poignant. In *The Pleasure of My Company,* the character is inherently poignant so you never have to play it. You can really find comic situations. And because the character is so sympathetic or frustrated, that humor just naturally arises.

A listener asks Martin about the relationship between his physical comedy and his comedic writing.

SM: All I can say is the writing came much later. You know, as a kid, I was influenced by movies and Charlie Chaplin and Laurel and Hardy and Jerry Lewis and Abbott and Costello. So all that physical stuff was to me the meaning of comedy. That's what comedy was. And then as I got older and went to college and read books, I had this horrible thought, which was, "Uh-oh. If I am going to be an original comedian I am going to have to write it all myself." So I tried to figure out how to write comedy. The first thing I did was to start to pay attention to life. When I laughed and—if I laughed out loud—I asked, "Why did I just laugh?" I would start writing it down either in my head or writing it down on paper to remember it. It was a natural progression just to start writing. Also, as a young man in college I found great joy in reading poets and poetry. So it was just a combination of a lot of things leading me to something else, I guess. But the humor, the physical humor was just to me a part of comedy.

LM: Are you one of those for whom the physical can be enough for you, or do you need a multi-layer of comedy for it to work most effectively for you?

SM: Oh, it can be completely by itself. The joy of doing a big physical gag or watching a big physical gag is just too exciting.

LM: You grew up here in Los Angeles; is that right?

SM: I grew up in Orange County—Garden Grove.

LM: And obviously living so close to Hollywood, there may have been some influence. Did you know anybody who worked in the movies at the time?

SM: Nobody, nobody knew anything. It's very different now. Everybody seems to know how showbiz works. There are backstage interviews from *Entertainment Tonight* that show everything. Then, it was just all in front of the curtain, and we did not know how to break into show business at all.

LM: What gave you the idea that you wanted to do this but also that potentially you could make a living doing this?

SM: I never thought of making a living. I just wanted to do it. I mean, I would perform for free anywhere I could, and the idea of being paid for it was at best four or five dollars.

LM: I read that when you wanted to perform as a kid you put together a variety show.

SM: Right, exactly.

LM: You've always been the guy that put together the vehicle to expose yourself.

SM: Yeah, so I could perform, yeah.

LM: Do you see that even in your professional career, that when it came to making movies, that you put it together to get it started?

SM: That's a little different. But we did. I say "we" because I had writing partners early on.

LM: So you created your own vehicles in films?

SM: Right.

LM: Why is it so many comedians have struggled in that transition to film?

SM: I thought when I first started doing movies, meaning acting, that it was a natural transition to go from stand-up comedy to acting. Turned out it wasn't; I had to actually learn a whole new thing. All I had was the ego, I guess, to get out there and perform—you know, the love of performing. Then I really did pay attention to other actors and directors and I learned a lot from them.

LM: Richard Pryor was an incredible comedian in his stage work. But he did some film work that was okay but nothing compared to what he was able to create before. Why, do you think?

SM: I think that's because Richard Pryor's stand-up was transcendent and it was so dependent on his monology. There is no natural transition from Richard Pryor's monology to film, whereas I was doing physical jokes and gags and I was all over the place and it was a little easier thing.

A listener asks how Martin bridges the tension between the literary and popular worlds, since his writing ranges from plays to films to the New Yorker *to fiction.*

SM: It's tough, because "commercial" has such a ring, especially in the literary world, that "commercial" is sort of pushed off to the side and kind of quarantined by the literary community. But I feel I'm an entertainer, and whatever sophistication there is in my writing is meant to be visible, to be accessible. But, you know, I think some of the great performing art of the twentieth century is the musical: *West Side Story, Oklahoma, My Fair Lady.* These are very, what we'll call, middlebrow. And yet to me they are high art because those songs are so appealing, so indelible in your mind, so emotional and so smart, sort of like Noel Coward lyrics. They are so smart. But I must say that literary work actually lends itself to great, great sophistication as opposed to, say, music. Because music exists in time, you take time to listen to it. It's better when it's appealing and when it starts to get into twelve-tone, it's intellectual. It's wonderful, but you don't go out humming it—or rarely do. Let's put it this way: there is a great niche in the literary world for extremely sophisticated works. Very commercial things become regarded as high art and very sophisticated things become regarded as commercial. So that's my lousy answer.

LM: No. It's an excellent answer. It seems to me that the writings that work best are the ones that have a smartness to them. They are informed by the things that the writer and other parts of the creative team have exposed themselves to during the course of their lives. You are obviously a well-read person and that comes out in very natural ways in your humor and in your writing.

SM: When I was in my teens I read a book on performing magic as a magician. And it made a point that stuck with me forever, which was: "Use everything." It said: "Use the lights, use the sound, use the costume, use humor, use drama, use color, use big, fancy boxes—everything." And I still do that today. I think, "Okay. I can write a book. I can make it sophisticated, I can make it funny, I can make it appealing, I can make it quirky, and I just want to use all of those elements to keep it alive."

LM: As you look back now at all the things that you have done to this point in your career, are you able to appreciate all of it? Can you turn on Comedy Central and be watching an old skit you were part of on *Saturday Night Live* or a hosting gig you did and appreciate it now, or does that seem like it was another lifetime?

SM: It seems like another lifetime. It's very hard to appreciate it. I was talking to a friend of mine, a painter, and he said, somebody made a comparison between psychiatry and artistry and they said they were similar. He said the main contradiction is that artists must abandon their work, and in psychiatry you try to hang on to the accomplishments.

John McCain

November 8, 2002 and April 19, 2004

I've included two of my interviews with Senator John McCain (R-Arizona), conducted a year and a half apart. The first conversation touches on his 1999 run for the presidency and disagreements with members of his own party. It also explores the major influences on the senator's life, including his more than five-year imprisonment in the infamous "Hanoi Hilton" prisoner-of-war camp in Vietnam. At the time of this interview, Senator McCain had just written *Worth the Fighting For: A Memoir.*

Part One
November 8, 2002

Larry Mantle: Can you be candid about what your relationship with President Bush is like? The perception that we have is that it's a rather chilly personal relationship.

John McCain: Actually, we have a cordial relationship.

LM: That sounds kind of chilly.

JM: I think the most overrated thing in Washington is this issue of being friends. Harry Truman said, "If you want a friend in Washington, go out and buy a dog." I do have friends: Fred Thompson and Chuck Hagel and Mike DeWine. I've served with them for a long time and we're friends. But what you really want to do in Washington, rather than go make friends, is get things done. And for that you don't need friendship. You need respect. I respect the president of the United States. I respect the job that he did on September 11, rallying the country. The American people strongly approve of his leadership of the country in that way. Do we have our differences? Yes, but those differences aren't personal; they're differences in policy, particularly on some domestic issues.

LM: You feel the respect is mutual?

JM: Oh, sure. I supported him a hundred percent on Iraq. I managed the bill on the floor of the Senate, the authorization of it, along with Senator Warner, and he was very appreciative of that. So we have a cordial relationship. That relationship will, I think, maintain us in working together on issues that we agree on for the good of the country. I believe that he's dedicated to the good of the country and I believe that's what my job is as well.

LM: I'm curious about how you feel within your own party. Are you like a fish out of water, a man who is not fully compatible with his party?

JM: No. I think that my party has strayed. I think we need to go back to the principles of Theodore Roosevelt and Abraham Lincoln. I still believe in my party. I know that I'm resented by some because of my advocacy of campaign finance reform and other reforms. But I also know, come election time, they all want me to come out and campaign for them. They all want me to come out there, particularly in close races. So they may not want to go out and have a beer with me, but when they're up for re-election or election, they like for me to come out and be part of their campaign. And I appreciate that. So I do work with my colleagues on a lot of issues. It's a shared desire to achieve certain results. There are people that I'd rather work with and rather not work with. But I'll work with anybody in order for us to do the public's good.

LM: You have a fascinating family background, with your father and grandfather both being four-star admirals in the Navy. In fact, there's a poignant story about your grandfather, who died just days after the end of the war.

JM: The day he got home. It took a few days to fly. He was on the *Missouri* at the peace signing at the end of World War II and flew home. The day he got home to Coronado, he was there having a big party and he had a heart attack and died. But he'd had a full life and had achieved what he wanted to achieve, and that was the victory for the United States. He was a crusty old guy, rolled his own cigarettes, swore all the time. He was a very colorful leader and a very charismatic one, very much beloved by the enlisted people who served under him. My father also had a lot of those traits, and he smoked big cigars. I don't smoke by the way. They were both very colorful people, big personalities.

LM: You lost your dad about twenty years ago?

JM: Yeah, about that.

LM: How influential were both men on your life?

JM: Extremely, but because of the lifestyle of a military family, my father was gone a lot. So my mother, who was a woman of indomitable spirit, was the major influence. But she kept my father around, you know what I mean? He was constantly in our conversations and in our thoughts, so he was kind of a distant figure but a very motivational one, obviously.

LM: Your parents met here in Southern California. Your mom was going to USC and your dad was stationed on a ship at Long Beach.

JM: Yes, they met and she was only a sophomore at USC. They eloped and got married down in Tijuana, which was a big scandal in those days. They had a very happy marriage and loved each other dearly, although my father also had his love of the Navy and it was also part of their life, which she understood and accepted. There's a great book by Herman Wouk I know you've read called *Winds of War,* and it describes the military culture prior to World War II in a very interesting fashion. Every officer came from West Point or the Naval Academy. They all knew each other, they all served with each other. In my second book, I write about a lot of my heroes and people who inspired me, both real and fictional. One of them was Army General Billy Mitchell, who just had this vision of air power and how it was going to determine the course of warfare in the twentieth century. He fought so hard for it, and it alienated so many people, he got court-martialed and thrown out of the Army. By the way, there was a movie made of it with Gary Cooper called *The Court Martial of Billy Mitchell.* It's a pretty good film. But anyway, I asked my mom, "Didn't my grandfather know Billy Mitchell?" She said, "Of course. They used to play bridge together down at the Army-Navy club in Washington. Of course, he knew him well." And I said, "Well, did he like him?" "Your grandfather liked him but the other admirals hated him because he taught that airplanes could sink battleships," and in the Navy in those days, everything was "The Battleship." Anyway, he was willing to put it all out on the line. You can imagine what it was like to be court-martialed and thrown out of the military in those days. You were in total professional and social disgrace.

LM: How prominent is the time that you spent as a POW in your life today? Your love of your country, your connection with your family, are these things that you still reference on a regular basis? Or do they end up getting kind of distant as you're doing the day-to-day grind of being a senator?

JM: My friends—those I know best and love most—are those I served with in Hanoi. They sustained me. They made me realize that if you're a loner, if you're totally self-sufficient, if you want to be left alone, cussed, then you're just a punk. They taught me what the Naval Academy and my family tried to teach me, that you've got to be part of a cause greater than yourself, something that you are fighting and struggling for with others. I observed a thousand acts of courage and compassion and love in prison, and I'll always be eternally grateful for those who I had the opportunity of serving with. But what it did for me was also give me a certain confidence in myself, that I am comfortable with myself. People were astonished a couple weeks ago when I hosted *Saturday Night Live*.

LM: You got rave reviews.

JM: It was risky, and I was nervous. You never know when you're going to cross the line, which I have done a few times with my ill-timed attempts at humor. But I'm comfortable enough with myself. Before I was always wondering whether it was my father's influence or my good works that made me succeed in the Navy. Well, he couldn't help me there in Hanoi. Just briefly speaking about my youth and my father, I write about the first hero of mine outside of my father and grandfather. He's an entirely fictional character, and that's Robert Jordan, the protagonist of *For Whom the Bell Tolls*. I was twelve years old; I found two four-leaf clovers, and I was going to press them in a book. I pulled a book off my father's library shelf, and I just happened to catch part of the book. I started reading it. I was engrossed; I read the whole book at one sitting. I believed that this was my hero, Robert Jordan, willing to fight and die for what he believed in, die for his comrades and, by the way, also have a wonderful love affair with a beautiful Spanish girl along the way. When he's about to die after making a sacrifice for his comrades so they might escape, he's got a broken leg and he says, "The world is a fine place and worth the fighting for and I will very much hate to leave it." That's where I got the title of my book because Robert Jordan, with his fearlessness, with his service to a flawed cause, with his courage and his self-confidence but yet his fatalism, was everything I ever wanted to be in life. And he was as real to me as any real person that I've ever known.

LM: And the image of the character stays with you for such a long time.

JM: Forever, forever. And he fought for a flawed cause. If you re-read it, Hemingway intentionally puts in parts of that book to show how flawed the cause was with these Russians leading this "Communist" cause. There were no good people, no good side of the Spanish Civil War. It was the fascists against the communists, both of them using this conflict as a laboratory to test their weapons. And it was a terribly bloody, terribly bloody conflict. And Robert Jordan was the idealist from Montana who, with the rest of those thousands of Americans—they called them the Abraham Lincoln brigades and the George Washington brigades—came and fought for an ideal. And even though Jordan found out that the ideal was not being implemented in the war by the leaders, he still fought.

LM: I'm wondering if you parallel that with your experience. Here's the unpopularity of the Vietnam War and yet the cause that you were totally committed to, and paying such a high price for the cause, your imprisonment.

JM: I'd like to believe that, but I think there's a couple other aspects of it. One, when I was shot down in 1967, the anti-war movement was not really going; it was not until about '68 and the Tet Offensive that it really got cranked up. And second of all, again in the interest of straight talk, I was fighting and flying in Vietnam because I thought that's what professional aviators and pilots do. That was my business, that was my job, what I was trained for. Of course, I believed that it was good guys against bad guys and that Ho Chi Minh's guys were communists. But the prime motivation was I was a professional military man. I trained all my career and I was ready to go out and do what fighter pilots do. So I didn't so much have a grasp of the ideology.

LM: Did you end up with resentment later about what you had to endure?

JM: Not what I had to endure. I was deeply disturbed and terribly, terribly angry about the divisions within our country when I came home, and about the way that the war was conducted. As long as there are fifty-eight thousand names engraved in black granite on the wall, we know that this war, that conflict, was terribly led by both military and civilian leadership. You never want to see lives lost in that way. Therefore I dedicated myself to the reconciliation process. First, I wanted to try to get a full accounting of the POWs and the MIAs, and then I worked with Senator John Kerry to get the normalization of relations between our two countries. I view that as something I'm very proud of because we really needed to do that. There were too many, and still are some Vietnam veterans, who have never been able to come all the way home.

LM: Who are some of your personal heroes that you write about in your new book *Worth the Fighting For: A Memoir*?

JM: I write about people who inspired me, real and fictional. My favorite movie that I saw at an early age was *Viva Zapata*. I thought that this guy Zapata must be incredible. He was a great leader and he sacrificed and died for what he believed in. And people like Theodore Roosevelt, my ultimate role model and hero. Also Ted Williams, the baseball player who served four years in the military, two years in World War II and two years in the Marine Corps in the Korean War, and he was a cussed guy. When I was very young, I remember going to Griffith Stadium in Washington, D.C., and everybody booed him. And so he waved at them. He didn't use all four fingers. I thought, here's a guy—he did it his own way, you know. But he was also, as we found out in later years, very insecure, very uncomfortable, and yet he loved the game of baseball. But he was willing to go in the military and serve his country. If I could tell you one remarkable story. He was in Korea. He was flying the early Marine Corps jet. He flew wing on John Glenn. John Glenn told me he was the best natural pilot he ever flew with. He was all shot up, his plane was on fire, he couldn't get his landing gear down and so he did a phenomenal thing. He landed at a field with his landing gear up and walked away from it. Some years ago I filled out a questionnaire from *Esquire* magazine. Last question was, "Who's your living hero?" I wrote Ted Williams. I went down and visited him down in Florida and spent an afternoon with him. I said to him, "Look, here you were, your plane on fire; you couldn't get your landing gear down. Why didn't you just eject from the airplane?" You pull the ejection handle and it throws you out, your parachute opens. He said, "I looked at the instrument panel and I looked at my knees. I knew that if I ejected, I was going to break my knees and I'd never be able to play baseball again." He said, "I knew then I would rather die than never be able to play baseball again." Isn't that a lovely story?

LM: Ted Williams, also known of course for being quite irascible. People say of you that you have quite a temper even going back to when you were a boy. How do you see your temperament?

JM: I see it, as you might expect, to have improved over the years. But there are still occasions when I get angry. The key to it is, if you lose your temper and lose control, then you're totally ineffective. I think I've been able to do a lot better on that. But there's nothing wrong with getting angry when you see bad things happening, when you see the wrong things happening, when you see injustice done. If we lose our capacity for anger then we really shouldn't be serving. So what I've been able to do ninety-nine percent of the time is not *not* get angry, because I *do* get angry. But I don't lose my temper and therefore my control and effectiveness. Early in my political career, and particularly early in life, I was ready to go at it at the drop of a hat. But I have been able over the years to recognize that that's not productive. You can't just get angry at anything, because then you lose your effectiveness as a legislator. So do I occasionally fly off the handle? Yeah, but comparatively speaking, it's a remarkable improvement.

LM: But in your 2000 presidential campaign you heard the whispers from some people, "He's a loose cannon" and "I don't know how solid he is emotionally." How damaging did that feel to you?

JM: Well, it hurts. I also made sure that during that entire campaign there was not one instance where I did lose my temper. Never during the entire campaign. So I kind of proved them wrong by that. But, yeah, it hurts when you hear that. My hometown newspaper, the *Arizona Republic,* accused me of everything from being mentally unstable to being an ax murderer. But look, you got to be tough when you're going through these things. And you got to understand that you can't give them any ammunition. I think it's a tough business, it's a collision sport. But the fact that a guy who stood fifth from the bottom of his class at the Naval Academy is able to run for president of the United States shows that in America anything is possible.

LM: And not only that but you came back from the Keating Five savings and loan scandal. Was that the most difficult time for you in your political life?

JM: Yes. But the thing perhaps I most regret and am ashamed of is when I went to South Carolina and I knew that the Confederate flag should be taken down, I waffled on that issue. I had gone in my campaign saying I'll always tell you the truth no matter what. That was our line. And then I didn't tell the truth about my feelings about the Confederate flag because I wanted to win the South Carolina primary. Now, after the campaign was over, I went down and said that I was wrong, but I think that was, by far, my greatest failing in my political life.

LM: Can a person be completely honest, speak the truth as they see it, and be elected to the presidency?

JM: I don't know the answer to that, but I know that if you don't strive to do that, you get on a slippery slope and you just can't maintain it. It's like any other evil or any other failing. If you say, I'll only not tell the truth about A, B and C then you just can't do it.

LM: Will you try another run for president?

JM: I don't envision a scenario where I would. We had a great ride but I don't envision it. However, my dear and beloved friend Morris Udall, who was a member of the House of Representatives, once said, "If you're a United States senator, unless you're under indictment or detoxification, you automatically consider yourself a candidate for president of the United States." I think being a U.S. senator is a wonderful job. I think it's a great opportunity because you have so much latitude. I think there are all kinds of ways to serve. I think maybe being in the Peace Corps would be a wonderful way to serve. I loved my service in the military. AmeriCorps is a wonderful, fulfilling experience. I think any service to a cause greater than your self-interest can be incredibly fulfilling.

Part Two
April 19, 2004

In this later interview with Senator McCain, we spent a lot of time discussing the conduct of the war in Iraq. The senator's book, *Why Courage Matters: The Way to a Braver Life,* had just been published.

Larry Mantle: You've supported the war and the removal of Saddam Hussein from power but you've not been without your criticism of how the war was conducted. As you look at it now, what would be the areas where you think decisions were well-made and other areas where you take issue?

John McCain: Could I start out with saying that it's awfully easy to be a Monday-morning quarterback, and that it is what I'd be doing except in one area. When I visited Iraq with several other members of the Senate and House last August, I talked to enough people saying over and over again that we don't have enough boots on the ground, enough special forces, linguists, intelligence people, marines to bring things under control and move forward. Otherwise, they said, you're going to face a very serious situation six months or so down the road. Well, those people were right. And obviously now we are going to extend some people there in Iraq. I hope that they will make plans for increases as necessary. I'm very sorry that there was a window of opportunity there that, I think, we did not take advantage of, and allowed the former Baathists and unhappy people, and the Sunnis, the ones who were better off under Saddam Hussein economically, to gain a foothold that we're going to pay a very heavy price for, both in

American blood and treasure. Now having said that, could I say, very quickly, that accidents happen in war? Things are done wrong. That's why we try to avoid wars at all costs. For example, in the Korean War, Douglas MacArthur pulled off the most brilliant military maneuver in modern times with the Inchon landing, which broke the back of the North Korean army. Then, when they were up near the Yalu River, he assured President Truman that the Chinese, that all those guys they were capturing speaking Chinese weren't going to come down. And of course, we paid a heavy price then because they drove us all the way down south of Seoul. In every conflict there are mistakes that are made. Another one, I think, that is obvious now is maybe we should have gotten closer to Ayatollah Sistani and tried to get a better relationship with him. Perhaps we should have announced earlier that we were going to turn over power. There are a number of other mistakes I think that were made.

But from my standpoint, now we've got to win. We can't afford to lose. I think victory will have enormous consequences both in Iraq and in the entire Middle East, which does not know a democracy, with the exception of the state of Israel. If we fail, I think the consequences are profound, beginning with the breakup of Iraq into ethnic or religious sectors and that can lead to tremendous migrations of people from one place to another and other problems.

So, I'm sorry for the long answer, but I really feel that it's important to get the government of Iraq to the Iraqi people, as faulty and as difficult as it may be. And I think most of all, that the American people need to be told that this is a very tough struggle we're in. It's going to cost us more, tragically, but I think it is a worthy cause. And I think the American people will respond affirmatively if told over and over again, very clearly, what the stakes are here and what we're doing, and if we don't give them any illusions as we did during the Vietnam War. Remember the famous phrase that the light is at the end of the tunnel. And as some wag said, yes, it turned out to be a train.

LM: I did want to ask you about the September 11 Commission and some of the very difficult testimony that has come out so far. Given what you have heard from the various participants, what do you think in hindsight could have or should have been done before the September 11 attacks?

JM: I think a number of things could have been done. I'm not positive that it could have been prevented and here's why. I don't think that anywhere there was the understanding of the gravity of the threat. That includes the Congress of the United States and the media. I'm not sure that we would have made some of the changes that would have disrupted Americans' lives before such a thing happened. And I think that there were indicators that, obviously, should have been passed up the chain of command, such as that guys were taking pilot training in my own home state of Arizona, for example. But Richard Clark was asked, "Given everything you know now, do you think that 9/11 probably could have been prevented?" And he said "No." So I think the 9/11 Commission is a good thing. I think that we need to focus a little more on what needs to be done rather than what happened. But we also have to hold people as well as institutions responsible. I'm not talking about a witch-hunt, but people obviously have to be held responsible because they're given positions of responsibility. And most importantly, out of this commission, I think will come a unanimous report that will give us a good blueprint for how to fix our intelligence services so that we can absolutely be better prepared and able to prevent a repetition of 9/11.

LM: So you're saying, in a certainly more statesmanlike way, that a head or heads should roll out of this.

JM: I think so, because I believe that there are people who are responsible, and I will wait until the 9/11 Commission finishes its report. But if someone is responsible, then obviously they should be replaced. You know, a funny thing has happened in America. All of us are responsible so no one is responsible. I'm not interested in hanging anybody. But you might remember the story back during the French/English Wars; there was a battle in Majorca where the British didn't win, and when the commander got back to England, they tried him and hung him from the yardarm. And when I believe it was Robespierre was told about it, he said, "They do that to encourage the others." Well, I'm not saying that we need to encourage the others, but I am saying that we need to hold people responsible.

LM: Are you interested in another presidential run?

JM: I envision no scenario where I would run for president again. I'm very happy in the United States Senate. And that's another thing about this business of the vice-presidency. I think I can be very effective continuing my role in the United States Senate and more effective than I could be as vice-president of the United States. You know, there's an old line about the vice-presidency: it has only two jobs and one is to break a tie in the Senate and the other is to inquire daily as to the health of the president. The reason why that's kind of funny is because it's largely true.

A listener asks McCain to explain why Social Security and Medicare are "fading off into the distance" without funding from Congress while "big business gets its tax breaks and subsidies."

JM: In Washington, we seem to be dominated to a large degree by the special interests. The last major legislation, this Medicare Prescription Drug Bill, had two provisions in it that clearly indicate the dominance of the pharmaceutical companies, not to mention the staffers and the administration officials that are now working for the pharmaceutical companies. One was the prohibition of importation of drugs from Canada. The other was the prohibition for Medicare to negotiate with the pharmaceutical companies for lower-priced drugs. By the way, the Veterans Administration is very proud of the fact that it saves hundreds of millions of dollars a year for our veterans' health care by negotiating for lower-priced prescription drugs. It's very disillusioning. All I can say is that we go through periods of corruption and reform throughout our history. Things are very wrong in Washington. We need to fix it and there may be a need for a reform movement in the United States of America. I believe that there are good and honest people working in Washington. The majority of my colleagues are good and honest people. But I'm afraid the influences are so strong and the polarization is such that it's very difficult for us to do business in the United States Senate.

LM: Not to discount the support that you have among some Republicans, but clearly there are many within your own party who detest you. You get under their skin. To what do you attribute that?

JM: I think it's clear that I won't be elected Miss Congeniality again this year. It's hard for me to divine all of the reasons. Perhaps it is the fact that I don't go along on a number of issues. Perhaps it's the fact that sometimes I'm very strong in my language. And perhaps there's a certain abrasiveness that is in my manner. I don't mean to be, but I feel very passionate about some of these issues. I try very hard never to get personal because people never forget when you do.

LM: Can someone be as opinionated and clearly spoken on your opinions as you are, as an elected representative, and be a viable national candidate?

JM: I think that probably if you looked at the numbers, my positive versus negatives with the entire population is quite high—higher than most anybody else, according to some polls. Although I think Colin Powell, very justifiably, is still the most popular person in America. I think it would be hard to win nomination when you are a polarizing figure, but I don't know. I think it would depend on the mood of the country at the time. If everybody is happy and satisfied with the status quo and somebody who breaks china comes in, then clearly that would be one scenario. But if there is a need for reform, then that would be another one. My hero, Teddy Roosevelt, was not the most popular guy in his party. In fact, they kept moving him from one place to another because they kind of wanted to get rid of him. But at the same time, I guess it would depend on the mood of the country at the time.

LM: In your book, *Why Courage Matters: The Way to a Braver Life,* you make the point that the real difference between being courageous or not isn't the level at which you experience the fear, but it's your willingness to move ahead despite the fear, to take action, to remain cool as best you can, and to go forward—not to be inactive.

JM: And even show a little bravado from time to time. Act a little brave to become brave and recognize it. Recognize that you're afraid. Get back on the horse that throws you. Eleanor Roosevelt said we must always try to do the things we think we can't do. And another thing about our day-to-day life, stand up early to those who lack virtues you were taught to love. The bully, the cheat, the snob, no matter what the social cost is. In other words, we can all learn to exercise courage, and moral courage is in many respects like a muscle that grows stronger with exercise. Look, the first time we stand up to an abusive boss, it's tough. The second time, it's a little easier. The first time I cast a vote against the majority of my party, it was tough. It gets a lot easier over time. So courage is there for all of us. We're born with a capacity to love and if we're raised to love virtue, we'll develop the courage and we'll pass that on to our children.

LM: Can you tell us a bit about your years in the prisoner-of-war camp, the "Hanoi Hilton?" You have spoken about how the other men, who were also captured along with you and imprisoned with you, were able to help each other and reinforce your ability to survive that experience.

JM: For the first several years that we were in prison, the Vietnamese kept us in solitary confinement or two or three to a cell, so we developed a way of communicating by tapping on the walls to each other. Over time you'd get so it's almost like carrying on a conversation. When we were taken to interrogation, one of the things I knew was that I was going to return to my cell and I'd be tapping on the wall and I'd tell them what happened to me and what I did or did not do. And when I failed and I came back, they did everything they could to strengthen me, to help me, to pick me up and help me move on. And that, to me, is the greatest privilege of my life, to have served in the company of heroes where I was privileged to observe a thousand acts of courage and compassion and love. And without that help and assistance I got from them, I may have survived, but I don't think with anywhere near the honor that I maintain to this day. It's because of them.

LM: Should the Patriot Act be renewed?

JM: I think it probably needs to be renewed. But I also feel, like any other law that's enacted at a time of crisis, we should examine whether there are excesses, whether it needs to be either improved or scaled back. We also know that things have happened in our history, the incarceration of Japanese Americans in World War II, and Abraham Lincoln did some things in the Civil War which were an abridgement, to say the least, of citizens' rights. I think it needs to be renewed, but I would really like to see it go through a very careful scrubbing and scrutiny on the part of the Congress.

LM: What are your views on the environmental policies of this administration?

JM: I believe that climate change is real. I believe that it's taking place. I'm deeply concerned about it. Greenhouse gases contribute to it. We've got to get it under control. Senator Joseph Lieberman and I got forty-three votes for a very minor, modest measure. But I am deeply, deeply concerned, and very frankly, I do not agree with this administration's lack of concrete and specific actions on the issue. And by the way, if you're worried about the price of fuel, maybe we ought to think about raising the CAFE [Corporate Average Fuel Economy] standards, which would reduce the use of petroleum and it would also help our environment.

LM: What do you think should be done about our immigration policy?

JM: I think the status quo is unacceptable, and those that think that it is acceptable have not visited the border in Arizona, where four hundred and some people died in the desert last year, where we are undergoing hundreds of millions of dollars in healthcare costs because of the treatment of people who have come to our country illegally, the shootouts on the interstate, and the list goes on and on. On the right they say it's all amnesty and they're against any reform. On the left, the so-called Hispanic advocates say they want nothing but amnesty. Neither of those positions is satisfactory. We need to work together and work out ways we can provide jobs for people that Americans won't do, an orderly return to the country of their origin, give everybody a chance to come to America. And for us to absolutely do nothing because of the controversy associated with this issue I think is an abrogation of our responsibilities. And if any of our listeners have a good idea, give it to me because I'm not saying that we've got the perfect answer. Congressman Kolbe, Congressman Flake and I have introduced a comprehensive immigration bill, but please, please, in the name of humanity, let's move forward on this issue and engage in a great national debate and come up with a solution to it.

I 've not only had the pleasure of interviewing this great mystery writer and creator of the beloved Easy Rawlins character numerous times, but Kristen and I have also enjoyed spending time with Walter Mosley over meals at the annual Sun Valley Writers' Conference in Idaho.

I am drawn to Mosley's writing, whether Easy Rawlins books or his other fiction, because he creates great depth and humanity in his characters, which allows the reader to become completely invested in their fates. For those, like me, who can't get enough Los Angeles history and culture, Mosley also recreates an earlier L.A. in all its great and awful contradictions. It's not just relations between races, but the overall feel that's so right. Perhaps this doesn't matter much to the many Mosley fans outside of Southern California, but I think it's a huge draw for those of us here. As a fourth-generation Angeleno, I long for depictions of us that feel true—whether present or past. Mosley knows the people and the place, and has the talent to recreate it in words.

This conversation with Walter Mosley took place while he was touring the country to promote his eighth Easy Rawlins mystery, *Little Scarlet*.

Larry Mantle: Let's talk a little bit about the Easy Rawlins character because this is the character who has brought you fame. What are your feelings about Easy?

Walter Mosley: That's an interesting notion. How do I feel about Easy? I'm not quite sure. I like writing about him very much. I really like his voice. I find his voice very interesting and very different from my own. I'll be writing, and Easy'll say something. I'll go, "Wow, that's really wild." I know that Easy's not separate from me, that he comes from in me, but I get into his face and I write about him. I love writing about Los Angeles and the different moments in Los Angeles. In *Little Scarlet,* I write about the Watts riot and its impact, not only on black and white people in Southern California, but over the whole United States, and from there, over the whole world. I think, "What did that mean? How did that impact us?" I'm working on the new Easy Rawlins, and he runs across hippies for the first time. And that's this wonderful thing.

LM: So you feel a closeness to the character, even though he's very different from you?

WM: Very, very different. But yeah, I feel close to him, but you know, really, one of the places that I come from as a writer—not all writers do or have to feel like this—is I really love all my characters. I love writing about them. I really like getting into their minds and feeling where they're going and how they got there. Even the really bad ones.

LM: Even someone as tough as Mouse?

WM: Yeah. Mouse is tough, but he's not bad. There's a bad guy in this book, but I try to get next to him a little bit.

LM: One of the things that you've handled so well in these books are the ambiguities about racial issues. This book is just loaded with ambiguity, deep emotion, conflicted feelings that Easy has as the city is blowing up around him. Though he doesn't take part in the riots, the rage that he has largely kept bottled up throughout his life becomes much more tangible in this book.

WM: It became tangible for the world. The black world knew how upset they were. But I think the riots even surprised black Los Angeles at that time. People couldn't take any more and said, "I'm going out in the streets and I'm going to shoot at people and throw Molotov cocktails. I'm going to burn down my own neighborhood, my own stores. If a fireman tries to put out a fire, I'm going to shoot at them." That kind of intense rage caused a different notion inside the black community and certainly outside the black community. People outside are saying, "My God, I never realized that these people felt like this, or that they felt anything different than what I feel." Many people were completely unaware of what's going on. There are a lot of echoes in America today, both internally and externally, about being unaware of passions outside of your own community.

LM: You were a little kid at the time of the Watts riots.

WM: Thirteen. I was down in Watts during the riots, but the biggest impact on me was when I was with my father. We lived in West Los Angeles at that time. One night I came into the room during the riots and he was drinking heavily and he was very upset, almost crying, if not crying. I said, "Dad, what's wrong?" He says, "It's these riots." I said, "Are you afraid?" He goes, "No. I'm not afraid. I want to go out there and do it. I want to go out there and shoot and throw rocks and Molotov cocktails. I know why those people are mad, and I want to do the same thing." I said, "Are you going to?" I was very scared. He said, "No. No. I'm not going to, because it's wrong. It's wrong to hurt people you don't know. It's wrong to burn down your own businesses. But that doesn't mean I don't understand and that I don't feel like doing it." That had a real impact on me. And coming at this point of Easy's life, it was really important for me to write, not about the days of the riots, but the days right after the riots.

LM: You set this mystery story in that immediate aftermath, when literally, at the beginning of the book, the embers are still smoldering.

WM: Right, right.

LM: I was six years old at the time of the riots and vividly remember that we evacuated the apartment building that we lived in one night at the height of the riots, when there were rumors that rioters were going to be in that area of southwest Los Angeles.

WM: That kind of fear had never really existed anywhere in the country before, you know, a worrying about that kind of violence, where it was coming from and what it was doing. It was an amazing moment for the city. It's funny, because black people before were invisible in mainstream America. They were there, and there were problems and there were marches, but people weren't really thinking about it. All of a sudden, they were visible. And still, nobody knew their names. They weren't yet fully persons, but they were now visible. It was an interesting transitional moment.

LM: It was odd for me, because I'd lived in one of the few areas where there was a fair amount of cross-racial communication. I remember being so surprised that there was so much anger that was coming out. I think you get into that in *Little Scarlet* about how black Angelenos, up to that point, really kept this rage from being out there on the surface, undoubtedly because there was no place to put it.

WM: No. There are a lot of problems with that. And I want to say, because it's really important, because I love this conversation. But *Little Scarlet* is a mystery and a crime novel. Very often people start to say, "Oh, Walter Mosley writes these sociology books." It's not true. One of the things that I've learned, though, in writing crime fiction, is that if you're going to write a mystery with a plot that's going to be exciting, you have to base it on something real, something that people can sink their teeth into. Because very often people will write a crime fiction that has no basis to it. It's just a crime, you know, and people are floating in space.

LM: And the art of it is that you have the story and this character rooted in something very real.

WM: Right. Thank you. I try very hard. It was a great deal of fun to write this book; it's fun to write. I love writing books. I'm always writing.

LM: Let's talk about the particular story in *Little Scarlet,* because you've got Easy being enlisted by the Los Angeles Police Department, because of the color of his skin.

WM: Yeah, that's what you have. The story of this is that the riots have happened. Easy is stunned by it and he doesn't really know what to think and he doesn't know how to really act, how to talk to people. He's in conflict, in between people a lot. But the police come to him and they say, "Listen, there's been a woman murdered. There's one extra murder that nobody knows about. We're pretty sure that a white man did it, but we can't go down and investigate. We feel that if we go down there and start investigating the murder of a black woman and ask about a white man, the riots will flare up again, and we'll be in riots for another few days or weeks, or whatever." And of course, Easy's pretty cynical about that. He says, "Oh yeah, you don't want your tourism to go down, right?" And they say, "You don't want people in your community to be hurt, either." He agrees with them, and he starts to go. The problem, of course, is that he has questions of whether or not this white man has committed the crime. And Easy, being the kind of guy he is, wants to find out who really did the killing. This unearths another level of racism in the community that nobody ever suspected before. So he takes up the case.

LM: He has this ability because of the document that he carries to go places that he otherwise wouldn't have access to. Can you talk a little bit about the mixed feelings that the character has over this.

WM: He's been given this letter by the deputy commissioner of police, who's a guy that Easy doesn't like, and who doesn't really like Easy. He likes Easy because he can use him, but he doesn't like him. So Easy now all of a sudden has entrée, and he's confused about this entrée. But the confusion is part of how the whole world has changed. Up until now, I've had Easy as what they call an amateur sleuth since 1948. He solves crimes; he gets involved with crimes; he works, you know, not with the police, but parallel with them on many things. But he's never been a real detective. But all of a sudden, things have changed so much that he can no longer hide in the shadows in between things. He has to answer to this higher authority and, to some degree, to become a part of it. And of course, he questions this. Is this the right thing? Is this the wrong thing? Am I going to do what they want me to do? And is what they want me to do the right thing?

LM: This is at a time in Los Angeles's and the country's evolution where more and more African Americans are starting to move into positions of some power and some authority, and are being allowed a kind of responsibility that wouldn't have been given them before.

WM: And this causes a split in the community. How do you respond to that? Do you claim fealty to the people who are giving you this power? Do you start to take on what they think is right and wrong, or what you've always known was right and wrong, up until now? Easy sees this as the beginning of a split in the black community, where you have some people who are taking up what you might think of as "the white side" and "the black side." Easy understands that it's much more subtle than that. There are people who will stop him on the streets and say, "Listen, I understand why you people rioted. I would've done the same thing. If you want to come do business with me, here's my card." On the other hand, people are afraid of him and say, "What are you doing here? What are you doing in my community?" and immediately call the police. In the meanwhile, Easy has this letter. So whenever the police stop him, he pulls out this letter and he shows it to them. He even commits a couple of crimes with that letter. It's a very complex issue, though. In the beginning of the book, he goes downstairs. There's a white, German cobbler who owns a store. The store has been torched. A black man has come into the store and is angry at the cobbler. He says, "Listen. I gave you my shoes. If I owned a store and my store got burned down, I'd still have to give you your shoes." Now, Easy comes in. He's a friend of the German cobbler, but he understands what the other man is saying. So this is where his heart is broken, all throughout the novel. He's torn between one side and the other, the side that he thinks is right, and his side, which has been victimized for so long.

LM: How much additional research did you do on the riots, as a part of telling the story?

WM: I didn't do any research on the riots themselves, because I finally decided to write about the middle of the riots. Mainly, what I do is to read newspapers. There's a scene in here that is taken right out of the newspaper. A group of policemen was going down the street and somebody took a shot at them from the top of a building. The building was a Muslim mosque. The police opened fire on the building and broke every window in the building. And nobody was shot, but something like forty people were cut, some of them seriously, by flying glass. You wonder, if somebody was on top of the May Company, on Wilshire and Fairfax, and took a shot at the police, would the police open fire on the May Company? Or from the top of a Catholic church. Would they have opened fire on it? There were a lot of things that happened which weren't even questioned. The thing that I found the most interesting was right after the riots, Martin Luther King came to Los Angeles to speak to the mayor and the police chief and all the powers that be. Twenty-four hours later, or thirty-six, he left the city. And they said, "Well, what do you think?" He says, "With the people you've got in charge here, there's no hope for Los Angeles." Martin Luther King gave up on Los Angeles after the riots. This is an astonishing thing. He didn't give up on Selma. That was really sad.

LM: You mentioned that you're already working on the next book, which takes Easy into territory where hippies reside. How long do you see the series going? Do you have an end to it that's outlined at all in your mind? Or are you just riding with it?

WM: It'll most likely end at the turn of the century, the year 2000. Easy will be eighty and who knows how his life is going to change between, you know, 1965 and 1980. But it is going to change, and probably that'll be the last case for him. Yeah, after eighty, it'd be hard to be a private detective. But you know, in America today, I was talking to somebody the other day about retirement, and the truth is, people of my generation, we're not going to retire. Easy is in the same thing. If you don't have any money, what are you going to do but work?

LM: A very good point. Now, his day job as the school custodian is an important part of his character as well, even though the focus is on his work as an investigator. How do you see that issue of his day job playing into who he is?

WM: You know, I'm in a genre when I write these books, the noir genre. And in the Forties and the Fifties, the genre was like this: There's a man. He had no wife, no children, no parents, no relatives; he never owned a house, only lived in an apartment. His car is always falling apart. Nothing is steady in his life. He is completely a loner. And that's why, if he gets arrested and thrown in jail and they say, "Listen, until you talk we're keeping you in jail," he says, "Well, keep me in jail, because I'm true to my existentialist ideals." That's all good and well. I like those very much, you know, the Continental Op and Marlowe and Archer and all those people. But I'm writing about a character who's deeply connected to the world and who even has middle-class aspirations. He wants to own a house, maybe an apartment building. He has some kids. They're not his, but he adopted them. He's trying to cobble together a life that makes sense. And so it's important that he has a job, because he doesn't see himself as a part of this criminal world, as a part of this shady world. He gets involved when he feels he has to, but he doesn't really see himself in that way. And so the job is a way that he can be real. He's the supervising senior head custodian of a junior high school down in South Central. And he's read all of the study books. And a lot of the students, a lot of the teachers, come to him before they'll come to anybody else, to find out what's going on. He does almost a similar kind of job as a private detective, as the custodian.

LM: Did you grow up reading detective fiction? Was the genre appealing to you early on?

WM: Very much so. When I was starting, at the age of about sixteen or seventeen, Nero Wolfe, Dashiell Hammett, Ross Macdonald, all of those books, I just read them up. And then I stopped. I was about twenty-five. I didn't start writing my first mystery until I was about thirty-six. I didn't start writing until I was thirty-three. So it came back to me, you know, from a long way in the past.

A listener asks Mosley if he bases his characters on any specific people.

WM: They really are composites. When you come up with fictional characters, it's impossible to put a real person on the page. You have to abstract to some degree. You have to change things to fit in with what that character would or wouldn't do in certain kinds of situations. Certainly there are people that I've known and met who inform those characters, but usually there's more than one.

LM: How does your multi-racial background factor into your work?

WM: It's a very interesting notion. I'm not certain. Southern California is a multi-racial area. Most of the cities in the east and the south are very old. They didn't grow appreciably at any particular moment. Los Angeles starts off as a very small city and grows really quickly. So if it's your job to build the highway and somebody says, "I only want you to hire white people," you say, "Well, I'm sorry about that." You say, "I'm going to hire anybody who comes in here, because I need people to work. If it's Japanese, if it's Mexican, Korean, black, I'm going to hire them. And if they work well, that's good. And if you don't work with them, you're out of here." So there was a whole notion that integration had to happen. You couldn't keep people out. My parents met here. That's part of the reason they met. They both worked in the same place. They met each other: my Jewish mother and my black father. So partially their coming together was part of the character of Los Angeles. And in fact, I think that most or many people in Los Angeles are multi-racial. There are very few people who are not, at least in their minds, influenced by many, many different cultures and races. And certainly our blood is very, very mixed.

W ho isn't a fan of the classic TV sitcom, *The Dick Van Dyke Show*? It had a wonderful cast, inventive stories, and great chemistry among the actors. Thanks to the emergence of cable networks devoted to classic TV, new generations have had the opportunity to enjoy the show.

Carl Reiner is the man responsible for *The Dick Van Dyke Show.* Forty years after its launch, it still stands as one of the best. Reiner got the opportunity to create the program after many successful years writing and performing on Sid Caesar's various network shows. In addition to his many television successes, Reiner has written and directed feature films, and is the author of many books. He is also the father of director and actor Rob Reiner.

I have included two interviews with Carl Reiner that touch on many aspects of his long career. The first conversation was December 6, 2002. We talked again on May 14, 2003.

Part One
December 6, 2002

Larry Mantle: What are you most proud of?

Carl Reiner: I have three non-toxic kids, very nourishing, wonderful human beings, and I think that's about it. You can't do better than that. To have three kids that you like and that people like and they make you wonderful grandchildren and they do wonderful things for humanity, I can't imagine anything to be more proud of.

LM: Of course, Rob Reiner, your son, is a well-known film director and actor as well, going back to *All in The Family.* You have two other children. One is a psychotherapist, is that right?

CR: My daughter Annie is a psychotherapist. She is everything with a P. She's a psychotherapist. You know it begins with a P even though it doesn't sound like it. And she's a painter, a poet and a playwright. She does psychoanalysis for a living. She has three books of poetry out and a couple of plays produced. She's also one of the smartest people I know. I also have a wonderful young son, Lucas Reiner, who is an artist and a filmmaker and a father of two and just about as good a human being as you want.

LM: Let's talk about your career going back to Sid Caesar's *Your Show of Shows,* in which you were not only a writer but a performer, a regular part of that cast. Share with us what that atmosphere was like in those early days of television, being around such a celebrated group of writers and being part of what was really an embryonic art form.

CR: Well, you don't know what you're doing at the time you're doing it. You don't know what you're creating at the time you're doing it because you don't know that someday they're going to call it the Golden Age. All we knew was that we had to get to work every day at ten o'clock and go home at seven and get a show on every week. We did know one thing: we did know that we were doing something special because there was nothing on television like it. Max Liebman created *Your Show of Shows,* and he was able to people it with the most extraordinary talent. The writing talent, almost every one of them who ever wrote on *Your Show of Shows,* became an important entity. We're going all the way from Mel Brooks to Neil Simon to Larry Gelbart, and the list goes on.

LM: Even Woody Allen had a stint as a writer on that show.

CR: Yeah, Woody Allen in the ninth year. He was a nineteen-year-old young pup; it was the year I left. I had been with Sid nine years, four years on the *Show of Shows* and five on *Caesar's Hour* and *Caesar Presents.* Sid did a series of four or five specials and I remember coming to visit him. We always had a redhead in the room, somebody with red hair. He said, "Here's my new redhead." It was a nineteen, eighteen-year-old kid sitting in the corner and who knew he was going to turn out to be Woody Allen? Every writer who was worth his salt, when they saw what Sid was doing, said, "Oh, I want to be part of that" and they gravitated to them. That's the reason there were so many great writers coming into that.

LM: Obviously the influence was tremendous on your life when you created *The Dick Van Dyke Show.* You recreated that kind of an environment, albeit with the smaller writing staff, with the character of Rob Petrie apparently being a stand-in for you.

CR: Well, the funny thing was that I didn't know I was going to do that. That was one of those lucky happenstances. When the *Show of Shows* and *Caesar's Hour* ended, the review format was *persona non grata.* There were not any around, I think, until Carol Burnett came around a few years later. The half-hour situation comedies and cowboy westerns were the norm on television. They were offering me situation comedies to do, and none of them was terribly good. My wife said to me, "You can write a better one than this." I had never written a situation comedy. I had written sketches and things. You know how you ask yourself a question sometimes and if you're pretty smart, you'll give yourself a good answer? I remember the revelatory moment on the westside drive in New York riding down on 96th Street in my car going home to New Rochelle. I asked myself, "What piece of ground do you stand on that nobody else stands on? That's what you should write about." And I answered myself. I really did, out loud. I said, "Well, you used to work on the *Show of Shows,* a variety show. You went home to New Rochelle. You had a family and you split your time between New Rochelle and Manhattan." And I said, "Well, that's what I'll write about." I'll write about a guy who works for a variety show and has a home in New Rochelle. And I went home and I swear I sat down and within two days I had the basis of the Dick Van—well, it was really called *Head of the Family* and I was writing it for myself. We did a pilot. It didn't work. I mean, it worked well enough for people to say, whoa, this is good. Let's put it on. But they never did. That was the year of the horse and the gun. There was *Bat Masterson* and I remember a couple of others. So I put it aside, but I wrote thirteen episodes. That was my pilot. Nobody has ever written a thirteen-episode pilot. I put it aside and I said, "Well, this is the best I can do." Luckily I started a career in motion pictures. I wrote a movie for Doris Day and James Garner [*The Thrill of It All*]. I thought that would be put to bed and my agent, who was dogged, said, "You can't let these thirteen scripts go to waste." He gave them to Sheldon Leonard, who was a big executive producer with Danny Thomas, and they forced the issue. They said, "You've got to put this on again." And I said, "No, I'm not failing twice with the same thing." He said, "No, we'll get a better you than you. We'll get somebody to play you who is better than you." And he suggested Dick Van Dyke. I went to New York, saw him in *Bye Bye Birdie.* By the way, you didn't expect such a long answer to a short question, did you?

LM: No, that's all right. I love hearing the chronology of the show's development; it's very interesting. It's very circuitous, particularly compared to how most shows come and go so quickly. Now there's really not a chance, it seems, for a show to develop naturally as *The Dick Van Dyke Show* did.

CR: That's true. As a matter of fact, the first year we foundered as far as ratings. The second year we almost didn't get on, and Sheldon Leonard actually ran to New York and got us half a sponsor. We were missing a half of a sponsor. But what saved us is that somebody suggested that we go on in the summer. I remember being the hero of that because I said, "I don't care what it costs or what they're going to pay," because they weren't going to pay very much. I said, "Let us go on in the summer with reruns and maybe the people who see *Perry Como* will watch us and what we're doing." Then the second year when we did go on, we made it. So if we had been living today, with today's rules, we would not have gone on the second year.

LM: Did you have any sense of where television would be several decades later? Could you have envisioned that it would be as large a medium as it is today?

CR: No, absolutely not. We knew it was an important medium when the coaxial cable joined the two coasts. We said, "Whoa, this is big." Now, however—I'm looking at a television set right now that is not on and I realize if I turned it on, there are 365 stations I'd get. I think at the time we could get seven to thirteen stations, and that was it. See, I still call them stations, because we were honed in radio. But I can't believe what's on, what is being said on some of the cable channels. We were talking about that yesterday. I played poker with a bunch of nice buddies, Johnny Carson and Steve Martin and a couple of other people you know, and we were talking about the fact that we could not believe some of the things being said on cable. There was a roast on and we couldn't believe that this language was coming over the air, and these were all sophisticated people who knew all the words. They've even used them in public, but not in that kind of media.

LM: Yeah, it's pretty shocking. I'm curious if you find yourself distressed at many of the things that you see on television. Does the content of what's in the box concern you?

CR: Absolutely. As a matter of fact, sometimes you get distressed enough to call somebody and say, "Hey, what are you doing?" We talked about that yesterday. Self-censorship is the best thing. There's no question about it. We did that. From the very first days of *Your Show of Shows* we were censoring ourselves, because there was somebody looking over us. It went too far sometimes. I remember on the *Show of Shows* we had a sketch about war, and one of the people in the trenches when the bomb is bursting overhead said, "War is hell," and they said, "You can't say that." We said, "Wait, war isn't hell?" Of course they won, and we actually said "War is heck."

A listener asks two questions: first, was there any significance to the Dairy Maids sheet music that was prominently displayed behind Rob Petrie's desk in his office, and second, did Reiner ever get into any trouble or receive negative feedback about such episodes as when Morey Amsterdam's character had a bar mitzvah, or when black actors were featured?

CR: On the first question, the Dairy Maid poster, that was just the set decorator putting it up to make the place look nice. And once it was up there it had to stay, and we didn't even know what that was. We got more questions about the poster—and we're getting them to this day, as you see. About getting flack, as a matter of fact, we got no flack about those. We got lovely letters about Morey's bar mitzvah. There were no problems about that. We did a show where Laura and Rob think they've taken home the wrong baby, and it turns out there's a black couple who come in and tell them that they got their right baby. The biggest laugh you've ever heard. But CBS was worried that we'd be making some kind of an anti-black reference. I said, "No, wait a second, if your heart's in the right place, the audience will know that." I said, "Did you notice in the tag when the parents are discussing their two children, and the black couple said their child grew up to be a wonderful kid? He's seven years old and he's top of his class." And Rob and Laura say, "Yeah, maybe we did get the wrong kid," suggesting that a black child could be smarter than a white child. I said, "But you know, the people are not going to notice that. And of course we got the biggest roar we ever got. By the way, one of the good things about having a studio audience is you know right away what kind of water you're in, that the behavior of the whole of America will be very similar to those two hundred people who are in the audience, and they applauded and screamed and all of that. But that's the only problem we ever had.

A listener asks how much of Your Show of Shows *was improvisation, and how much was scripted.*

CR: The improv happens in the writers' room during the week. On Monday we came into the office after having done a show on Saturday, and we'd sit around and decide what forms to fill that week. You know, a situation comedy form, a pantomime form, a take-off of a movie, a silent movie, an opera, and then we'd fill those forms during the next four days. The writers would split up into groups, and we'd meet on a Thursday and say, "Okay, what have you got? What have you got?" The improvisation aspect came in those rooms. That's what writing is, improvising on paper. There was very little improvisation when the show got on the air, because you were constrained to a certain amount of time. You had to finish the show. There was no snipping the way you do if you have a taped show or a filmed show. This one had to go off on time. So there wasn't a lot of time to ad lib, and you wouldn't ad lib, because the material was pretty good. What you would ad lib is attitudes, because you never had an audience before, and when the audience would start laughing very hard at something, you had to fill it in with something. Sid was an awfully great attitude ad libber. He would create new ways to get laughs with the same material because things were happening in the audience.

LM: Just as an aside, it seems to me that Imogene Coca doesn't get her due. As someone who knew her so well and worked with her so closely, I wonder if you could speak about her talent, because it seemed to me that she was every bit the talent of Sid Caesar.

CR: Well, she had a different talent, but her talent fit so well, tongue and groove with Sid's, that it made him funnier than he ever would have been with anybody else. She had been in a lot of reviews in Broadway before. She had more experience than Sid. But there was a symbiotic thing that happened there. I used to describe Imogene as the strongest human being in the world. She looked so frail, but she was able not only to do the sketches with us, she also had musical comedy ability. She could sing and dance, and she used to do wonderful take-offs of ballets. In one particular episode she did a strip tease dance with a big overcoat. It was hilarious. But she didn't have the same kind of comic talents Sid did. Sid was a more creative comic talent. She was more a performing comic talent. As far as her due, I think she got her due. She was America's sweetheart for four years while we were on the show, and we all loved her.

A listener says most comedy writers and comedians seem to be "tortured, tormented souls full of neuroses," but Reiner seems "like a pretty down-to-earth and common-sense kind of person." The listener asks where Reiner thinks the source of his comedy is, since he doesn't seem to be that kind of tortured, neurotic person.

CR: Well, I don't know. There are a lot of comedians who are only mildly tortured, and they do well. I do not consider myself a comedian, because I never really was a very good stand-up comedian. I did stand-up in the army and I did it after I got out of the war, but I don't know where it comes from. I think there is that funny bone that is born in people. I think having been born during the Depression and lived during the Depression and being deprived, and in the case of ethnics like Jews and black people, I think a little bit of persecution goes a long way in making a comedian. You can fight back with your fists, your gun, your knife, or you can fight back with your mouth.

Part Two
May 14, 2003

Larry Mantle: You obviously have no interest in retiring. You continue to speak to groups and write books.

Carl Reiner: Retiring means when you can't breathe and you lie down and your eyes shut and you can't open them. Then they either bury you or burn you. No, I have no thoughts of retiring.

LM: You must love your work.

CR: Yes, that's the trick. Nobody retires from something they love to do. As long as they let you do it, as long as your brain and your tongue keep working, you can work.

LM: The other thing that leads people to retirement is because they have to be so separated from their families that they want to recapture some kind of a family life. But it seems that you've been able to integrate your wife, Estelle, and your children into your work.

CR: I've been very lucky this way. I can't take credit for it. It happened accidentally, but in my history as a father, husband, actor, whatever, I have never been away from home for more than two weeks. How about that?

LM: That's shocking in this business.

CR: When I did *The Russians Are Coming,* I was away for—I'm lying now—for four weeks, but I came down every weekend.

LM: So you performed in that?

CR: Yes, I did. The only time I ever got above-the-title billing was in the Bronx, because I lived in the Bronx. My mother says, "Look, look, on the marquee, it says 'Carl Reiner in The Russians.'" They took a picture with a Polaroid; I have that at home.

LM: That's great. It's funny, all this other stuff, your fame, but getting it on the hometown marquee, that's the big deal.

CR: Everybody wants to first please their mother and father. And if they please their mother and father, then the neighbors next door, then the people down the block, then strangers and then finally, hopefully, the radio and television world.

LM: You obviously love talking about your work. Johnny Carson always said that you were one of his favorite guests, that he always enjoyed talking with you so much. I don't know whether you're friends.

CR: Oh, yes, we're still friends. We're both quiet, loners, we go about our business. But we do meet every six or eight weeks and play poker at Steve Martin's house, and we have a good time talking about what we've done and what we want to do.

LM: We'd all like to be flies on the wall for that. I'm sure there are some very funny comments. Or does the fact that you're funny in your profession mean that these poker games aren't very funny?

CR: Oh, no, mainly they're to reminisce. They're to put into the pot not the money, but the things that have happened lately that you want to tell your friends about, the funny things that have happened lately.

LM: How does it make you feel when you have very talented young writers or comedians be so thrilled to meet you, and then tell you how much they admire your work and how influential you are?

CR: It feels terrible. No, it's the best feeling you can get. Those are the residuals. Yesterday I was on *The Wayne Brady Show* and a young writer came up to me and said, "I'm a writer because of you." This is said to me many, many times. As young kids they watched *The Dick Van Dyke Show,* where somebody got paid to sit in a room and make jokes. If it's a funny kid who has seen this, he said to himself, "I make jokes, my friends laugh, maybe I'll do this, sit in a room and get paid to do this." And I'm not kidding you, at least a half dozen kids have come up to me and said, I'm a writer because I saw *The Dick Van Dyke Show.*

LM: It did look like so much fun. Was that a fun program to create? Working with that cast, Rose Marie, Morey Amsterdam and of course Dick Van Dyke and Mary Tyler Moore, was that a fun set to be on?

CR: You know something, fun wasn't the word, the operative word is exciting. You can't have fun if you're under pressure all the time. And in those days, I was alone for the first two years, I was the writer and story editor. I wrote the first forty out of sixty. So I didn't know I was having fun, but I did know that I was doing something good, and I went after the possibility of this being rerun someday.

LM: In the opening of *The Dick Van Dyke Show* you didn't know if he'd fall or step around the ottoman. It was always funny to see which way it was going to go.

CR: That was because somebody at the network said, "How do we keep them tuned at the beginning of the show to stay through the main credits?" I came up with the idea, let's have him fall over the thing one week and not the other. By the way, it didn't matter. The people who tuned in and get to know your show, watch your show. Then we stopped. I think he only fell one time every thirteen weeks or so, because we said that if he fell every week, then he's just too big a goof, a klutz.

LM: I was wondering about that great group of writers you worked with on *Your Show of Shows*: were you all first-generation Americans, or had your families been here longer?

CR: Yes, Sid Caesar, Mel Brooks, myself, I think Neil Simon's parents, were second generation.

LM: So you're all products of that immigrant experience, but of a very Americanized childhood.

CR: We were also products of early radio and early motion pictures, and of knowing that first-generation immigrants like George Burns and Jack Benny could make it. We had all these heroes, Eddie Cantor, the Marx Brothers, Bob Hope, he was here from England. He was a different kind of immigrant, but absolutely we knew that it was possible to do that. It was a venue open to us.

A listener asks Reiner what he thought was important to teach his son Rob.

CR: Rob is a self-made man. I'm not kidding. What he took from my wife and me are examples, mainly. I never told him, do this, do that. He and Albert Brooks would come down to the rehearsals of *The Dick Van Dyke Show* every summer. They were around fourteen, fifteen, sixteen at the time. They sat watching rehearsals. He told me he heard me talk and he heard how I behaved, but he also was very curious. He was a very curious child from the time he was born. He hung around when our friends came. He always sat on the steps and listened. Mel Brooks—he made him roar. But I never told him anything. I think kids learn by example.

LM: He saw how much fun you were having, clearly he wanted a similar life.

CR: My wife and I are very neurotic, and I think we gave that to all of our children. They're all very alert people because they are nervous, excited, and very in-the-world people. I must say, I don't know how it happened. Our kids said the other day, "You never disciplined us." And we said, "We didn't have to." They always did their homework. I don't know what it is, they saw ethics. They saw me working in the house. My father worked in the house when I was young. He was a watchmaker. And for all my young life I saw him working, so I got a work ethic just by example. So did our kids. We didn't goof. We just did our job.

A listener asks if the role of Rob Petrie boiled down to the choice of two actors, Dick Van Dyke and a pre-Tonight Show Johnny Carson.

CR: You know something, it really didn't boil down. Those two actors were mentioned. A producer had mentioned Dick Van Dyke. I mentioned Johnny Carson. I said we need the kind of a guy who can perform. Writers all can perform, but they choose not to. They choose to write it and let somebody else get in front of the audience, mainly out of shyness. Woody Allen is a perfect example. He was a writer long before he stood up, and when he stood up he was still the shy writer. Johnny Carson was that kind of a person. I mentioned Johnny Carson, but we never talked to him about it. And by the way, if it hadn't been Dick Van Dyke, I don't think we'd be talking about the show today. Dick Van Dyke is the most talented situation comedy performer in the history of television.

LM: As you look at other classic comedies, which other ones also struck magic?

CR: It certainly struck with *All in the Family*. It certainly struck with *Friends*. It also struck with Ray Romano.

LM: What about *The Mary Tyler Moore Show*?

CR: Oh, *The Mary Tyler Moore Show,* my God, did that strike. It struck for seven or eight years; I'm glad you mentioned it. How would I forget that one? I didn't, actually. I was still talking. I would have gotten to it.

LM: That's right, I interrupted before you got to it.

CR: No, no, thank you for interrupting. And look at those people, they're still friends to this day.

LM: What about your cast, did they stay close?

CR: Not really. They moved to different parts of the world. Mary moved to New York, and Dick is another loner. He sits at his computer a lot. He's not quite a loner because he loves to sing barbershop quartet harmony, and he's got a group of guys who sing every day.

A listener asks about other TV shows and plays that portrayed Sid Caesar as "less than a tolerable person."

CR: Sid was very strong and did some things that were really nutty, but he behaved nicely to his writers. Like any person who was in charge of his own life, he wanted the best and he would fight for the best. But I worked for him for nine years, as did Mel, and nobody works for anybody nine years unless they like them. Sid was a very giving person in many ways, and as a matter of fact, I wouldn't be here today if it weren't for Sid saying, "Let Carl do it. He can do that better." He said that quite a few times.

LM: I've had the pleasure of interviewing Sid Caesar on the program. What a remarkable man, given the battles that he's had with the difficulties in his life. Have you talked to him about that period after the show?

CR: Not only after the show but during the last parts of the last few years of each show, *Caesar's Hour* and *Caesar Presents*. He was so gifted, but they didn't gift him with the one thing he needed. He didn't believe in himself. He didn't believe that he deserved what he was getting. He tried to get out of his own body; he was in pain. He drank. He never drank at work; he thought it was impossible. How could anybody drink at work? But on his way home he would drink and get out of it, and then he started taking drugs. He wrote a book that made me cry, how his kids got him on the straight and narrow again. They didn't know him, and they finally threw his pills away. He suffered very, very much from not believing in himself. It all starts with your parents. Your parents either tell you you're okay or you're nothing, and I think he got a lot of nothing from his parents. I hate to say that, but in my book I write about my mother always saying I'm the best one, and saying, "Why don't they give you more to do—you're the best one."

LM: It's hard not to believe that when your own mother is saying it. I wonder if this is part of the challenge of creative people. I think very often people who are performers come from that kind of a background, where they are overcoming very difficult childhoods and parenting. I wonder if that feeling of "I'm a fraud, I don't really deserve my success," is a rather common thing in Hollywood.

CR: As you're saying it, I realize I really felt that way when I started as an actor. I wrote a book when I was thirty-five, thirty-six years old. In the last line of it the main character is on stage for the first time in front of a big audience, and they applaud, and he thinks, "I got away with it. I'm a fraud. Will they ever notice that? Will they find that out?" So I felt that, too. I don't feel it anymore.

LM: If you're a fraud, you're the most incredible fraud in history.

CR: You know something, I have an epigraph here which I'd love to read: "Inviting people to laugh with you while you're laughing at yourself is a good thing to do. You may be the fool, but you're the fool in charge."

sa-Pekka Salonen is not only considered a great conductor, but during his tenure as music director of the Los Angeles Philharmonic, he has helped move the orchestra into the elite of classical music. The young Finnish conductor/composer came full-time to Los Angeles after garnering attention for his work in Scandinavia, and in guest-conducting appearances with the Los Angeles Philharmonic. The Philharmonic's international tours under Salonen have given the orchestra its highest profile in history. That's further enhanced by the opening of the Walt Disney Concert Hall. Salonen is also a critically acclaimed composer, whose work has been performed by his and other orchestras around the world.

I talked with Esa-Pekka Salonen at the newly opened Walt Disney Concert Hall.

Larry Mantle: I'd like you to compare and contrast Disney Hall with the Dorothy Chandler Pavilion. The acoustics there were heavily criticized. Here you're in a building where you were so heavily involved in how the building was designed, in the acoustical design as well. Is there a big difference?

Esa-Pekka Salonen: There is a huge difference in every way. This hall sounds fantastic. It really is. It's one of the best concert halls acoustically in the entire world, I daresay at this point. In the few concerts we have done so far, the acoustics are very unusual in the sense that they seem to be able to combine totally opposite ends of the spectrum, i.e., it sounds warm but clear at the same time. It's very powerful but yet transparent at the same time. The sound blends very well but yet you can hear the details. It is a very rare kind of acoustical environment.

LM: Are there any halls elsewhere in the country or in the world to which you would compare it? Does it have something unique about its sound?

ES: Well, every great hall has a unique personality. There is no question about that. If you want to name a sort of sister hall in terms of aesthetics, if not in terms of details and design, it would be the Philharmonie in Berlin, which was designed by the German architect Scharoun in the Sixties. That hall has something that vaguely reminds me of Walt Disney Concert Hall. It has got this amphitheater kind of idea where the orchestra is in the middle and it is surrounded by the audience. The sound has the same kind of lively quality to it, but of course in terms of acoustics and the architectural design, they are very different in character.

LM: What is your sense of how the orchestra is responding to it? Obviously what they are hearing reflected back to them is going to sound different than it did in the more cavernous Pavilion. There's also the natural human excitement about performing in an architecturally significant building and a new hall. Has that led to any changes in the orchestra's performance?

ES: First of all, they are very excited about this, and moved, because we don't take this for granted. We realize what an incredible thing it is to have been given this hall to perform in. While we are incredibly excited about it, we also see this as a challenge. We have to rise to the occasion, and somehow the quality of the playing has to match the quality of the building. Everybody is expecting some kind of a quality leap in the Philharmonic's playing, but also on a deeper level, the ideology of what an orchestra is all about has to develop. We cannot think of moving into this fantastic building with this radical design and just carry on as usual. We also have to redefine our existence the way this building has redefined the idea of a concert hall.

LM: It was said before the Philharmonic moved into this building that it was an orchestra that had become superior to the building in which it had performed. And now you talk about the orchestra raising its performance further because of the extraordinary building into which it's moving. I wonder if this relates to the musical choices that you make for programming here. Are there kinds of music that you are going to be comfortable doing here that you wouldn't have been comfortable doing at the Dorothy Chandler Pavilion? Are there risks you can take here given the size or the sound of the hall that you've been longing to take?

ES: The truth is that there are lots of goodies I have decided to save for this hall, both the big ones and the smaller pieces. I wanted to wait with some of the more massive, more complex Late Romantic works, for instance, until we were safely in Walt Disney Concert Hall. For instance, *Gurrelieder* is something I haven't done in the old hall, and we have programmed it. Mahler's *Eighth* is something I would like to do in this hall because it can take the most tremendous amount of sound. This hall is also incredibly sensitive in terms of the lower end of the dynamic scale. So we can do the beautiful, almost chamber scale Mozarts and Haydns and so forth. There is a lot of stuff that we are going to be doing now that we didn't do in the old building.

LM: You mentioned the back wall and how acoustically that provides a kind of bass response that is rather remarkable in this building. You are also surrounded by people. And I am curious, when you are up there as the conductor, you're seeing people behind the orchestra, they are literally wrapping around you. When you are in that intensely focused state of conducting, are you even aware of the people who are there? And if you are, what is that like for you?

ES: I like having people around the orchestra. Ultimately, what we are doing is communicating. We are communicating the thoughts and the ideas of composers to the audience. It is nice to have it verified at the very moment of performance, that there are people close by and that this has to do with a dialog between people and not just some kind of abstract thing—like we do our thing and then we hope that somebody in the other part of the room would understand or would somehow be moved by this. I very much like the idea of having this close contact.

LM: When the audience is responding in a particular way, can you feel it? Can you feel an audience being emotionally moved?

ES: You can always tell. The signs are usually subtle, but you can tell by the degrees of silence. When things really get going, those moments when the performance really lifts off and something special happens and the audience gets it and they sense the magic, those moments are very clear. We all feel it and it becomes like an amplifier in a way. When the audience and the orchestra are completely in sync, on the same frequency, then the effect is that of amplification.

LM: As a noted composer yourself, do you have any sense that conducting in this hall will have any effect on music you are writing?

ES: I'm sure it will generally have a big effect on everything I do musically, but it is more difficult to say exactly how. I'm sure that the particular sound in the hall will affect my orchestration choices. There is also a more concrete thing coming up, which is a new piece I'm writing, based on Frank Gehry's architectural language on some level. That's going to be premiered in May 2004. Of course that piece has a lot to do with the design of this hall.

LM: The Philharmonic has expanded its outreach to kids, bringing them in to hear the orchestra, doing educational programs, music in schools, attempting to fill in gaps where there have been budget cutbacks that have removed many of those programs. What do you see as the Philharmonic's role in music education, and for you as someone operating at this very highest level of music? What do you see as your obligation to younger potential music fans?

ES: Now we have a perfect vehicle to spread the word. It's this hall. For those kids who come in, it is going to be an unforgettable experience. The combination of the building, the architecture, the visuals, the sound, the orchestra, the performance, the performers, I think it is something that even if they never come back to a classical music event this will be something that they will always remember. So now we have the perfect thing to offer to kids around town: come to Disney Hall. We will bus them in rather than going to schools and playing these concerts where they have to go to a gymnastics hall and listen to the orchestra. That's not an event in the same way. For a child or a teenager to come into this building and experience all of this is going to be a major, major event. I think we will have a big success in this.

LM: Like so many of our listeners, I still vividly remember as an eight-year-old my first visit to hear the Los Angeles Philharmonic in the Dorothy Chandler Pavilion; it is like it was yesterday. It is so indelible, the memory, the power of being in the presence of a live orchestra. Then to add to that this new hall, this is going to be a very rare opportunity, as you say, and obviously a time when you are going to be able to attract people who might never have considered going to a classical music concert before.

ES: I meet those people almost daily. I bump into people in bars and cafes and supermarkets and gas stations, and they say, "Well, you know, I've decided to come and hear you guys in your new hall." These are people who have never, ever been to a classical music concert, but now this is the moment for them to come and check it out. I'm very hopeful that the experience is powerful enough that they keep coming.

LM: As you look to the future, whether you are the music director, conductor, or you have moved on to other things, what do you hope will have happened with this orchestra in ten or twenty years' time?

ES: I hope classical music and orchestral music will become an essential part of the L.A. identity, so that in addition to Hollywood and the entertainment industry and the surfing and the cardboard Hollywood signs and the Hollywood Hills, there will be something else that defines L.A. life—the Philharmonic, Disney Hall and classical music.

LM: Does any of that involve moving across barriers between types of music? It seems like in new music, there are opportunities to broaden what is considered classical music. Is that an important part of making classical music even more vital, getting beyond the customary repertoire?

ES: I think it is vitally important to do all of the research, to see where classical music is going, what are the new composers writing, what is the current thinking of aesthetics and styles. Is there an era of repertoire we have neglected? Are there undiscovered masterpieces in the older repertoire? It is a dynamic process. And it should continue. We cannot simply say, okay, this is the canon. These are the masterpieces and these are the works we are going to play forever and ever. It has to be a constant process of self-analysis, of research and quest for new ideas and points of view.

As any parent knows, this is the era of the children's book. Rapidly expanding bookstore space devoted to the genre, celebrity-penned bestsellers, and an emphasis on reading to children have driven the business to heights never seen before. However, if you ask most parents which books are their favorites to read to their children, and which ones their kids respond to most, I suspect they would list the gems of the mid-twentieth century.

In 1963, Maurice Sendak wrote and illustrated the classic *Where the Wild Things Are.* This Caldecott Prize-winning work was enormously popular, and offered a tone that was far different from typical kid fare. From this book, and others that would follow, Sendak's respect for children's ability to handle reality, coupled with his extraordinary artistic ability, set him apart from his peers. Sendak's artistry further expanded into sets and costume designs for several prominent operas.

In 1993, I was excited to learn that Sendak would be talking with me about the publication of his book, *We Are All in the Dumps With Jack and Guy.* As one of Sendak's many fans, I was looking forward to hearing more about his childhood, and how he came to his approach of writing for kids. However, I'd never heard Sendak interviewed before, and was told by an acquaintance of mine that he did not suffer fools gladly. I didn't think much about that characterization at the time, but certainly laughed about it later.

My conversation with Maurice Sendak is among my favorites, not only because of my admiration for his work, but because of how much I enjoyed his personality. I was very impressed by both the clarity of thought that was reflected in his remarks, and his willingness to probe so deeply into his art. I assume that every creator of children's books loves kids. What Sendak also has is a perhaps unmatched respect for children's intellectual and emotional honesty.

Larry Mantle: I'd like to talk about your view of kids, because to me that is fundamental to what you do. One theme you come back to time and time again is that we don't give kids an awful lot of credit for being able to handle the real world.

Maurice Sendak: No, I don't think we give them much credit at all. This is a subject that's been part of my work since the Sixties. When *Wild Things* came out there was a huge hullabaloo. It was a controversial book. And why? I think primarily because it seemed so strange that a book for children would have something vital in it like a child's temper tantrum. It was considered an inappropriate place to show real emotions. I think the real problem is that anything related to children in the publishing industry called "art" is placid and tepid. I speak generally, of course.

LM: And in more modern times also, because certainly historically, works that have been aimed at children have had levels of reality, of poverty, of violence, and strong emotion.

MS: Yes; if you go to the nineteenth century and Charles Dickens, a book like *We Are All in the Dumps* would have been a very commonplace book. Every character in a Dickens novel is looking for a home; every kid is lost; everyone is making up a family as quickly as they can count on their fingers. It was commonplace that children were homeless and children died in the streets. Somehow that's been smothered in our society, and we kind of have amnesia about it. We don't like to think about it; who does? It's a grim subject.

LM: In a lot of ways, this kind of literature introduces kids to the real world, the world that they are already beginning to experience.

MS: Yes, kids know all about it, and we underestimate them painfully. Children are so polite that they don't like to frighten their parents by telling them how much they know.

LM: What they really know, yes.

MS: Of course they know and they confirm it out in the street, in the backyard, in various ways that their parents would really not approve. But parents, generally speaking, largely hide their heads in the sand. And the presumption that kids don't know is ridiculous; they know. When I was a kid I knew, and there wasn't even any television to know by, but I knew by watching my parents' faces. I knew by their anxious voices. I knew by newspaper headlines and horrible pictures on front pages of the *Daily News,* I knew more than I ever should have or wanted to know.

LM: And if you or I knew that as children, certainly kids today are bombarded with it in multimedia.

MS: Yes, what's curious to me is that they're confronted with things like television where they see incredibly horrible things about other children in the world, and then when you do a book, you're not supposed to show that. It's a dichotomy and a silliness which baffles me, but doesn't trouble me anymore; it's simply the way things are. And, when people say, "Well, should kids know this?" Well, they've been watching television and they've seen the Somali babies, they've seen every day and heard every day about kids coming home from school—or not arriving home because their brain's blown out in crossfire in New York City and other big metropolises. So what don't they know?

LM: So it's almost an irrelevant question.

MS: It's even worse; it's criminal to not inform them that you know what their situations are like and to not help them. You have to help them. If you don't tell them, you are not helping them.

LM: That's interesting; so in your view, if you don't acknowledge it, in a sense there's a deception there?

MS: A terrible one because you're leaving them vulnerable, without defenses.

LM: You mentioned the display of temper and how controversial that was in *Where The Wild Things Are.* To me, it wasn't the issue of the tantrum itself, it was the starkness of the tantrum. Because I think we've seen kids act out in other children's literature, but it's so Dennis-the-Menace-ized, it's so smoothed off.

MS: Cleaned up.

LM: Yes. But this was real—the sense of hatred of the parent came through. And that's how kids are, they hate their parents in that moment.

MS: Yes, yes. And what they're counting on, which is what Max, the hero of *Wild Things,* is counting on: that although his mother is furious, and she might even at that moment hate him, she's going to love him within minutes and she's going to feed him. And it's going to happen every other week or every other day of every other week, probably until he's thirty and gets married and moves out of the place. It's a normal occurrence in everybody's household; kids freak out this way, get very mad, say desperately bad things to their parents, and occasionally parents say them back. We are only creatures after all. To not acknowledge that is to not acknowledge the child's right to hate or to feel these desperate feelings, and yet know that underneath all that is comfort and love. That wasn't the point of *Wild Things.* The point of *Wild Things* was, I was happy doing a book that excited me very much. All these manifestations and all these subtexts came much later.

LM: That's what I was going to say. Using your new book as an example, *We Are All In The Dumps With Jack and Guy,* it seemed to me that there are very clear and thought-out themes: homelessness, children who were abandoned, lack of care, and all these things that are very real-world. But I got the sense that the underlying tone of the book just comes from you very naturally, that there's nothing that's really thought out about that. The tone just is what it is. The themes are conscious.

MS: And they are contemporary, but the tone, or the basic underlying theme, is always the same in all my books, which is the vulnerability of children. How do they make it from one minute to the next?

LM: And that's automatic with you, isn't it?

MS: It's automatic. It's just the way it is; only the form changes. So when people say, this is a book about homeless children, well, yes, in a sense it is, but it also isn't. That's to reduce the meaning of the book. The book is about kids and how tenacious they are, how tenacious that baby is to have a family come hell or high water. They have to survive. And they will follow those kids and they will follow until they get home. They must live—they want to live—that's the healthy impulse. And that, probably crudely put, is the theme of all my books, just the tenaciousness of children.

LM: It sounds simplistic to put it this way, but to me it's about how kids are real. That may sound fatuous, but I think that that's the problem we have, that we don't accept that kids are real.

MS: Oh, yes. We don't know how to interpret real, because it means things that are disturbing. Children do think disturbing thoughts and feel disturbing feelings, and act in disturbing ways. We don't like to think of them that way because we have television-ized them and movie-ized them and kiddy-booked them to such a degree that we have drowned them in a kind of soporific state, so that we simply don't allow their animal natures to manifest themselves anymore. We don't like it; it's troublesome. It's understandable to a degree; every parent who has a child wants to protect that child. The sad truth is, there's a limit to that protection.

LM: When we look at the dark side of kids it's in such an over-blown, malevolent, unrealistic way.

MS: Yes, which does hurt as far as I'm concerned. It does damage to the concept of children having these opposing emotional forces in them, to exaggerate them to either sweetness and light and desperately insipid, or malevolent and crazy, Charlie Manson. Those are enormous extremes. It's using kids in a terrible way, I think. It's really using them and not showing them for the complicated little incredible creatures they are.

LM: The book that you have just written is your first in ten years that is in the genre that you are most commonly associated with. Does it take that long for the whole process to take place, or have you just been so busy working on all kinds of other things?

MS: I have been very busy. The last book I finished—the last picture book I finished—*Outside Over There,* was the one I was trying for and waiting for and I accomplished it, and I was very happy with it, and that was 1980. There were many other things I wanted to do, like sets for operas. I started a children's theater. I have a production company here in California. I wanted to do other things that were outside things, as if the title of my book, *Outside Over There,* was a directive to me. But oddly and paradoxically, *We Are All In the Dumps With Jack and Guy* was inspired by two nursery rhymes that I have been desperate to solve since 1964. I didn't know what they meant. I fell in love with them in '64, and I did a dummy based on them in '65, but it failed, and I abandoned it for twenty-five years.

LM: Before I read the book, I didn't understand them, particularly the first one.

MS: You know why? Can I tell you why? Because these were nursery rhymes, these were satires probably in the eighteenth century, a political satire or social commentaries. That's what nursery rhymes were: they were jokes that everybody understood. When those meanings were lost, they were dumped into the nursery where the kids could play with them, because we didn't know what they meant anymore. We have lost every inkling of understanding of what these were composed for. So they end up as being kind of strange haiku-like images, which the kids love because the kids can make up their own stories. Kids don't need logic the way we pedantically do. So I love these two rhymes that have nothing to do with each other. As I said, I did the book in 1965, but I didn't do it right. It was a sweet little funny book, but it didn't measure up. I mean, the rhymes are tough and strange and beautiful and lofty. I just hadn't reached that height. I put it away. It wasn't the book I wanted to do. It was in 1990 that it was solved. I got the idea hearing about cities that are ringed with shantytowns, where only children live, where children run away from families where they're abused, where little girls are sold into prostitution and they form their own little villages and towns. And they live in garbage cans and shanties and cardboard houses. What suddenly struck me was, this is what *We Are All in the Dumps* is about. In 1965 I thought dumps meant anxiety or depression. Everybody in the Sixties who was anybody was in therapy, so what else could it mean? "Dumps" now means dumps; you can take it quite literally. People living in garbage. Then suddenly the book sprang to life.

LM: So the world had devolved to the point where the United States was having some of the same characteristics of Latin American countries, where you had poor children without any sort of caretaker. And you come face-to-face with that. You live just north of New York, but I'm sure you spend a lot of time around Manhattan and you see it there, and then you see it when you come to L.A. or any large city.

MS: Yes. Every city I've been in on this tour . . . shocking experiences. You can't not see it anymore. You can't push it out of your line of vision—it's right there blocking your path. And that stimulated the whole concept for me. Also seeing the whole thing with Somalia over the past year, the wars in Bosnia, and the photographs that you see in papers of children clutching each other and kids, kids, kids, always in the line of fire. It was going to be a book about those kids and how tough they are.

LM: What's interesting is that, as you were looking at this earlier, you didn't take "dumps" other than to be some sort of depression. And yet as you look at it now, the connection, if you look at "dumps" in a literal sense, seems very clear. Not to make more of it than it is, but do you think there was something working long before at an unconscious level that maybe you didn't recognize?

MS: Very likely, because I don't take much credit for how these things happen. There is a computer that works all by itself that is, I hope, permanently plugged in. Then finally when it's ready it pushes little buttons that say, "Hey Maurice, listen, copy it down, here's the stuff we did for you." That's how it happens.

LM: Because what else would have been the connection except that very point?

MS: I agree with you.

LM: And since you saw these two as a set, even though there wasn't anything obvious about it, it seems as if you must have known it without knowing it.

MS: It's almost as though it had to wait until it became critically clear. We are living in the Nineties, and we are by and large living in the dumps. We read about it all day, we see it every day. Suddenly, these two antiquated verses are immensely contemporary. So I always wanted to bring these together and bind them so they would be forever linked, and I think I've done it, and I'm very pleased with it.

LM: I'm going to read the two rhymes, and then we'll talk about the story that results from the connection. The first one is: "We are all in the dumps, for diamonds are trumps. The kittens are gone to St. Paul's! The baby is bit, the moon's in a fit, and the houses are built without walls." And the second nursery rhyme: "Jack and Guy went out in the rye and they found a little boy with one black eye. Come says Jack let's knock him on the head. No says Guy let's buy him some bread. You buy one loaf and I'll buy two, and we'll bring him up as other folk do."

MS: Jack and Guy are like a kid's version of Jimmy Cagney and Pat O'Brien, who live in the dumps. They're the two tough kids who rule this tiny community of lost children living in garbage. A little black baby enters the scene saying help, but they just dismiss the baby; there's no place; there's no time. They just don't care; they're tough. The moon watches pathetically all during the opening part of the book because I have to prepare dramatically for the line, "The moon's in a fit." What does that mean?

So the moon right from the start is grieving, watching the helpless children, not being able to help. Then these two rats come in, and homeless children and poor children and rats, alas, are companions; we all know that. The rats steal the little baby, and they steal all the kittens, which are going to have to go to St. Paul's for that line. They run away with them, and Jack and Guy say, "No, no, no, you can't do that, you guys." So the rats say, "Okay, we'll play a game of bridge; we'll see who wins the kid and the kittens." I had to play bridge in this book, because of the line, "For diamonds are trumps." They play the game of bridge and the rats win.

The moon is so disgusted and distressed at what is happening on this planet Earth. She's so angry at Jack and Guy for being so passive that she forgets they're only kids. This is too much for the kids. So she comes into the scene, grabs the two kids, brings them up into the heavens, carries them through the heavens and drops them in the rye, very close to St. Paul's bakery and orphanage, which is what I turn St. Paul's into. We know St. Paul's is the cathedral in England, but it doesn't make any sense to us. So that's where the kid is incarcerated and the kittens are incarcerated. The kid has been dropped on the way, however, and Jack and Guy find the little kid in the rye. They embrace the little kid. They go off to get the other kittens and save them. It's perfectly clear to the moon that they can't manage this, they're only children. So the moon transforms herself into a *Moby Dick* cat. Herman Melville is my other hero, along with Mozart.

LM: Mozart and Melville.

MS: Anyway, the cat appears, charges into the bakery and orphanage, cruelly dispatches the two rats, saves the kittens, brings the kittens and Jack and Guy and the little baby back to the dumps where they came from. And they bring up the baby as other folk do. That's about the best they can do. I think it's a really happy ending, happier than is most often the case. But it's curious and funny because when my sister came to visit me when I was finishing this book, she was very moved and she said, "It's very nice. It's very nice. But why, if the moon is bothering, couldn't it move them to a nicer neighborhood, like the Upper West Side?" And I said, "Natalie, the moon's not into real estate, this is not a problem that the moon has. The moon is helping those children survive."

LM: And the sad truth is, that as much as this is fantasy, of course, the reality is the kids would go back to where they had been.

MS: It's like what that man said about reality and fantasy, a very good statement he made. Fantasy is meager and pointless if it isn't rooted in reality.

LM: But to me it's a very happy ending because the closing line is a real affirmation of the fact that these kids aren't like everybody else.

MS: Yes, just look at the baby's face that's smiling in its sleep. The baby started off by crying in the very opening pages of the book, screaming for help. And it ends up in the arms of these children safely sleeping and smiling, as other folk do.

LM: I wouldn't assume that when you set out writing and illustrating that you have an idea in mind of an upbeat or downbeat ending; it just is the ending that seems right.

MS: It's the ending that seems right, but I prefer happy endings because when they're bad endings they scare and depress me. So I don't really like to end it unhappily; I end it as truthfully as I can. And very often that appears to be too sad for a lot of people, but for me it's as good as it can be.

LM: I'm curious about the page, there's no text on it, but the page where the moon returns with Jack and Guy and the baby. There's the Jesus image where the baby is removed from the bottom of the moon.

MS: Right, that's interesting, a lot of people said it's Christ coming off the cross, which is very beautiful. I see it now. It's curious because I didn't see it at first, because I had a very particular image in mind when I did that. They're bringing back the baby from the moon, and they're putting him to sleep. That triggered a memory which is one of my favorite in my childhood, which is we were rather poor and there was one relative who was well-to-do, and they, the husband and wife, had an automobile and once in a great blue moon they would come and take us, the Sendak kids, for a drive. Well, I can't tell you what that meant when the car was out front and we'd all go roaring down the stairs and I'd go into the backseat and the worst thing that could happen was within seconds I was falling asleep. The movement of the car, everything, and I desperately tried to stay up, because this was a rare adventure. But I couldn't—I couldn't. And then the next thing I knew the drive was over, the door was open, and my father was reaching in to the backseat and taking me up in the air. That's the memory in that picture, the wonderful delight of being half-asleep and knowing your papa is picking you up out of the car, is going to put you in his arms and take you upstairs. I wasn't thinking of Christ, but somewhere in my consciousness perhaps I was, because it's a great favorite subject in terms of painting. It's one of the most beautiful, beautiful moments in art, so who knows what sifts into the mind.

A listener asks about censorship of Sendak's In the Night Kitchen, *and what should be done to combat censorship of children's books.*

MS: Fight. We're talking about some few librarians, as opposed to the majority who are repelled by this kind of thing. It's happened frequently to me, especially with *In the Night Kitchen,* which was published in 1970. It's a book that I put so much into, emotionally speaking, and it was so fatuously reduced to a little boy's penis. I mean, it was incredibly embarrassing that we could all still ponder such a thing. It seemed to me any number of people have never seen one. There was no other explanation for this kind of excitement. It was ugly and silly, and the book is still banned in parts of the country. It is not permitted in some libraries unless the teacher or principal takes a Magic Marker and covers poor little Mickey in very kinky little outfits. I've seen some of them, so then you have a bunch of kids holding the book up to the light and drawing their attention to the very thing that, of course, the teacher or principal had opposed. And that's happened to other books, too. It's a very, very serious problem we have in this country, which is the secret, or not so secret, censorship of children's books.

LM: I think what drives it is the view that children are either non-sexual, or that when children are sexual, there's something to be afraid of.

MS: It's embarrassing, it's embarrassing. Why in God's name do we teach them so quickly to be ashamed of their bodies? We've all seen children, I was just in San Francisco, and it was a hot day and we're sitting in the park, and some kid just slipped out of his clothes and jumped around naked. His mother pounced on him as though he'd done the most incredibly criminal thing, and practically strapped him into a box with hooks in it. Why? Why? It was just beautiful and innocent and perfectly natural. Why do we do this? We allow our children to go to the museum and see the Christ child naked. But we won't let a kid be naked in a book for children. It's benumbing.

A listener says she lets her child get angry at her, and wonders why other parents don't.

MS: You are a good mama. You're a rare one. I don't know—I can't answer your question because I think a kind of amnesia takes over. I think once you get married a deep amnesia takes place. Then when you have children, you start worrying so much about taking care of them and not losing them, and nourishing them, and I think you push away thoughts that are frightening to you, even thoughts that you know you had as a child. You are unusual in that you can talk about it so openly and freely; most people can't do it. They can't do it because they don't want to remember. Thus they're out of sympathy with their children; it's a paradox because they love their children. It's a scary thing to remember and you're describing it and you know you're right; it's a scary feeling, it's an overwhelming feeling.

LM: You referred earlier to children's animal nature. Do you think society tends to not give credence to the fact that we are animals overall?

MS: Yes, it's always amazing to me. We're so curious about what the dolphins are saying and what various creatures are saying, and we don't seem to be interested in what babies are saying. I think infants are talking their heads off the minute they come out. We are very complicated, wired creatures. Just watching a baby is so fascinating, simply because they talk with everything but language: with their eyes, their nose, their mouth, their fists. Watch a baby who is held by a careless slipshod person, that baby is purple with anxiety. Get me out of this guy's hands. In listening to babies talking you see the animal struggling to live, the little animal that hasn't got any strength, whose screaming says, "Get back in this room and feed me! Pick me up!" The means they have are so small, are so weak; it's so poignant to watch a baby. I think we could invest much more time in figuring out what they're saying, in decoding the language.

LM: Do you pick up any of your books and read them just for your own pleasure?

MS: No, once you're finished, you're immensely finished. It's such an emotional gust, you know, to do the book, that one is almost permanently exhausted. I don't know if that's true of other authors; actually, I've always been rather curious about that. But no, it's very hard for me to be interested once it's finished. I'm proud of it, I take great pleasure in it and I love hearing the effects on other people. But it no longer has that effect on me.

LM: It does sound, though, like you do consciously think at certain times about the impact that your books have.

MS: I must be honest. To a very small degree, there's one pleasure principle which is basic to this whole thing, which is the solution of a creative problem. That is so exciting and so thrilling and so preoccupies me, it fills a year or two of drawing and redrawing and composing and redoing. It's such a personal assignment that there's only a peripheral sighting of what it might mean to other people. That's a fact. It's there, but it's not major to my thinking. What is major to my thinking is fairness to the kids. Being as honest as I know how to be to the kids. I will not condescend to them. I will not treat them like little idiots. I will tell them what I think I know about the situation. It's the way my parents treated me. My father used to invent stories at night to put us to bed and they were "inappropriate for children" stories. I would tell them at school and my teacher would scream and send me home to have my mouth washed out. I obviously take after my father. Because they were wonderful stories; they were real-life stories. Like the Grimms' are real-life stories. They aren't censored; they aren't foolish; they're tough. Kids are tough. They have to be tough; it's another aspect that scares people, that toughness. Kids will hide it because they know it's inappropriate, and they finally get all the signals that nobody likes this in them. And little girls will act like little girls and little boys will act like little boys, and they'll put on the show, probably, alas, for the rest of their lives. But that initial raw toughness is the beauty of childhood. If it could be harnessed, encouraged, loved, I think we'd have a hell of a lot more interesting people in the world.

LM: Let's talk a little bit about your background, since you gave us a little look into it with your father telling you these "inappropriate stories." What was your childhood like?

MS: Ordinary. Both my parents were immigrants. They didn't speak English, only Yiddish, when they came to this country. They were very proud to be here, like all the immigrants who came before World War I. I'm the third of three children, much younger than my sister and brother. I was part of the Great Depression; I wasn't desired any more than the Great Depression, but once I was there, it was great. It was like moving into a business, everybody was writing stories and drawing pictures and binding books. There was no choice in my life. My parents did not want us to be artists. My brother and I grew up to be professional artists. My sister couldn't because girls didn't have a chance. She was groomed like a racehorse—because she was extremely beautiful—to be married and do well that way. So all the educational facilities and hopes were abandoned for her. My parents were deeply disappointed that they had, as my father always said, two greenhorn sons. Meaning we read and we drew, and we'd rather stay in the house than go outdoors. They were appalled. What they didn't recognize was that we took after them.

LM: I was going to say I assume this is not coincidental, and this probably goes back in the family generations.

MS: We don't know that it goes back because, alas, when my mother and father came here their first job in life was to earn enough money to bring the relatives over; that's all they did. And one by one the sisters and the siblings came and all lived on top of each other in our house and nearby. When we got to my father's family, it was too late. There are no survivors, none. We're the last of the Sendaks.

LM: So the stories of who they were and what they were like—

MS: —were precious. I wanted to hear them ad nauseum over and over and over. I wanted to know about little Stedla. I wanted to know where every house was. I wanted to know every day of my father and my mother's lives. Happily I was so curious as a child I asked constantly, so I have a repertoire of stories. That is all that's left of us. That's an important part of my history.

LM: Are your parents still living?

MS: No, they're gone.

LM: Did they live long enough to see the kind of acclaim you received?

MS: Oh, yes. They were thrilled—especially when I illustrated a book by Isaac Bashevis Singer.

LM: Then they really knew you'd made it.

MS: They couldn't figure out why he wanted me, but he was, for a short time, connected to the family, and he was so good to my parents. He called them and sent them his first editions in Yiddish; he was marvelous. That was a high point for them; I had made it; I had made it.

W hat must it be like to receive the adoration of millions of fans, while very few of them actually know your identity? That's one of the highly unusual aspects of Caroll Spinney's more than thirty-year career as *Sesame Street*'s Big Bird and Oscar the Grouch. Though I was already past the age of its target audience when *Sesame Street* started on PBS, I've long been impressed with the stronghold the program has on adults who did grow up with it. Big Bird has certainly played a big part in that relationship. In talking with Spinney, it's clear that he has a great love for his character and its ability to connect so strongly with preschoolers. As a parent, I've scored points with my son Desmond because of my acquaintance with Big Bird. Hopefully our conversation will give you the feeling that you know the man inside the world-famous bird.

Larry Mantle: You've been a huge celebrity in American households for more than three decades, and yet your fans don't know what you look like.

Caroll Spinney: That's right. But that never bothered me. I'm often asked if I don't feel a little jealous of my own characters, but I'm a puppeteer, and most puppeteers are quite content to have only their puppets seen. Although I used to watch *Kukla, Fran and Ollie* when I was young and it always ended up with a nice shot of Burr Tillstrom with Kukla on his hand. And I said, "Gee, I'd like to end that way." So I wouldn't mind being seen a little bit, and now I am being seen a lot because I am pushing my book.

LM: I love how you share interacting with various celebrities who were on some of these shows, for example Raymond Burr and others, and how some seem to be so gracious and great to deal with, while others didn't necessarily treat Big Bird so well.

CS: That's true. Oscar doesn't treat Big Bird very well, either.

LM: So you get used to that?

CS: Yeah, Oscar has his own approach to life and it's quite contrary, and people who don't see eye to eye, he is a little hard on them.

LM: Is Big Bird a manifestation of you, and Oscar more of an alter ego?

CS: I'd like to think of it that way. My wife Debra says that when I am in traffic at some point when you see silly things, I sound an awful lot more like Oscar. But in my heart—

LM: But the uncensored Oscar I am sure.

CS: Yeah, I guess it could be as colorful as you want. There are only the two of us in the car, but I really feel that Big Bird is a child of mine. I am not him, but he is like a child of mine, and I feel very protective of him as you would with your little boy, Desmond.

LM: So you have this relationship that has grown over thirty-four years, and the character has evolved, too.

CS: Yes, he has. I didn't know who he was when Jim Henson designed him in a cartoon form. His puppet builder used to work for Burr Tillstrom, and he gave him a much nicer look. Jim was an incredible genius and really hard to work with.

LM: That's clear. I love how you describe how he works and some of the developments he made, for example, making your Big Bird suit more able to move and the eyes more responsive.

CS: Yes, there were a lot of steps. So I asked Jim, "How should I play the bird? Does he talk like a parrot? What's he going to be like?" And he said, "I've been thinking more about how to build the puppet, creating a thing that's really a costume." And he's got bird feet and most puppets don't have working legs. They're my legs. But the whole top part's a great, big hand puppet. Jim had thought of that because he created that genre of compiling a human with a puppet. But he hadn't really thought about his character. So I said, "Well what's he like? What's he do?" And he said, "Hmm, I don't know. Maybe he's like Mickey Mouse's pal, Goofy?" You know, a country bumpkin. I had done a voice like that.

I had a dog in my own show, which he had seen. His name was Pistachio. He was a not-too-bright follower of Pickle Puss, my feature character, who is a cat. So Big Bird, when we first got to know him, sounded like this: "Well, hi, here I am." I sound a lot like a purple dinosaur. He didn't say that, though. There was no purple dinosaur.

LM: You got there first.

CS: Yeah, but it wasn't long before a script came down and we said, "You know, it really seems he should be a kid. He's a little kid and he hasn't learned the alphabet yet." And once we had that, he could grow. And he did. He grew. The first year he made his biggest changes, and before that first season was over, which took six months to tape, I had learned he was a little boy and he sounded very much lighter and less of a bumpkin.

LM: Would you mind just saying something?

CS: Well, Big Bird happens to be right here now.

Big Bird: Yeah, I'm right here. What would you like me to say?

LM: Big Bird, I understand that you went through quite a bit of a mobility change for the Emmy Awards of 1970; is that right?

Big Bird: Yeah, well, one of my problems is that sometimes when I'm in a crowd, particularly away from *Sesame Street,* I can't see so good and I tend to trip over things a lot. And I sat down on somebody's lap when I was running down the aisle to go up on the stage with Dick Cabbage.

LM: Cavett.

CS: Dick Cavett, right.

Big Bird: Oh, yeah, I sat down on a lap and I discovered I was sitting on Cliff Robertson's lap. Then I went up and I guess I did pretty good because Hollywood called. And I got to go on the *Flip Wilson Show* and that was my first visit out west here.

LM: You became a big star. And now, you relate so well to the children who are watching. You're really one of them.

Big Bird: Yeah, because I'm six now. I can read and write and I know every letter and I can count way beyond twenty.

LM: Big Bird, in some cases, is kind of a big brother to a lot of the kids watching, too.

Big Bird: Yeah, I think so. Because we've discovered the kids are younger and younger every year. And so we got my little pals, Elmo and Zoë. And they're three-and-a-half. It seems the kids really identify with them. They're always trying to learn stuff. I'm sort of the big brother now.

LM: I think so. And your voice is something that kids connect to so much. I know for my son, Desmond, there is just something so soothing, so calm, so reassuring about your voice. That's a huge part of the character.

CS: Yeah, once in a while we get out of the place and I was waiting to go down into the "Pirates of the Caribbean." It occurred to me that maybe Big Bird should be with me and so he started yelling—

Big Bird: —Hey, Snuffy, where are you? It's hard to see. It's getting dark here.

CS: And all the kids were looking around. They couldn't spot him. He was hiding very well.

LM: Very funny. Do you think you've grown in a different way because of these characters?

CS: Yes, because I have personally met so many children. And knowing that Big Bird and Oscar are seen by millions every day, that's got to have some affect on your psyche, I suppose. Matter of fact I've noticed the book, I went looking for it yesterday, it was at Brentano's bookstore in Beverly Hills, it was listed under religious books.

LM: How did that happen?

CS: On the inner flap it says, "An inspirational message," and they must have looked at that and said, "Oh, it's religious." No, it's not a religious book. It's more of a memoir. I think that anybody who has watched the show all these years, I mean, we have the grandmothers now because they were young mothers when their children were watching. And they often watch with them. So it meant a lot to them and to their children, who are now mothers and fathers, and to the children. It's not a children's book. And it's not one you'd even read to the kids, because it's more about the physical problems of being a puppeteer and how I got there. Although at an awful lot of the signings I've been doing at bookshops all across America, there are a lot of kids there. And I have a friend with me, too, who is extremely grumpy. But I can't tell you who it is.

LM: You can't?

CS: Yeah, it's a secret who this grouch is. I mean, oops, did I say grouch?

LM: Does a trash can have to come along?

CS: No. He appears over the podium.

LM: When this program started, you couldn't have guessed that here you'd be thirty-four years later and the show would be not just extremely popular but iconic.

CS: Yeah, he's actually become part of the fabric just like Mickey Mouse—his image is known all over the world. Our show is now seen in over one hundred forty countries. So while there are a lot of countries that don't have him, he is also even seen in Russia occasionally.

LM: Incredible. You really grew up seemingly meant to do this. You took an interest in puppeteering very early on.

CS: I did; I saw a couple of puppet shows when I was five and then again at six. F. Lee Bailey, the lawyer, I used to play with him, he was a real brat. What a surprise. His mother ran a very expensive daycare center, and my mother would make costumes for their pageants and stuff. They had a puppet theater there and I saw my first real puppet show there. I was really impressed; then a few people came out and bowed at the end, and I realized that they were the ones who did the show. They had their characters on their hand and I said, "That would be really great. I could do a whole story all by myself." For Christmas my mother made me a "Punch and Judy Show." She used to see shows in Blackpool, in England. She was a little girl there. So she looked up Punch and Judy in the library, built me a bunch of lovely puppets and even the theater, which my brother helped her build. And so for my ninth birthday, which is also Christmas, that's why I'm named Caroll, believe it or not.

LM: Really? That's very appropriate.

CS: Yeah, I was going to be Douglas. I said, "Mom, you got a bad sense of humor."

LM: Well, it could have been Noel so—

CS: Yeah, that's right, that would have worked. So anyways, she gave me a career that morning.

LM: So she clearly was really behind your interest in this, and even more than that, had the talent to set you on your way.

CS: Yeah, she was born an artist. My oldest brother, who is now my late brother, and two of my children, they have gone to the Art Institute of Boston, where I went, and they are very good artists.

LM: What did your father do?

CS: He was a screw maker at Waltham watch factory. He made tiny little screws, some so tiny for women's watches it would look like a piece of dust, and with a strong magnifying glass you could see the little threads screwed in. So he was going to get me a job helping him make screws too. And he couldn't see why I wanted to go to art school and also develop my puppet show broader.

LM: It gives you a lot of good lines out of that, given your father's work. We won't go there because it would be inappropriate for Big Bird.

CS: No. I know I am thinking of those. As I said it, I said to myself, "Hmm, what will they make out of that?"

A listener asks whether Stan Freberg's early work had any influence on Spinney.

CS: I've always been a huge fan of Stan Freberg, and so was Jim Henson. As a matter of fact, Freberg had a huge influence on Kermit the Frog. Kermit is sort of an imitation of Stan Freberg's stuff.

LM: Largely because of an erosion of ratings and competition from all of these different children's programs on cable television, *Sesame Street* has evolved in the way it's formatted. Share with us this process of reformatting.

CS: The show right from the start was experimental TV. We have never put on anything that we thought would be controversial without first testing it on four-year-olds and even younger, putting them in a room with things that would distract them and our show too. Some things didn't work; some things did. Lately they had to analyze why our ratings—which we never even worried about for twenty years—have dropped, because now, you flip around the dial any hour of the day, there is children's stuff, even late at night on the Cartoon Channel. So they analyzed and studied the children, what they were doing, and discovered what we were doing wrong. In the old days it was all very slam bang, with quick changes, like short-attention-span theater. We were really based a lot on *Laugh-In*. So they edited some of the stories together without those little cartoons about the letter "A" into one long story, and the children stayed with it more because they weren't distracted in between. Some of the little three-year-olds didn't remember when we'd go back to the storyline, the street scenes, that it was the same story. And so now the stories are eight to ten minutes long and the rest of it is broken up into parts and finally ending in *Elmo's World*.

LM: How are you feeling about this new format? I have to say as a viewer, the show seems to be working creatively very well.

CS: Yeah, our ratings jumped thirty percent the first year of that. So they seem to know what they're doing. I think probably I'm a little nostalgic. I miss Jim Henson and the jokes he put in. We were always encouraged to go crazy with the jokes as long as we stuck to the storyline. Perhaps it was a little bit more grownup oriented. Now we're really aiming at a much younger audience, because we discovered that a lot of the children go away rather quickly at seven. By then they are watching *Pokemon* and *Power Rangers* and things.

LM: So you are aiming at the preschool through seven-year-old, that's your population?

CS: Yes. We still put in a lot of humor that the kids may not get. It's important to us that you hopefully are watching with your child, at least parts of it. So we try to put some zingers in there for you as well. That's one of the fun things to do. We laugh all day. We've got great writers. We stick to the story, but if you can think of something that's funnier, you can do it your way—I like that.

LM: I wonder if you could describe what it's like working inside the Big Bird suit/puppet? What was fascinating to me in reading your description is how it is a hybrid. You can't really call it a costume because it really isn't, and it isn't fully a puppet. Describe how he works.

CS: Jim conceived it. He was such an original thinker. Generally with most costumes, say you're playing a polar bear, you then put a big polar bear head over your own head. Jim dispensed with that idea. My head is inside of course, but it's not the head. Big Bird's head is held in my hand high over my head.

LM: Where does your head line up, chest level?

CS: Yeah, the same height I am now, which is five feet ten inches.

I can't really see out. A couple of feathers are on Velcro so I can see where the door jamb is and I won't just walk into the wall. I wear a tiny television set. I look down at it. It shows me the same picture you and your little boy would be watching. I can see this way if Big Bird is looking down at Elmo or whomever. Also on our show we talk to the kids at home, which means you've got to have Big Bird looking right into the camera. I can't see the camera. I'm watching my little TV set. I have to wear magnifying glasses because my picture's only an inch and a half across. They don't make them anymore, either. It's a real Vidicon tube. Because the new LCD things, they're not good to watch. I need to see specifics, not a bunch of pixels.

LM: When you're straight on the camera that seems less of an issue, but when you're turning, then you have to react to the opposite of what you are seeing on the monitor.

CS: Yes. It's not quite the same as looking in the mirror. You automatically know that your left hand looks like your right hand. But looking at a television set, the things to my right appear to be to my left. Several times I've headed off left and walked away from Gordon rather than toward him. So often, when I know I'm going to make a move, I'll make a little subtle move, and I'll see which way Big Bird is going just to straighten out my head, because after thirty-four years I still can get mixed up with that.

LM: I was going to ask if you still have that experience, or if it's become second nature to shift into that sort of opposite reaction.

CS: Some of it has become second nature; for instance, running his head is. One of the important things about manipulating Big Bird is to make sure he looks like he is thinking. Often he gets unhappy, and his eyelids lower. Everybody is watching from that one eye, the camera. So if I tip his beak up and lower his eyelids he can look very unhappy and then if I quiver the lower jaw he is about to burst into tears. Then if he is happy, if you tip his beak downwards, the line is now going up to create a smile. And if his eyes get wide open, which I run with a little lever in my little finger, he can be very happy looking. But his beak is a lot like a porpoise; it can't change shape. And a porpoise always looks like it's smiling at you. So you don't want Big Bird to always look like he is smiling, especially if he's miserable.

LM: So all of these subtle things you do portray the emotions of the character.

CS: Yeah, the emotions do play across his face; you can see his thinking pattern. That's why I think so many children are able to identify with him as if he is another kid, even if he looks like an absurd bird.

LM: What do your hands do? You mentioned that you have a monofilament you're able to move the eyes with.

CS: The eyes actually move with a little piece of bent coat hanger. That's good stuff to work with.

LM: Oh, very high-tech.

CS: Yeah, very. The most high-tech thing about Big Bird is inside the eyes. Gee, I hope kids are listening. It looks like a little clock because there are little gears inside and they make his eyelids move up farther. The little finger is the only useful one for that because the others have to hold up the weight of the head. It only moves up about an inch-and-a-quarter or something. You don't have much strength either.

LM: And then you have one hand that's in the beak of Big Bird?

CS: That is my right arm, which I am holding straight above my head, hopefully straight. Actually, I'm stronger than I was in the early years. He used to have more of a buzzard's neck. That meant I was get- ting tired and my elbow was bending. But my left arm is in the left wing and the monofilament you mentioned, it's such a fine fish line we often break it. But we don't want it to show. Once in a while the light will glint off it. But if I lower my left hand, the right hand will travel up. That way it isn't inert.

LM: So the arms don't move independently; when one moves, the other automatically moves.

CS: Right. But it's far better than it just being inert. People used to say, "What happened to Big Bird's wing? Did he break his wing?"

A listener asks if Spinney was on the TV show, The Muppet Show.

CS: It was done outside of London while I was mostly doing *Sesame Street,* but they did run past our season. So once the Muppets called me, that's my boss, and said, "Guess what? Do you want to go to

London and be on *The Muppet Show*?" I got back to the phone after doing the cartwheels. They always had a famous person, mostly movie stars or big TV stars, and the featured human was Leslie Uggams. Big Bird did a dance bit with Leslie. It was one of the biggest struggles I've ever had. They had a real great dance group, the Paddy Stone Dancers. Paddy Stone, he looked like he was a pirate and he looked like he'd kill you. He was the scariest choreographer I've ever seen. They had the most elaborate dance and I couldn't do it. One of the Muppeteers, a young man named Richard Hunt—he played Janice, part of Dr. Teeth's Electric Band, and he also played Gladys the Cow on *Sesame Street,* who was the most elegant cow—anyway, he gave me great advice. He said, "I notice you're having a lot of struggles trying to dance." I had burst into tears; it's in the book. Because it was Jim Henson, I wanted to please him. He asked me to go all the way to London and I was doing a lousy dance and Richard said, "Why don't you pretend Big Bird can dance? Have him show what you want, as if Big Bird thinks he is a great dancer." I did a great job thanks to his advice. The book is based a little bit on that all the way through, because I learned that you can engineer an awful lot of things that are going to happen to you if you believe in those dreams.

LM: Is it a similar feeling on the set of *Sesame Street* today as it was in the early years, or is it hard to recapture that feeling?

CS: Those were the learning years. But it's nice to get to know the character and relax, because you do now know what he is doing. It becomes like touch typing. You know you're going to get this look if you do that. So you can get lost in the acting. And so in those moments right after they say, "Action," I actually think I am truly living a bird's life—an unusual bird, sure. He talks and cries and all kinds of things.

I had an incredible experience once. I used to conduct symphonies all over America. There was a woman who was backing the orchestra in Michigan, I wish I could think of the name of the town. She gave a million every year to them. She heard me talking about it in a little wine thing just before the big show and she said, "Wait a minute, you're talking about the bird like he is not a real bird?" And I said, "Well, he is eight feet tall and sings and talks." She said, "Oh, I know, but you can train birds to do that." She said, "I can't believe he is not real," and I am thinking, "and she gives a million dollars every year."

LM: She meant this literally. I'm sure there's another program in that for us to do. One other fun thing, in the introduction I believe it is, you actually take us through being picked up at your apartment in Manhattan and being driven the half-hour out to Kaufman Astoria Studios where the show is now done in Queens. Could you recreate that from the book, what you see as you walk into the building and the various sets?

CS: Right. I get in there and I look at my scripts I have already prepared for the day. If it's an opening scene with Big Bird I climb into the hip boots, zip them up and I'm all ready to go out. The rest of them are waiting on stage. But in order to walk I have to waddle, because he's got these toes facing inwards, three toes on each foot. So I have to walk with the middle toe facing quite a ways out so I won't step on the other toes, which would get them dirty. Sometimes I wear slippers. Boys love to step on Big Bird's feet. It costs a couple hundred dollars to clean them because you have to dissect the whole thing. So I waddle on out there and we run through the scene and I've got the script in hand. After doing it a couple of times, we'll do a run-through. If it's a difficult thing I'll climb into the bird and we go through it while dressed. (Sometimes it's going to be rather simple, you're only going to be standing in one place. I don't have to put the bird on and I can breathe a little freer.) So we're finally ready to go; I put the script in and it's held on with Velcro up against the inside of the costume.

LM: And it's little cards you put the script on.

CS: Yeah, I have to fold, do a lot of origami to get the script small enough to get in there because I'll have five or six scenes. I've got to get it within a five-by-fifteen-inch panel and there's not that much room in there. And so then we're ready to go and all of a sudden action and—

Big Bird: "—I'm living, I'm a bird."

LM: And is it like being in another place when you're in that character?

CS: It is, because you want to put all your feelings and emotion into it. It's like a child listening to a story being told, they get lost in it.

A clip of Oscar the Grouch is played.

LM: Let's talk about how the character of Oscar has changed. Has he gone through a transformation comparable to Big Bird?

CS: No. Not at all. What you just heard was recorded at least thirty-two years ago. Oscar sounds pretty much the same right from the time I was on the way to do the voice for the first time and the cab driver said, "Where to, Mack?" I stole his voice and he sounds pretty much the same today, don't you, Oscar?

Oscar the Grouch: Yeah, except I still don't like you.

CS: I have a problem with him.

LM: Did the tragedy of September 11 have an effect on Oscar and his presentation?

CS: I don't think so. I think in a way it's good that evil doing doesn't make us lose a lot of things that we like.

LM: Do you end up taking the costume on the road with you very often?

CS: The bird I am not able to. I have a handler and he has to arrange the shipping because he goes in cargo. It's huge and so I can't travel without a lot of work. People say, "Can't you bring Big Bird along?" "Sure, you got a couple thousand bucks?" A grouch enjoys being crammed into a suitcase.

Oscar the Grouch: I love it.

CS: He's right in this room.

LM: The excitement level in our master control area, when you came in and you picked up Oscar the Grouch, it was like the greatest rock star in the world had just arrived.

CS: I hope Henry Winkler doesn't mind what I said in the book, but I assumed from his own real appearances that, while he is a very brilliant fellow, he was not the coolest dude in his class. And I sure wasn't; I was at the end of the line. But when he put on the Fonz, "Yeah." He was one of the coolest characters in all the years of TV. And Oscar somehow has found a coolness.

LM: Isn't that funny?

CS: I think he knows it.

LM: Yeah, the cranky guy ends up being the cool character. You worked with the late Jim Henson so closely and you described what was really a close working relationship and friendship.

CS: Yeah, he was such a gentle, good friend. He'd call Deb and me once in a while and say, "I've got to get away from it all," which was rare for him. He loved to work. And he'd say, "Let's go to the movies." So, oh boy, we're going off with Jim. He was definitely the most intelligent man. Sometimes intellectual people are harder to know; he was that, but also he was not guarded about himself. He was very thoughtful to people. He really was worrying about whether this was good for someone else, too.

A s any regular *AirTalk* listener knows, I'm thrilled to talk with musicians whose work I admire. However, it can be a challenge to get someone who is gifted at communicating through music to put what he or she does into words.

That is clearly not the case with Sting, one of the most articulate musicians with whom I've ever spoken. Just as I and many *AirTalk* listeners are fans of many genres of music, Sting synthesizes a huge range of influences into his work.

In this interview, I spoke with Sting shortly after he received his second Academy Award nomination for best song, this time for "Until" from the comedy *Kate and Leopold.*

Larry Mantle: I want to ask you first about your work on films, because now you've had two straight years of Academy nominations, and clearly you must enjoy the challenge of writing songs for a film.

Sting: It's extraordinary to be nominated again so quickly. I didn't really expect it. One of the nice things about writing for film is that you're told really what the brief of the song is, whereas normally I'm walking around in my garden wondering what the hell I'm going to write about. The director or producer will show you a film and say, "This is the plot." This is the mood of the film. These are the characters. Go ahead, write a song. So in many ways it's a little easier.

LM: Now you actually had a chance to see *Kate and Leopold,* did you not, before writing the song for the film; so you had a sense of where you wanted to go with this?

Sting: I wouldn't have done it otherwise. I mean that's the way I want to work. Interestingly enough it was screened for me in October of last year. And as you remember, that was a pretty fraught time for all of us after September 11, with the terrorism and the anthrax attacks and the impending war in Afghanistan. So to see a rather delightful and romantic movie about love was a wonderful release from all of that mayhem and misery. I was completely taken by it and was very happy to write a song for the movie.

LM: The song is very reminiscent of a waltz.

Sting: It is a waltz. The last scene in the movie is Meg Ryan and Hugh Jackman, the lead characters, dancing in a nineteenth-century drawing room with a string quartet in three-four time. I thought, well, that's my lead. And the film would finish and then my song would begin, taking it from that. So I wrote a very old-fashioned waltz. When you're normally asked to do this kind of work, there's always a suspicion that you're just being used so they can get you on MTV.

LM: Sell a soundtrack, etc.

Sting: Get bits of the film on radio or whatever. I was determined I was going to send them a song that was radio-proof, at least for rock radio. So half of me was expecting them to say, "No, we can't use this song, Sting." But they turned around and said, "We love it. It's absolutely what the film needs and what's more, today is the last day you can qualify for a Golden Globe nomination, so we've sent it in." This was even before they cut a deal with me, so I was very flattered and I said, "That's great." I didn't expect much more, but lo and behold, in January we won. We won this Golden Globe and I'm thrilled. I'm thrilled to still be in the game. We've got the Oscars next week. So I'm keeping my fingers crossed. I'd love to win.

LM: You're performing on the telecast?

Sting: Absolutely. I think it's great to perform. I performed last year. Before the other show someone asked me on the television, "Sting, are you going to win?" I said, "No, I'm not going to win, but I'm going to sing well enough so that everybody wishes they had voted for me."

LM: So that's what motivates all the performances on the award shows. If they don't win, they want to be able to show that they should have been the winner.

Sting: Well, there you go. Who knows?

LM: You said that when you delivered this waltz to the filmmakers you wondered whether they would like it because of the possible lack of radio airplay. But I've always seen that as one of your strengths, that the kind of music that you do is not easily categorized, because you borrow from so many different styles.

Sting: I think that's part of my job, really—to try and avoid all of these categories, all these labeling things, because I really think they're ultimately destructive of music. Music borrows from everything. And it's a great mongrel that grows because of that. And when you put it in a box that's too tight, it just simply wants to get out. So part of my job is to use my success to ease those restrictions, you know, to de-Balkanize music, which is a serious problem.

LM: It seems to me that often English musicians are the ones who are most interested in incorporating different musical influences. I'm curious if that's the case for you, that as you were growing up you were exposed to jazz and to classical and to different kinds of music, and therefore it's very attractive to use those elements?

Sting: I was educated musically by, first of all, my mother, who was a very good piano player, but then by the radio. We had the BBC, which was just one radio station. And the BBC played everything from the Beatles to Beethoven's *Fifth*. And so you didn't get that sense that music was in a box. Music was a continuum and it was the shared language between classical composers, between folk musicians, between pop musicians and ethnic blues musicians or whatever. So in a sense I'm very grateful for that. My mother, too, had a very catholic taste in the universal sense in that she played me a lot of Rodgers and Hammerstein as a child, a lot of show tunes: Lerner and Loewe, *My Fair Lady*. I played those records to death and loved them. And, you know, I can sing a lot of *Oklahoma* if you made me.

LM: That'll be a future album, no doubt. Has that, in a sense, informed the theatricality of your presentations, that you were exposed to music designed for the stage?

Sting: I like to tell stories in songs. I think it's a wonderful thing to be able to do. I have a theory that if you structure music correctly, then it's already telling you a narrative story. All you have to do is translate that abstraction into words. And so often the music, if it's constructed well, can be translated into something that you can say, that's a story. It goes from A to B and then moves onto C.

["Fragile" is played.]

LM: This rendition of "Fragile" has extra significance, given the timing of its recording. The performance was taped on September 11, 2001 in front of an invited audience of about two hundred at Sting's home in Italy. The concert was both Webcast and being recorded for Sting's latest CD, *All This Time*. Why were you recording a live CD in front of such an intimate audience of friends and family instead of the typical arena crowd? Was this a creative decision?

Sting: I wanted to celebrate a massive, very successful tour we began in late 1999. We played to something like 3.6 million people, and our record had done extremely well. I wanted to thank the fans in a much more personal, quiet way than a big, live album in a massive stadium. I thought, let's go into my backyard (it's a very nice backyard in Italy) and invite people from all over the world—fans, friends—and we'll just celebrate. We'll rearrange the songs in a very improvisatory way and it'll be more of a love letter than anything else. The date that I chose for this wonderful celebration was September 11. By the middle of the afternoon as we were preparing the show and people were arriving, we heard the terrible news and saw the awful footage that everyone saw and we had to make a decision. My instinct immediately was that I didn't want to sing at all. I was miserable. I thought singing would be a total waste of time. But I put it to a vote. I'm very democratic. My band and I sat around a table. Most of them are from New York, had family in New York and didn't quite know what had happened to them, and each one of them said, "This is what musicians do. We play. We express our emotions this way and we want to play." And I said, "It's all very well for you playing an instrument, but I have to sing. It's a different mechanism, you know. I'm not sure I can do that." They said, "No, people are arriving. They want some kind of contact and we have to provide that." So I said, "Okay, I'll go out there and we'll do one song. We'll play 'Fragile' because 'Fragile' seems to have the right kind of sentiment for what has happened, and then we'll shut down the Webcast as a mark of respect. Then we'll ask the audience what they want, but I've no guarantee that we can go on." We did that and it was probably one of the most difficult performances of my life. We sang "Fragile," turned off the Webcast, and then I asked the audience what they wanted. They all seemed to say they wanted some form of music to soothe them, to heal them. We began very tentatively again, and after a few songs I think the mood became more and more defiant, and we realized that we had a perfect right to express ourselves in this manner. We kept the tapes rolling and it wasn't the concert we planned at all. It was completely different from the one we planned, a completely different mood, a completely different choice of songs, a completely different way of playing them. But at the end of the day, I listened to it and I thought I would dedicate it to those who had lost their lives, including a friend of ours, a very close friend. And we put this record out *All This Time* and there you have it. I wish it was not the case. I really wish it was something different, but it's not.

LM: One of the things I really like about the disc is that these songs are all very familiar to us. We've heard the studio recordings so many times. But to hear them fresh in this kind of environment and with some different instrumental focuses in the music, there's a real intimacy to this that really can't be captured in the same way in the studio.

Sting: That was always the intention, but then it had this extra dimension which came from the context of what was happening in the world that day. So it is quite an extraordinary record, a record that I'm very proud of. But as I say, I wish it was different.

LM: We talked earlier about your use of many different musical styles and the many different influences that you had growing up. We hear so much in the music business about Balkanization and music that's very age-specific, and how it's difficult to get radio airplay if you break certain genres or if the music is overly complex and borrows from too many influences. This seems to me to be very much at odds with the way that people listen to music, that most people do listen to very different kinds of styles. I'm wondering, as someone who is so familiar with the business side of music, is there any way of reforming the recording industry that really takes into account how people listen to music?

Sting: I think we can sponsor radio stations like this one. You know, where there is more freedom, where there is a sense that music is more important than research. I never believed in computer-programmed radio. It's simply against music, ultimately.

LM: What is it that keeps you going creatively, that really excites you? You've traveled so much; you've performed live so many times. What excites you? What makes you want to either get back into the studio or get out on another tour?

Sting: One of the things that really excites me is that I'm still a student of music. I'm still learning my craft. I'm still learning about how to be a better singer, a better songwriter, a better lyricist, a better arranger. If you think you know about arranging, go and listen to Ravel and you realize you know nothing about arranging. There's an infinity of knowledge out there, and that's what excites me. Until my dying day I will be involved in this mystery we call music. It's a wonderful thing to be lost in.

LM: It seems that as musicians age, they're able to bring something extra. For example, I think your voice is richer now than it used to be, and maybe part of that, as you say, is this ongoing learning process and part of it is just that the instrument develops a kind of richness as you age. That must be one of the things that you like, that this is not perfectible. Do you see yourself continuing to perform and to record well into old age?

Sting: I'd love to. You know, I'm fifty. I was fifty last year. This age is probably the Golden Age, whereas in rock and roll you tend to be washed up by the time you're twenty-two.

LM: There's only so much to be rebellious about.

Sting: Exactly. But to have stayed in it this long is very heartening, very satisfying. And I need to continue to be honest to myself and honest to the people who listen to me. This is me and this is what I believe, and I want to do it with dignity and grace and gratitude.

LM: Given the things that come your way because you live, in some sense, a kind of unreal life with the level of celebrity, the wealth that has come your way, the acclaim that you get, how do you stay sane, so to speak? How do you stay a real human being given the fact that you're in this very challenging environment, which really doesn't bear much resemblance to the reality that most of us live?

Sting: I think we're all real human beings. I was fortunate that I didn't enter celebrity until I was twenty-six, and by that time I'd had a family, I'd paid a mortgage, I had a job as a schoolteacher. So I lived in what most people regard as the real world before this roller coaster of fame and stardom happened to me. I'm very grateful for that period in my life.

LM: And it sounds like you knew who you were. By that point you'd had a chance to develop enough as a person. You had a sense of yourself as separate from what you do.

Sting: Even so, I forgot pretty quickly who I was. But having had that experience, at least I could go back there.

LM: How long did it take to recapture yourself?

Sting: A while, believe me. I really have a lot of sympathy for people who never had any other experience but celebrity. That is a very difficult position to be in. They are real human beings with real problems.

LM: When your head was turned, and you were in this world of unreality, did you find that you liked yourself less?

Sting: Absolutely. That's the main problem. You don't really like yourself. You have to relearn to love that soul inside you that was in love with music in the first place, and that takes a while.

Jack Welch

November 14, 2002

B efore KPCC made *AirTalk* programs available online, we offered listeners an opportunity to buy tapes of interviews they wanted to hear again. This interview with Jack Welch was one of our most requested tapes ever.

Regardless of some coverage Welch has had in recent years, his accomplishments as the longtime CEO of General Electric are legendary. In this post-retirement conversation with Welch, he describes his entrepreneurial way of running GE, and what he thinks others in business can learn from his approach.

Larry Mantle: You were an only child, growing up in a household where your mother took a great interest in you and not only encouraged you, but really prodded you to achieve excellence. Talk about your relationship with her and how that helped form you.

Jack Welch: I was the only child of a mother who was in her late thirties when I was born, and that, in those days, was quite late. I became the rising sun and the setting sun to her. She focused much of her attention on me. I had a speech impediment that I still carry a bit of with me. I'd come home from school, and she would say, "Jack, don't worry about that; it's just because your mind works so much faster than your tongue." So that'd be another of those supportive things. I'd go home at lunch when I was in the first grade and play gin rummy with her. And there was nothing she liked more than to put the cards down and go, "gin," on me. I wanted to beat her so badly. So that got some competitive juices going.

LM: She was a very competitive woman?

JW: A very competitive, very competitive woman. She only had an eighth-grade education, but she did the taxes for the whole Irish neighborhood we lived in. She was sort of the major-domo of the block, if you will. She would yell at me about things like, "Jack, that's the way it is—face it. See it the way it is; don't kid yourself." She told me that all the time. And I carried that for life.

LM: It sounds like she used some of the same tools that successful managers would use in grooming employees.

JW: You know, I hate to admit that. I'm a manager without an MBA, without all the tools. At my mother's knee I learned most of the things I practiced for the next forty years.

LM: One of the things that's really impressed me about people who are very successful in business, or in most things, is not how they deal with the successes, but in the ways they're impacted by defeat. I'm wondering if, in your experience, this relationship with your mother gave you such extra confidence.

JW: You have touched on what management's all about. Every manager's job is to instill self-confidence in every person who works for them. Give them opportunities to fail, give them opportunities to reach, let them stretch, dream, try things. And in doing that, each time they succeed, they'll try further. A manager's job is to walk around with fertilizer and a watering can, and throw it on a seed and get that seed to grow. That really is a big part of the job. Celebrate every little victory, make people feel it's very important when they win, no matter how small the victory. A pizza, a keg of beer, something—but always letting them know victory came. That's so important. Some people get it at their mother's knee; some people get it in school with great grades.

LM: Some people seem to be born with that kind of resiliency that they don't experience their setbacks at a deep core level. They're able to brush it aside and move on.

JW: Get back on the horse. I always told people, it's not how you fall off the horse; it's how you get back on the horse.

LM: You went to the University of Massachusetts at Amherst to get your undergraduate degree, and then on to the University of Illinois at Champaign-Urbana for your master's degree and your advanced work. When you came out as an engineer, you had two companies that you could go with. Share with us the decision-making process that led you to GE.

JW: Well, I had a PhD, and I liked to sell. I liked the commercial aspects of business. So I tried to look for a place that had a product-development place where I could launch new products. GE had one in Pittsfield, Massachusetts. Exxon had one in Baytown, Texas. Those were the two best jobs I saw that fit my skill base, a combination of technology and selling. I ended up going to Pittsfield. I guess I went back there because I came from Massachusetts. I was the first employee of the new plastics business. That was a great break. So I was the number-one employee, I was king, emperor and bottle washer at the same time. We started a new business, and I hired employee two and employee three and employee four. We were off to the races, and we built, over a number of years, a multi-billion-dollar business.

LM: You had the luxury of being in a very small environment of a much larger company, where you were establishing yourself.

JW: My personality might not have worked, had I started in the middle of a bureaucracy in one of the bigger locations. I might have blown myself up. I was fortunate to be outside the mainstream, in a little shed in Pittsfield, Mass., with a bank supporting me, basically, a big company. And no one really caring much about plastics. So it was sort of an ideal situation. Plastics was an outlier in the General Electric company.

LM: So, you were able to be a boss from the beginning. And, as you say, you never ended up in the middle of the bureaucracy. You were always in the position of leadership as your career progressed.

JW: That's right. I stayed away from headquarters for eighteen years. I ended up operating out of a hotel suite in Pittsfield, Mass., with businesses all over the country, rather than move to headquarters.

LM: Why?

JW: The politics, the stuff, the environment. It wasn't right for me. It wasn't right for my personality.

LM: Was part of it that you are by nature a star, and to be in an environment where it's tough to be the star, wasn't comfortable for you?

JW: Well, that's a hell of a good question. I never thought of it that way. I'd say it was more I couldn't be myself. I mean, I never wore neckties; I was a bit of a rebel. I loved challenging business ideas. I loved the excitement of being an entrepreneur. I thought I was an entrepreneur. But I wasn't really an entrepreneur like you have out here. All the entrepreneurs are looking for money every day. I was lucky. I had the best part of entrepreneurship. I could be an entrepreneur, but I always had the backing of a big company. So it was one of those luxury jobs. I was very lucky in where I ended up.

LM: As you began to establish yourself at GE, sort of off to the side with this plastics company, what did you start learning about the larger General Electric? Did you do an assessment of the larger company at that point?

JW: After several years of being in the plastics business, and growing it, people started to recognize the success of our team there. They added a number of businesses to ours: a motor division, a medical division, an electronic components division. And I started to see, in these larger, older units, a rigorous bureaucracy, layer on layer. Now, this was not untrue of many corporations in the Seventies. We had come out of the postwar era; growth was in the air. We had built organizations to manage growth, not to create it. So all these hierarchical companies were sitting there managing. There was no Japan; there was no Germany. And as they started to come along in the late Seventies and early Eighties, we were in real trouble. But I saw that early in the Seventies. I was in this little garage running this plastics thing, and I couldn't believe the formality, and the parking spaces that people had, and the offices, and the meetings, and all the stuff that took place. It was incredible. I just hated it.

LM: Is part of it that you're most comfortable in a face-to-face environment where you're the seller, or you're making the deal, and you consider all these layers of bureaucracy as distancing a person like yourself from being able to do what they do best and enjoy most?

JW: Look, I think the job of a leader is to get in the skin of every employee. Jump right in, and help that person understand the mission, the goals, and give them the tools to get there. And with all these layers, the way corporations worked, in those days, it was incredible. Bureaucracy always wants to come back. It's like a creeping disease. There's always somebody wanting to be the boss of somebody else, and somebody else. A flat organization gives you speed: rapid communications and response time. It's the whole game.

LM: But don't you feel, in a sense, you're fighting human nature, that we are largely hierarchical beings, that we take comfort in knowing to whom we report, and who reports to us, and what our role is?

JW: No, I wouldn't necessarily agree with that. I think people want to know they count. It's absolutely critical that we make sure everybody in the organization comes to work knowing we want their best ideas—not their hands, not their feet, but their minds, and that we'll listen, and they count.

LM: Is there something in American culture that is perhaps an advantage over what you see in Europe or in Asia when it comes to the individual counting?

JW: I think in Japan, they did a very good job with that. Toyota Motor, Sony, the best companies there have done a great job of that. I think Europe has that problem; it's a disadvantage. In America, some do and some don't. Basically, though, we had a company whose whole culture was built around getting up every morning and believing that an organization's ability to learn, share that learning and act on it, was its ultimate competitive advantage. Not some product, not some service, but this thirst for learning with great people.

LM: In fact, GE products and services changed dramatically under your tenure. Let's talk about situations where a single decision, like the acquisition of RCA, could have meant financial disaster or the incredible success that it ended up being. How do you get yourself to the point where you can make those kinds of decisions, knowing the stakes?

JW: I think that an organization that's open to change, that sees every change as an opportunity—glass half-full versus glass half-empty—is absolutely critical. I'd like to tell a quick story about a fellow from Vail Resorts who was on television the other morning. He had just bought fifteen properties, resort properties. And he was so excited to have bought these after 9/11. He got them at prices that were a fraction of what he could have bought them for in August. On the other side of that trade, somebody sold those properties. Now, two different lenses were looking at the same 9/11. One said, people are going to travel again. People are going to go to resorts again. On the other side of that lens, somebody was saying, the world's fundamentally changed. Resort living is not going to be the same, and people aren't going to travel. That's happening today, all over America.

There are opportunities from this terrible tragedy. People are looking at the same situations in totally different frameworks.

A listener wonders, given the pressure to get results, how much rope Welch gave to employees who were not doing their jobs adequately.

JW: Look, the biggest thing a company has is a candid appraisal system. It is the most valuable tool it has. As I go around and ask people, how many people have gotten candid appraisals, the number of hands that go up are few and far between. I ask if they work for a company with integrity and a hundred percent of the hands go up. I ask if they've gotten an honest appraisal. Five percent go up, at most. I say, "How do you justify saying you work for a company with integrity if you haven't gotten an honest appraisal?" If you have a candid appraisal system you will be able, within a very short time frame, to get people to understand where they stand, where they fit. And hopefully, early in their career, you will be able to tell them that this isn't the right place for them, and move them on. As you build that garden, you'll have some weeds; there's no question. And weeds have to be cut out, as your flowers grow. That's how you build a beautiful garden.

LM: How much of a right fit is because a person comes to work every day energized? How do you weigh the drive to do the job, versus being smart, being organized?

JW: You need both. But I'd buy passion every time. Energy counts big. Ability to energize others counts enormously. I always evaluate people by four E's. Do they have energy? Can they energize others? Do they have the edge to say yes or no and make the tough decisions? And do they execute? And I wrap those four E's in a big P. And so, for me, I err on the side of heat.

LM: But that's something you often don't know until the person is actually in the job and you can see whether it is just an employee's infatuation for being hired, or you have someone who can really go the distance, because every day they're excited to do the work.

JW: Runway's a big question. How much have they got ahead of them? It's easy to look at what they've done; it's harder to predict runway.

A listener asks if Welch considers himself a rule breaker.

JW: I wouldn't be considered a maverick among a series of entrepreneurs. But I was probably a maverick, or rule breaker, in a big bureaucracy. I didn't do the conventional things. But I played within the rules of that institution. It would be silly to think that I could get to the top by throwing mud in people's faces every day, to be different. I was different, but just different enough.

LM: You're different enough to stand out for people to see you, but not so different as to threaten them.

JW: I think that's a perfect way of putting it.

A listener asks if Welch ever found a difference working with people in rural areas versus big cities.

JW: No, I don't really think so. I think it's all about energizing people. And I think you might have a sharper-talking, faster-talking person in a big city. But in the end, the question is, can you excite them to reach further than they ever dreamt they could reach? Can you create an atmosphere in them? And I think you can do that in a rural farm, or in downtown Los Angeles. I don't think it makes much difference. I think it's all about how you can get in the skin of those people, as I keep saying, to raise the bar of excitement about the job, the curiosity, the ability to learn. The thirst to win.

A listener says he worked at NBC in Burbank when GE bought the company, and claims that management was not only "mean and hard to deal with," but also "dumb."

JW: To the best of my knowledge, Burbank was run by the same people that had it before, Brandon Tartikoff, Don Ohlmeyer, Warren Littlefield, etc. To the best of my knowledge, a GE person has never managed the Burbank property. So I don't really understand this. I'm sorry that you felt that whatever happened there wasn't fair, wasn't done smartly. That certainly wasn't our intent. And if we did it wrong, shame on us. There's nothing I can say other than, I'm sorry that your experience was not favorable. I mean, our whole role in life, as you've heard me say here, is to not have people feel like you felt.

And thank God we don't have 300,000 people who feel like you felt, or we wouldn't have become the best company in the world.

LM: How involved were you in the management of the RCA/NBC division of GE, or did you feel like it was best to leave that to people who'd come up in that business?

JW: The star of this NBC story is Bob Wright, who was a pots-and-pans manager in housewares who basically came to run the network. People laughed, how could this pots-and-pans guy run a network? Well, he's the longest-serving network president in history now, some thirteen years. He succeeded Grant Tinker and he took NBC to No. 1 in most of these years. He was very, very reluctant to ever get involved with talent. His strength came from picking great people. So he picked people who were in the industry, producers. The newsmen came from CBS. The people out here were great talent, like Don Ohlmeyer and Warren Littlefield. We never put GE people near these properties. They may have been in finance jobs or something like that, but they were not near the creative process.

LM: How did you make this NBC acquisition work in the mid-Eighties? Here you are, GE, this major manufacturing company, and you're acquiring what is a large creative and social force. How did you get the cultures to work together?

JW: In the end, we don't manage businesses; we develop people. That was our core competency. You couldn't, if you think about it, possibly design a *Seinfeld* show, build a jet engine, build a power plant, build a medical scanner. So we got to understand our job clearly. Our job was to develop great people. So we pick a leader. A leader then is responsible for picking the talent to run that business. As far as picking shows or getting involved, we'd be involved in some salary negotiations and things like that, some of the financial aspects of the business. But as far as the creative process is concerned, I never sat in on pilots to see which one we'd pick.

LM: One of the criticisms of network news these days is that it's looked at by its corporate parent as a source of great revenue, and that much of the public affairs or public service aspect of network news has diminished in the process. According to this argument, now that news makes so much money, that becomes the focal point, not depth, not providing news in a way that really tells people what they need to know. How do you respond to this concern?

JW: I don't buy it at all. I think the facts are that news has plenty of resources, that cable has offered all kinds of new news outlets. We have twenty-four-hour news now, the quality of which we can debate at different times, but with the same people, many of the same people who were there before corporate ownership. The anchors, for example, were all the same anchors on the networks that were there prior to corporate ownership. The cable outlets have been expanded by corporate ownership and are giving more news. So, you know, I just don't buy it. I find news, whether it's on NPR or whether it's on cable, or the networks. There's plenty of it out there.

LM: One of the arguments is that it's in abundance, but it doesn't have the depth that it used to. So, yes, there's twenty-four-hour MSNBC and CNN and the like, but the argument is that international news has declined significantly, and analysis of social and political issues has declined in favor of personal stories.

JW: That might be true. There's no question that ratings play a part in this; let's not kid ourselves. What the public gets is determined by ratings. The public decides what they get. Ratings drive the business. There's no question about that. And if you don't get ratings, your show doesn't last long. Those are realities of the television world.

LM: Critics argue that one of the problems with the American business culture today is that you have to work such long hours that it makes it very difficult to be a well-rounded person. You could be said to be Exhibit A of this man who has lived for his job. How do you respond to those who say, that's too high a price to pay?

JW: Well, let's talk about the alternatives. We're playing in a global world. We're fighting for a standard of living. Only winning companies are worth much. A losing company is worth nothing. A losing company doesn't pay taxes. Its employees aren't energized. They're scared about their job security. They don't give back to their community. In GE, we have fifty-five thousand mentors who volunteer in the inner cities all over this country, and all over the world, to teach the less fortunate, on their own—with no credit from GE. We don't promote them because they do it; they do that because they volunteer. We can do that because we're winning. If you don't win, despite what your critics or your other friends might say, there is no game. Now, you've got to decide for yourself, on a very personal level, how much commitment and how much excitement you have in each frame of your life. I happen to be somebody who has great kids, who always took a vacation, who worked my tail off, did all those things. But I wanted to win, and I wanted to win for our company, and I wanted to win for thousands and thousands of people. Our largest shareholders are our employees.

LM: But there are only twenty-four hours in a day, so you had to make decisions about how you were going to manage and live your life. What are the things that you gave up to be who you are?

JW: Nothing I wanted to do. I had four great kids; they went to great schools. I've got nine grandchildren. I did have two wives. But guys that didn't do anything had two wives, too. I mean, it isn't because of how hard I worked that I had two great wives. Both the first and second are terrific. That's life.

LM: So you felt you were able to balance your life, despite the demands of being the CEO of GE.

JW: I loved it. I mean, I loved it. I loved doing the job. And I wanted so much for every person that I touched to feel the same way about it. To live life to the fullest. To work hard and play hard. I just thought that was part of it. Passion for everything you do. I hate dabblers—reading a little, painting a little. Dabblers, to me, don't add much. They might have a nice time for themselves, but dabbling does nothing for me.

LM: So you don't see that as a spur to creativity. You think the passionate, clearly focused employee is the more creative employee?

JW: Well, I also think great artists have great passion. I don't think they sit around and dabble and then read a book one minute, and crochet the next and do something else the next. I think they're focused.

A listener asks how much influence a mega-corporation like GE wields over our government and the making of its policies.

JW: I think a mega-corporation like GE has a voice. And it expresses its opinion. But the interesting thing in today's world is that lots of constituencies have a voice. Labor has an enormous voice. The environmental movement may have the largest voice today, in unity, whether it be the Sierra Club or any other group like that. So there are voices being expressed on all sides of all issues. And politicians are going to have to take into account all sides of the argument. But there's no poor group that isn't being listened to.

LM: So you feel like the lobbying that corporate America does is just balancing out other interests that in some way might have an effect on the bottom line of American businesses?

JW: I'd say corporate lobbying is no larger than the environmental movement, than the labor movement, than Common Cause and all the other things that are out there. I'm saying they're balanced.

A listener talks about companies frequently hiring incompetent "friends of friends of friends," and asks what can be done about this.

JW: Getting cronyism out of a company is a full-time job. And it's something that has to be policed and looked at all the time. You fight every day of your life to build a meritocracy, to build a diverse—by race and gender—organization that is able to cope with anything and operates as a meritocracy. Now, I can't solve the problem. I know that's what leaders want, but if you're going to have some crony hire a friend and cause a problem, it's probably going to happen. It might happen in GE; it might happen anywhere. But it's not the norm; it's not what anybody wants, and you fight as hard as you can not to have it.

LM: But one of the problems is that, since business is so relationship oriented, having an affinity for someone is an important element in this.

JW: Absolutely. But hopefully the person that I hired is smarter than I am, more energized than I am, more creative than I am, bringing more to the party than I am, and I also like the hell out of him.

LM: So let's take the example at Disney of Michael Eisner and Michael Ovitz. Is that an example of where a relationship, in your view, took precedence over someone's preparation to do the job?

JW: Larry, Mrs. Welch didn't bring up a fool. I'm not answering that question under any circumstances.

LM: All right, well, that says something right there.

A listener who is CEO of a small company asks Welch if his method is still applicable to small and midsize companies.

JW: I think the culture I'm talking about is even more applicable. Forget the zeros on the back of it. You have the opportunity in a smaller company to really get in the skin of people, to really excite them, to make their jobs so exciting that they can hardly wait to get there. You can give them vision; you can give them rewards. You can celebrate more. Bureaucracies have trouble celebrating. You can set the tone. Setting the tone of an organization is absolutely critical. You as the CEO of a small company are totally responsible for setting the tone, creating the environment, getting the people to reach and stretch like they never have before. And to have more fun. Don't forget, you spend most of your waking hours at work. How do you make that the most pleasant? How do you make it the most fun? It's a big assignment. But in a small company, you really have that responsibility.

LM: Well, it seems to me, one of the ways you do that is by the employees not only having passion for the tasks, but a sense of ownership. Putting stock options aside, how do you engender a sense of ownership so that when the GE employee comes to work, they feel somehow a sense of ownership in this large, publicly traded conglomerate?

JW: Well, one, they want to win. Two, GE employees are our largest share owner; thirty-two billion dollars of stock are owned by GE employees.

LM: So that's a major tool in giving that sense of ownership?

JW: Absolutely. When I'd have a management meeting, I'd look at the top five hundred people, and I would say, look, don't think about Wall Street when you think about your performance. Don't think about some pension fund, some faceless thing. Think about your factory. Go out in your factory and look at those people who are counting on their retirement and their 401(k)s, based on you. That's whom your obligation is to. It's not to some faceless investor in some office in L.A. or in New York or anywhere else. You look to that person in your office. You have a responsibility to deliver for those people.

A listener asks Welch to compare the longer-term view of business in Japan and Korea with the American point of view of, "What have you done this quarter?"

JW: There's no question, the Japanese view for years was longer than the American view. The interesting thing to me now is that the Americans think in days, the Japanese think in decades, and the Chinese think in centuries. So you now have a new force called China. In the Eighties, you'll recall, many feared that Japan was going to take over American manufacturing. Well, that in the end didn't happen, even though they have great companies today. But China, going forward, is thinking long term: billion people plus, bright. We have companies over there. Anybody who's in business today has got to find a way, not just to sell to China—they've got to find a way to partner with China, to participate with China going forward. I use this simple thing. Draw a pie chart. Fill in half of it with your normal competitors. Leave the other half blank for companies you haven't heard of in China. If you think about one thing, most Americans go to China, they fly to Hong Kong, then fly to Shanghai, and then go to Beijing, and then come home. They've missed eight hundred million people, out to the left, if you will. And out there are enormous factories doing enormous things that we've got to find ways to participate with for the long haul.

Acknowledgments

This book truly has been a collaborative effort, with many people providing extraordinary time and expertise to make it happen in time for our twentieth anniversary year.

There would be no *This is AirTalk* without the vast time commitment that KPCC News Director Paul Glickman made to this project. From his editing of my words and our interview transcripts, to tracking the gathering of our interviewee releases, he has been integrally involved in all aspects of this book. He's done this at the same time that he continued to lead our large news department, including *AirTalk*, through the 2004 election season and many other day-to-day challenges. During his four-plus years at KPCC, Paul has led us to ever greater success and growth. He is committed to journalistic integrity and the values that make KPCC such a highly respected source for news. I deeply appreciate all that Paul has done for this book and how accomplished he is as a manager.

Paddy Calistro and Scott McAuley of Angel City Press are absolute delights to work with. I was very excited when they expressed interest in publishing *This is AirTalk*, as I've been a huge fan of their work for years. I appreciate all the guidance they've offered me. Amy Inouye's graphic design is incredible. All Southern California readers should be thankful to Angel City Press for its high-quality books, devotion to literature of the West, and care for the future of our region.

I appreciate Jonathan Kirsch on so many levels. Not only has he been a frequent guest on *AirTalk*, both as a book critic and as the author of acclaimed books on religious themes, but he is also a highly regarded intellectual property attorney. I am deeply honored that Jonathan represents me and am so thankful to him for his friendship.

Though Paul Glickman edited the majority of interview transcripts, he received tremendous assistance from Carla Lazzareschi, the former general manager of Los Angeles Times Books. To have someone who ran a highly respected publishing division happily give hours of her time to edit interviews speaks volumes about her love of public radio, KPCC and *AirTalk*. We are extremely fortunate to have her journalistic and editing experience shape so many of these interviews.

I'm grateful to Lynette Johnson, who spent hours securing the necessary releases from our interviewees.

KPCC volunteer Freda Lin spent many hours, including weekends, overseeing the copying of the interviews we considered for the book, and then shipping them out to Rapid Text for transcribing. I cannot thank her enough for how quickly she worked on such a short deadline. Bijal Shah also contributed many hours working with Freda on the pre-transcription process. Like Freda, Bijal has also spent many hours helping to produce segments for us on *AirTalk*.

I am incredibly fortunate to have the best production team in radio: Senior Producer Linda Othenin-Girard and Producers Jackie Oclaray, Polly Sveda, and Chumi Paul. Linda and I have worked together for more then twelve years, during which time we've established a close professional relationship. This mutual understanding and respect is an incredible advantage when producing *AirTalk*. Linda, Jackie (who also produces our *FilmWeek* segments), Polly and Chumi seemingly work twelve hours a day, often on weekends, and are as devoted to *AirTalk* as I am. Listeners frequently express thanks to me for the program, but it is our producers who make this unwavering commitment to quality who deserve every bit as much credit, if not more. Their families are also extremely understanding of the demands of this job, and I thank them for their sacrifices.

I am indebted to the KPCC production and operations staff, led by Doug Johnson, for their tireless pursuit of audio engineering quality. I am particularly grateful to our daily *AirTalk* engineer Tony Federico, who is always on the ball and creative in his approach to the sound of the program. Our *FilmWeek* engineer Jeff Krinock brings the same qualities and commitment to his work.

We have a terrific team at KPCC and Southern California Public Radio, led by CEO Bill Davis and General Manager Mark Crowley. Bill and Mark are extremely supportive of *AirTalk*, and all of the work done by our news department. They were also enthusiastic about this book, and I appreciate their support.

I extend my thanks to everyone on the KPCC/SCPR team. You are deeply appreciated for all your hard work and dedication to the station, whether in the public eye or not. KPCC is an interlocking unit, requiring all of us to work toward fulfilling the same mission. We share in each other's successes, and I'm so proud to work with you.

Over the years, I've been lucky to work for general managers who had great trust in me and belief in the quality of my work. Thank you, Rod Foster, for your years of KPCC leadership and friendship. My thanks, also, to the man who hired me, John Gregory, and to Bob Miller, who suggested I create the new program that ended up being *AirTalk*.

I must credit and thank my friend Kathy Spilos for coming up with the program's name when she was a valued KPCC news employee and volunteer.

I also offer my personal thanks to those closest in my life. My wife Kristen is so understanding and supportive of my work that words fail me in appropriately thanking her. Since *AirTalk* requires an average four hours nightly of reading and study, it takes a selfless and highly understanding partner to help me do this job. Kristen is also a great sounding board, lovingly challenging my assumptions every step of the way. I've also learned so much from my three-year-old son, Desmond. There's nothing like an inquisitive child to help a parent examine his or her deeply held beliefs or automatic assumptions. Thanks, Des.

My parents John Mantle and Carole Morse have given me incredible love, support and counsel, not to mention a terrific childhood springboard to what I'm doing now. I love my parents very much, and I also deeply value their friendship. I owe them more than I could ever articulate.

I offer my thanks, as well, to so many other family members and friends: my in-laws Dan and Maria Hernandez, stepfather Dick Morse, close friend and colleague Steve Julian, and all those who surely know their importance to me.

Finally, thank you *AirTalk* listeners and supporters. What a great twenty years. May we have many decades more together!

Larry Mantle, Southern California Public Radio and the publisher wish to thank the following individuals, estates and organizations for their permission to publish the interviews contained in this book:

Alexa Albert, M.D.
Milton Berle Enterprises
Peter Bogdanovich
Ken Burns, Filmmaker
Michael Caine
President Jimmy Carter and the Carter Center
Estate of Divine
George Foreman
Anne Garrels
Frank Gehry
Chuck Jones Center for Creativity
Meadow Lane Enterprises, Inc. and SteveAllen.com
Steve Martin
U.S. Senator John McCain
Walter Mosley and the Watkins/Loomis Agency
Pasadena Area Community College District
Carl Reiner
Esa-Pekka Salonen
Maurice Sendak
Caroll Spinney
Sting
Jack Welch

ANGEL CITY PRESS